MAKING
SENSE
OF

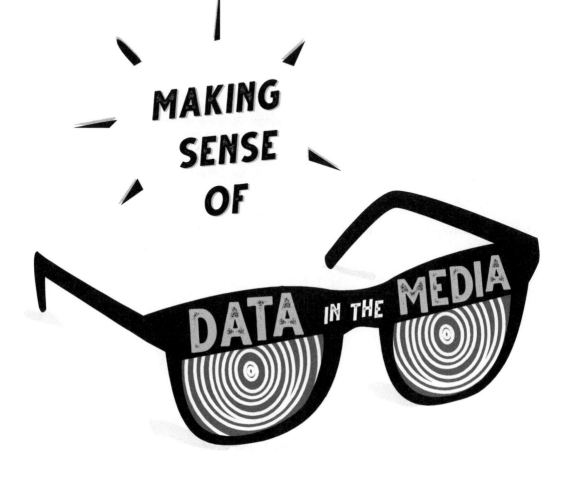

MAKING SENSE OF

DATA IN THE MEDIA

ANDREW BELL, TODD HARTMAN,
ANETA PIEKUT, ALASDAIR RAE
AND MARK TAYLOR

Los Angeles | London | New Delhi
Singapore | Washington DC | Melbourne

Los Angeles | London | New Delhi
Singapore | Washington DC | Melbourne

SAGE Publications Ltd
1 Oliver's Yard
55 City Road
London EC1Y 1SP

SAGE Publications Inc.
2455 Teller Road
Thousand Oaks, California 91320

SAGE Publications India Pvt Ltd
B 1/I 1 Mohan Cooperative Industrial Area
Mathura Road
New Delhi 110 044

SAGE Publications Asia-Pacific Pte Ltd
3 Church Street
#10-04 Samsung Hub
Singapore 049483

Editor: Michael Ainsley
Editorial assistant: Amber Turner-Flanders
Production editor: Imogen Roome
Marketing manager: Susheel Gokarakonda
Cover design: Lisa Harper-Wells
Typeset by: C&M Digitals (P) Ltd, Chennai, India
Printed in the UK

Library of Congress Control Number: 2019940551

British Library Cataloguing in Publication data

A catalogue record for this book is available from the British
Library

ISBN 978-1-5264-4719-7
ISBN 978-1-5264-4720-3 (pbk)

At SAGE we take sustainability seriously. Most of our products are printed in the UK using responsibly sourced
papers and boards. When we print overseas we ensure sustainable papers are used as measured by the PREPS
grading system. We undertake an annual audit to monitor our sustainability.

Contents

Acknowledgements

We are extremely grateful to the Nuffield Foundation, ESRC and HEFCE for funding the Q-Step programme that has allowed this work to take place. In particular, we would like to thank Dr Simon Gallacher at the Nuffield Foundation for his tireless work, constant support and enthusiastic advocacy for improving quantitative skills in the social sciences.

Also, thanks to Dr George Leckie, Professor Charles Pattie and Professor Ron Johnston for looking over previous drafts of chapters, as well as the anonymous reviewers who gave us excellent feedback. Thanks also to the students of our class 'Lies, Damned Lies and Statistics' in Sheffield, and our Futurelearn 'Making Sense of Data in the Media' MOOC, for letting us test some of these materials and ideas out on them. Thanks also to the audience at the Research Methods Festival 'Innovations in Teaching Statistics' session, in Bath in July 2018, for your helpful suggestions.

1 Introduction

Statistics are everywhere in the news media. And yet they are widely misunderstood, poorly reported and often downright false. Not only that, but consumers of the news are not well prepared to understand the figures used by reporters and journalists. Just consider how many people openly flaunt their poor quantitative skills. Maths teachers regularly hear phrases from parents like, 'We're terrible at Maths, we can't help at all.' Why is it that English teachers rarely get told by parents, 'We can't read very well, so we can't help Delila with her homework'?

Politicians in the news haven't helped remedy this quantitative skills deficit. In the run-up to the 2016 EU Referendum in the UK, Conservative MP Michael Gove defended Brexit by arguing that 'people in this country have had enough of experts'. In the United States, President Donald Trump routinely attacks the news media when they don't report favourable coverage of his administration. For instance, he once tweeted that 'any negative polls are fake news, just like the CNN, ABC, NBC polls in the election'.

Part of the problem is that people think statistics should provide an objective truth – one that can be used to definitively prove things. In fact, this is far from the case. Sometimes statistics are blatantly misused. But there are many other examples where figures can actually be interpreted in more than one way. As it turns out, statistics are sometimes as fuzzy and subjective as any other research methods.

Given this state of affairs, perhaps you can forgive Trump and Gove in the above examples. With so much bad statistics, isn't it best to just ignore them entirely? We can't trust the experts because of all the bad statistics, so surely we're better off just going with our intuition? An extra bonus of this course of action is that our views are never challenged, so we can continue believing whatever warm, fuzzy thing we want to believe.

This is one option. The problem is that it leaves us open to being manipulated and used by people who have their own, often sinister, motives. Corporations, news organisations and governments have realised that there are ways to subtly change and undermine public opinion, and to encourage people to buy a certain product, believe a certain viewpoint or vote a certain way. If we leave statistics in the gutter, and just go with our gut feelings, we leave ourselves open to those feelings being manipulated.

So what's the other option? The other option is a bit more difficult, requires a little more work and starts with reading this book. It involves learning how to understand statistics. It involves learning how to spot when statistics are done well, and when they are done poorly. It also involves reading news articles and poll results with a critical eye, and coming up with your own, sometimes subjective, fuzzy conclusions. And it involves being willing to let your preconceptions about your beliefs be challenged.

Fortunately, all this isn't as difficult as you might think. It turns out that by learning this one neat trick, you can understand everything that is written in the news and …

OK, maybe it's not that easy! But the ideas behind statistics don't need to be shrouded in complex equations and impenetrable language. Statistics are really just advanced common sense. That means there aren't any tricks that will immediately give you an answer about the world or about statistics, or about anything else. But it also means that the same abilities you have in thinking critically about other things in the world can be applied to statistics as well.

Having said that, there are patterns in the things that people often get wrong in statistics, and it is some of the more common issues that we focus on in this book. Over the course of the next 250-or-so pages, you'll see examples of statistics being used well, as well as being used badly. You'll see what people did right, and what they did wrong. And by doing so, you'll see the sorts of things that will help you spot good and bad statistics in the news and media in the future.

As a result, this book will be useful for people who want to be journalists, so they know how to report data in the news in a way that is responsible and effective. But it will also be useful to anyone that reads the news, or watches adverts, or goes on the Internet. In other words, it is potentially useful to anyone. Understanding data is not a niche thing that should be left to a few nerds in universities. It is everyone's responsibility to be able to understand the information that is thrown at us, and to critique it when it is used badly. We all need to do this to stop businesses cheating us out of money or politicians lying to us. In other words, understanding statistics helps our societies and our democracies to work properly.

That's the other thing about this book – it contains few equations. There will be some numbers, and occasionally there will be an equals sign, but for the most part we're going to tell you things in words. This is not because we think that equations are unnecessary. Sometimes, for some people, they make things easier to understand. But usually those things can be explained in words too, and that's usually better for most people who shy away from mathematics and complex equations.

Throughout this book, you'll see some boxes on a variety of different things. Some of these present examples that are relevant, but not essential, to the topic of the book. Some present interesting stories that help put some flesh on the bones of the overall points in the book. Others deal with advanced topics that many won't need or won't want to know, while some more advanced readers might like to learn more about them. So if you don't understand the content of some of these boxes, you shouldn't worry too much (but also, don't feel afraid to give them a go and see what you can get out of them!).

The rest of this introduction will give an example of bad statistics – just really a bit of fun. It will then go over what the rest of the book looks like. We hope you enjoy it!

1.1 '30,000 PIGS FLOAT DOWN THE DAWSON'

It might surprise you that, in a book about data in the media, we would start with the Rockhampton (Australia) *Morning Bulletin*. However, in February 2011, the *Bulletin* gained a brief moment of fame as a result of an unfortunate and comedic error. At the time, Queensland was struggling with flooding affecting hundreds of thousands of people, leading to the evacuation of a number of towns and cities. However, it also affected farming and livestock with, according to the *Bulletin*, 30,000 pigs being washed away from one farm alone.

Hang on, though: 30,000 pigs? In a book about being sceptical about numbers, here's a starting point. That number doesn't sound right. Even the biggest pig farms in the world have only around 2,000 animals. 30,000 pigs would, if lined up curly tail to snout, stretch about 50 km: that is, about 500 football pitches. While the image of that many pigs floating down the river is an impressive one, it is, sadly, probably implausible.

It turns out that the mistake resulted from a miscommunication between a journalist and the farmer. While the journalist had heard '30,000 pigs', the farmer had actually said '30 sows and pigs' – sows, as in female pigs! *The Morning Bulletin* issued a correction the following day.

This mistake is perhaps not the most regularly encountered data error you will ever see. But it is a reminder that not all errors are disastrous – some are just a bit funny. This isn't always the case, however. Sometimes getting statistics wrong in the media can have quite scary consequences. In this book we'll see an example where people have ended up convicted of murder because of a misunderstood statistic. We'll see that statistics can convince people to vote a certain way, meaning that misleading statistics can actively undermine democracy. And we'll see that misinterpreted statistics can be used to stir up people's prejudices and potentially increase hate crime against certain groups.

In other words, while errors in statistics can be funny, they can also be important. As we will see in this book, they can lead people with a disease to get the wrong treatment, or put an innocent person in prison. They can literally be a matter of life and death.

1.2 HOW THE BOOK PROGRESSES

This book is organised in chapters based around particular statistical ideas. However, within each chapter, there are actually very few statistics at all. The book focuses on examples which will illustrate statistical concepts in what we hope is a clear and easy-to-understand way. So, unlike a more standard statistics textbook, where you might start with a statistical method, in this book you will examine some examples, and in the process learn some statistical concepts perhaps without even realising it!

Chapter 2 asks perhaps the most basic question we need to answer when seeing a number in the news: is that a lot? It's a surprisingly difficult question to answer, and numbers can be made to seem big or small simply by changing the way they are framed. So, 0.0001 might be very big indeed, and 30 billion might, in fact, be pretty small. It all depends on the context of those numbers, and what they are measuring.

While lots of statistics books consider carefully how numbers can be manipulated once we have them, Chapters 3 and 4 take a step back and focus on how data is collected. Chapter 3 helps us think about the sources of data because some data sources are more valuable, accurate and informative than others. The chapter will help you spot bad data and consider some of the ways that people collecting data can make their data better.

Chapter 4 focuses on representativeness – that is, for data about people, how can we be sure that it's talking about the people we want it to be about? A survey of men might not tell us much about the views of women; a survey of politicians probably doesn't tell us much about the views of people in the country more widely. The chapter will help you understand how researchers try to make surveys representative, and the problems that failing to do this properly can cause.

Chapter 5 is about graphs and shows that, even if your data is accurate, a graph can mislead the person looking at it if it's designed in a certain way (either deliberately or accidentally). The chapter goes through some graphs that have been used in the news media, and shows how easily they can mislead people. It will also show you how you can avoid being hoodwinked by such graphs, by spotting some simple but subtle tricks that can make data show something that isn't there.

Chapters 6 and 7 are about the geographic representation of data, or, to put it more simply, maps. The fundamental principle underlying these two chapters is that, almost without exception, everything has a location and the numbers we see in the media relate to real-world places. A good example of this is voting patterns, which tend to cluster geographically at the neighbourhood level. So, with this in mind, Chapter 6 is based on the fundamental question of where things happen and why maps matter. We also discuss what you might want to consider *before* making the decision to map something and whether a map is the right tool in the first place. Maps are only one way to represent data and we're careful to note that they are neither value neutral nor inherently 'truthful'. Yet they remain immensely powerful, so it's important to understand them. The example of political gerry-mandering is used to make this point.

In Chapter 7 we go into more detail of why geography matters and look at slightly more complex topics such as spatial aggregation and why the geographic units we use to analyse phenomena can have a profound impact on our results. The key message we want readers to take from these chapters is that mapping matters, but also that the way we make maps can influence what they appear to show.

Numbers are often reported in the media as absolute, specific and certain values, suggesting that they cannot be questioned. But uncertainty is central to statistics, and it should be central to the way that numbers are understood. Chapter 8 focuses on uncertainty: how sure should we be about numbers in the media? It will give examples of numbers that, though reported as truthful, in fact have a lot of uncertainty, because apparent patterns can occur simply by chance.

Chapter 9 takes an example to help illustrate this. League tables are often presented in the media, both in sport and in other aspects of life (schools, universities, hospitals, and so on). They are presented as if the top-ranked team/school/university is definitely the best, the next as second best, and so on. But it's rarely clear what the assumptions underlying these league tables are, or how certain we are that the rankings are correct. Chapter 9 considers how league tables are far from objective and are often manipulated for political ends, meaning they should be interpreted cautiously.

Chapter 10 considers relationships between different things. Is a particular drug related to better health? Do parks make people happier? Does mayonnaise increase suicide? You may be sceptical about some or all of these (hopefully at least the last one!), but as it turns out, it's very difficult to say that something causes something else. Chapter 10 gives examples of news stories that assume a relationship is causal, when, actually, it's likely to have been a result of something else.

Chapter 11 considers some of the more surprising results that statistics can produce. It will show that things that sound impossible actually can be very possible indeed. A drug can be 99% effective, yet a positive test result is probably wrong? Sure. Employment rates can simultaneously be going up and going down? Yep. Two people in your class share a birthday? Almost certainly.

Finally, we sum up the book in chapter 12, by using an example that illustrates many of the concepts learned throughout the book and shows how important those concepts can be. We finish with a call for all readers to help in fighting against bad statistics and misleading uses of data in the media.

Throughout the chapters, you will learn a lot about scary-sounding statistical concepts. But this book will hopefully show that they aren't that scary. In fact, pretty much all statistical concepts can be boiled down to common-sense ideas. If the idea of statistics really fills you with dread, we hope this book will help you do something impossible (or at least, very, very unlikely): you might actually enjoy statistics!

1.3 A NOTE TO TEACHERS

This book can be used in a variety of ways in teaching both about data in the media and quantitative methods/statistics, more generally. First, it could be the core text and basis of a class in itself – indeed the structure of the course came from such a class that we run at the University of Sheffield. But it could also be used to supplement a more standard statistics course. In the main, individual chapters stand on their own, so chapters could be set readings that would help students understand *why* the concepts they are studying are relevant and important, rather than just abstract things disconnected from the real world. They could be the basis of discussions in tutorials and seminars associated with statistics courses – to get students talking about and debating statistical concepts, what they mean, and when they are relevant to the world. This is something that, in our view, is currently lacking in a lot of statistics courses, and it could be a way to increase students' critical engagement with their courses. Finally, we hope the book is an interesting read in itself, and that you, and your students, will enjoy reading it for its own sake.

2 How to make numbers sound big, or small, even when they aren't: 'Is that a lot?'

Key concepts

percentages, percentage changes, percentage point changes, gross and net figures, absolute and relative risk, measures of central tendency, measures of spread

2.1 INTRODUCTION

We live in a world full of numbers. Yet it's impossible to stay on top of all of them. So we're guided by the media to figure out which numbers we should be paying attention to.

But what does it mean to be paying attention to numbers? Understanding numbers in the media isn't simply a memory test. If the media suggest we should be paying attention to numbers, the implication is usually that the numbers are either too big or too small.

For example, the *Daily Express*, which is a British tabloid newspaper, regularly runs front-page stories about migration, with implications that numbers are either too big or too small. If you go to expressbingo.org.uk, you will see a range of front pages over a roughly nine-month period across 2013 and 2014. Among the headlines on the *Express*'s front page over this period were:

- MIGRANT BEGGARS ON £36,000 A YEAR
- 150,000 SAY NO TO NEW EU MIGRANTS
- 98% DEMAND BAN NEW MIGRANTS
- ASYLUM SEEKERS COST £1.5 MILLION A DAY

- FOREIGNERS IN £70 MILLION NHS RIP-OFF
- MIGRANT NUMBERS 'OUT OF CONTROL'
- MIGRANT NUMBERS AT CRISIS POINT

These sound like some big numbers, right? We've got five big numbers in the first five bullet points: £36,000 a year, 150,000 people saying no, 98% of people saying no, £1.5 million a day and £70 million. Finally, we've got two claims that numbers are big: out of control, and at crisis point.

However, depending on who you ask, some of these numbers might be big numbers, or they might not be a big deal at all. This might surprise some readers. Given how big these numbers appear, how could they not be a big deal?

In this chapter, we'll walk through some of the tools necessary to answer the question 'is that a lot?'. We won't address all of them straight away – for example, to get your head round '98% DEMAND BAN NEW MIGRANTS', you'll want to read Chapter 3 on how defining a sample in particular ways can get you these incredibly high numbers – but by the end of this chapter, you'll have a good sense of some of the ways in which the media can make numbers look suspiciously big or small. We won't use any of these examples from the *Express*, but if you search for any of those headlines you should be able to find them, and figure out for yourself whether any of the techniques that we'll describe have been applied.

2.2 IS THAT A LOT? IS ONE THING BIGGER THAN ANOTHER THING?

Donald Trump was inaugurated as President of the United States on 20 January 2018. That morning, he and his wife Melania attended a church service; then they travelled to the White House where they met Barack and Michelle Obama, the outgoing residents. Later that day, they participated in a swearing-in ceremony, at which Donald Trump gave a 16-minute speech. Not one to ignore controversy, the main discussion following Trump's inauguration was around the number of people who had attended the event.

Trump himself claimed it would be 'an unbelievable, perhaps record-setting turnout'. But as you might expect, it's notoriously difficult to estimate how many people there are at major unticketed events: people aren't all the same size and they move around, meaning that taking accurate counts is quite tricky. Experts estimated that there were around 160,000 people at the inauguration (Wallace and Parlapiano, 2017), although they acknowledged that this wasn't a precise estimate.

Was this an unbelievable, record-setting turnout? Let's think about it in the context of the question 'is that a lot?'. It's probably fair to change 'is that a lot?' into the more specific formulation 'did a lot of people come to Trump's inauguration?' And as Trump's own prediction was that the turnout might be 'record-setting', we might define 'a lot of people' as 'more people than there were at Obama's inauguration four, or eight, years previously'.

While estimating crowd size is a difficult task fraught with complications, you don't need to be an expert to figure out which of an empty room and a packed football stadium has more people in it. Similarly, you don't need to be an expert to compare photos of the Trump and Obama inaugurations at their peak attendance to see which one had the better turnout. Among other places, you can do this comparison yourself by looking at Hunt (2017).

The following day, the White House Press Secretary, Sean Spicer, gave an angry speech attacking parts of the media which had claimed that fewer people had come to Trump's inauguration than Obama's. Among other things, he said 'photographs of the inaugural proceedings were intentionally framed in a way, in one particular tweet, to minimize the enormous support that had gathered on the National Mall' (Politico, 2017). He also used plenty of big-sounding numbers, for example stating that 420,000 people had used the Washington, DC metro that day, compared with 317,000 people for Obama's inauguration in 2012.

As it turns out, none of these numbers was accurate, with a spokesperson, Kellyanne Conway, claiming later that Spicer's numbers constituted 'alternative facts'. Whether you believe any of these numbers or not, sometimes the way to answer 'is that a lot?' is to reframe the question as 'is that more than the other thing?'. Comparing overhead photos of the two inaugurations makes clear that more people showed up to Obama's inauguration than Trump's, and by this measure, it wasn't a big number.

However, a big number isn't just a number that's bigger than another one: there's all sorts of other ways to make a number appear big than simply to compare it with something else. (It's also not usually as straightforward to demonstrate that a number's not as impressive as it sounds by simply comparing two photos side-by-side.)

So let's get into some more ways in which we can address the question 'is that a lot?'.

2.3 IS THAT A LOT, GIVEN HOW MANY PEOPLE THERE ARE?

If you live in the UK, you'll probably see quite a few news stories about Birmingham. If you live in the United States, you'll likely see a lot of news stories about Los Angeles. If you live in Australia, you'll probably see a lot of news stories about Brisbane. If you live in France, you'll probably see a lot of news stories about Nord. And so on. By the end of this section, it'll be obvious why these are the areas you hear so much about.

For example, on 24 April 2015, a story in the British *Daily Mail* described Birmingham as 'the rat capital of the UK', with 14,182 exterminations having taken place between 2013 and 2014 (Pleasance and Rahman, 2015). On 13 April 2017, a story in the *Daily Express* described Birmingham as 'the benefits capital of the UK', with four electoral constituencies in the national top ten in terms of how many people received 'unemployment handouts' (Reynolds, 2017).

Is this a lot? While both stories describe Birmingham as some kind of capital – in both cases, probably the kind of title that the city would be keen to avoid – whether these are big numbers is not an easy thing to work out.

Let's look at the rats story first. Following the first two sentences of the story, where the author explains that Birmingham is the nation's rat capital, it explains that the pest capital (including other pests like cockroaches and wasps) of the country is Newcastle, with 5% of people having reported problems; this was followed by the City of London at 4.9%; and Knowsley at 3.4%.

But hang on: the number associated with Birmingham is in the thousands, while the other numbers are all percentages. What's going on here?

The reason why Birmingham comes up so often is that it's easy to make numbers sound big if you don't acknowledge how many people you're talking about in the first place. In the UK, administrative data like the numbers of people calling pest control, the numbers of people with particular kinds of educational qualifications, the numbers of businesses that are registered, the total volume of recycling that happens in a year, or indeed any other number of things, is measured at the *local authority* level. And when we're talking about local authorities, Birmingham has the most people – around 1.1 million of them. Second-placed Leeds has around 350,000 fewer people. So it's not surprising that Birmingham is the place where the most rats have been spotted; it's the place with by far the most people. It would be reasonable to assume that there's also a lot of people with university degrees, lots of businesses and lots of recycling in Birmingham as well.

Let's look into this a bit further. The question 'Is 14,182 rats a lot of rat exterminations?' might be better framed as 'Given Birmingham's got 1.1 million people, is 14,182 rats a lot of rat exterminations?'. The story invited us to think about percentages, so let's look at them: if we divide 14,182 by 1.1 million, we end up with a figure of around 0.013, if we multiply that by 100, we get the percentage: 1.3%.

So is it a lot? Well, the number certainly sounds less impressive as a percentage than an absolute number. While the story doesn't say so, it's likely that there are other local authorities where a higher percentage of people called pest control due to rats. But the way to make the story sound exciting is to lead with Birmingham.

Now let's contrast this with the second story, about Birmingham being 'the benefits capital of the UK'. This leads with some dramatic statements:

> In total, four areas of 'Britain's second city' feature among a league table of constituencies with the highest proportion of claimants.

> Birmingham Ladywood topped the list – with 10.3 per cent of residents receiving unemployment handouts.

Sounds bad, right? Four areas of a city being on a league table sounds like a lot of areas, and 10.3% seems like a lot of people to be claiming unemployment benefits. (There's much more to come on league tables in Chapter 9, and if you want to know more about how the rate of benefit claimants varies across the UK, see McGuinness et al., 2017.)

So, like the story about rats, this story includes both percentages and numbers. We've learned from the top of the story that over 10% of the working-age residents in the Birmingham Ladywood parliamentary constituency receive benefits; later, we're informed that 6,125 working-age people in Birmingham Ladywood receive benefits. The story then produces similar analysis for the three other constituencies in the top ten for these percentages.

Is that a lot? In the previous example the missing detail was the number of people in Birmingham, so we could put the number of rats into context. Here, there are two missing details: how many constituencies are there in total; and how many constituencies are there in Birmingham? Given it's a city with a lot of people, it shouldn't come as a surprise that there's more constituencies in the top 10 than cities with fewer people. This is particularly important as cities often have particularly rich and poor areas, and as the number of constituencies in a city increases, the differences in wealth between different constituencies also increase. (You'll read more about this in Chapter 7, where we address why the ways people draw boundaries are important.) Similarly, having four constituencies in the top ten is more dramatic if there's a million constituencies than if there's a hundred.

The missing details are as follows. There are 10 constituencies in Birmingham out of a total of 650 constituencies across the UK. So is four constituencies in the top ten a lot? Probably yes. Is it enough to describe Birmingham as the benefits capital of the UK? Probably no. While four constituencies in the top ten might be a lot, other constituencies are much lower down: Sutton Coldfield appears in 441st place.

More generally, the point here is that Birmingham is an **outlier** in terms of its size: given its population is so high compared with the rest of the local authorities in the UK, it's likely to look unusual in all sorts of ways. Similarly, Los Angeles is the county in the United States with the largest population, Brisbane is the city in Australia with the largest population, and so they tend to score high on different measures as well. (If you're surprised by this, realise that, for example, just as London is made up of several smaller local authorities, Sydney is made up of several smaller administrative cities, and so on. What constitutes an outlier is often slightly random.)

And, in this context, outliers are often interesting in all sorts of ways. But if you see a story where there's a big number, remember that the big number might be a result of the large number of people in the place you're looking at.

2.1 Cherry-picking Outliers to Make Numbers Seem Big

Large numbers of people aren't always just the numbers of people in the biggest cities, most populous countries or something else. On 10 December 2017, the *Daily Mail* contained a story about how the BBC had spent almost £13,000 on taxis on the preceding Christmas Day, Boxing Day (the day after Christmas) and New Year's Day (Joseph, 2017); £13,000 sounds like a lot of taxi fares.

So is £13,000 a lot of money on taxi fares? Maybe, maybe not. The BBC is a big organisation employing roughly 20,000 people, but the news story goes on to explain that the total was spent on only 171 taxi rides. A better question to ask is 'how much do those taxi rides cost on average?'. Well, let's see: £13,000 divided by 171 rides is £76 per taxi fare. In this context, we might conclude that £76 is more expensive than we might expect. But it's also possible that most fares were smaller than £76 and there were a few really expensive ones, or outliers, that make it seem like the BBC spent too much on taxis over that time period. It's also important to note that plenty of public transport isn't available on these days, so the numbers are likely to have been outliers in terms of how much is spent on taxis throughout the year.

This brings us back to the question 'is £13,000 a lot to spend on taxis?'. As you can see, it depends. Though it might sound like a lot of money to spend on taxis, it's probably not as big as it initially sounds.

2.4 IS THAT A LOT, GIVEN HOW MUCH TIME WE'RE TALKING ABOUT?

Healthcare can be expensive. In the UK, healthcare is free at the point of delivery – unless you choose to pay for private healthcare, doctors' appointments and hospital treatments are free. (Medicines aren't free in England, but they're heavily subsidised.) The money needed to pay for the care provided by the National Health Service (NHS) has to come from somewhere: hospitals are expensive to run, and healthcare professionals shouldn't be expected to work for free.

Discussions of how the NHS is funded involve various different strategies and elements, but one thing is constant: keeping the NHS going is expensive, and it's getting more expensive each year. In 2017–18, for example, spending on NHS England was around £110 billion. During her speech at the 2016 Conservative Party Conference, Prime Minister Theresa May claimed that the Conservatives were investing £10 billion extra into the NHS. Sounds like a lot, right? Not only is £10 billion a lot of money by anyone's standards, but it also sounds like a lot of money even in the context of the NHS, at a bit less than 10% of its annual budget (for more on this case, see Full Fact, 2018).

Well, it turns out that the £10 billion committed by the Conservatives actually corresponded to six years' worth of money. While £10 billion sounds like a lot, and like a big fraction of the NHS budget, it's not such a big deal when you look at how much money it is per year: a bit less than 2% of the annual budget, rather than the almost 10% that it looked like originally.

Amounts of money, and other big numbers, can look impressive if you sum them up into single numbers, rather than acknowledge that they're being spread out over a long time. So is £10 billion a big number? Well, it depends on how much you think the NHS should be funded, and that will depend on your own subjective view of how the world should be run. And, of course, it depends on the time period that £10 billion is covering.

2.5 COMBINING TIME AND PEOPLE

Adding numbers up over long periods isn't the only way to use time to make numbers appear big. There was another recent case where we were dealing with big numbers and thinking about weeks, rather than periods of six years. The UK voted to leave the European Union (EU) in a referendum in June 2016. The two official campaigns, Stronger In and Vote Leave, both made heavy use of numbers in the run-up to the referendum itself, but one number stuck more than any other: £350 million.

Most prominently, a bright red bus drove around the country associated with campaign events for Vote Leave, with 'We send the EU £350 million a week, let's fund our NHS instead' in huge letters on its side. It wasn't just on the side of the bus, though; the number £350 million was a major part of Vote Leave's advertising, with Boris Johnson (one of the most prominent Leave campaigners) often finding himself in front of a poster stating 'Let's give our NHS the £350 million the EU takes every week.'

In addition to being the number that stood out most during the campaign, £350 million was also one of the most argued-about issues. Obviously £350 million sounds like a lot of money; £350 million a week sounds like even more, because we can imagine how quickly it adds up. But it wasn't uncontroversial, with plenty of people arguing that it was flat wrong, or at the very least misleading in a way that shouldn't be allowed in a political campaign.

In contrast with Vote Leave's £350 million a week, Stronger In had its own campaign, claiming that the EU cost 30p per person per day. This sounds fairly straightforward, right? We've seen that you can make a number look bigger by ignoring the number of people that it covers, and by using longer rather than shorter periods of time. So it shouldn't be a surprise that Vote Leave can generate a big number by taking the total amount contributed by the UK over a week-long period, while Stronger In can generate a smaller number by dividing it by the number of people and looking at days rather than weeks.

What all these issues have in common (how many people? how much time? how much money does the NHS spend in total annually?) is that, in order to understand whether a big-sounding number is genuinely a lot or not, we need to get a sense of what the denominator is: what is it that we're dividing the big number *by*? Just consider that £10 billion might be a lot of money in absolute terms, but it's not a lot of money to give to the NHS over a six-year period. So let's delve into a bit more detail.

Around the time of the referendum, there were approximately 65 million people in the UK. So let's multiply 30p by 65 million, and then multiply that by seven days. Surely that'll get us to the same £350 million number used by Vote Leave:

$$£0.3 \times 65,000,000 \times 7 = £136.5 \text{ million}$$

Something's wrong here: £136.5 million is more money than 30p, but it's still nowhere near £350 million. This difference shows that it's not just a question of how much money goes to the EU; it means we have to start thinking about gross and net figures.

2.6 IS THAT A LOT? GROSS AND NET FIGURES

How do we reconcile these wildly discrepant numbers? To understand what's going on here, we need to unpack the difference between **gross** and **net** figures. The gross amount that the UK was sending to the EU may have been £350 million a week; this is the amount that, officially, left the UK and went to the EU.

What this gross amount doesn't take into account is the money that went from the EU to the UK. For example, the EU paid around £4.5 billion per year to the UK for public sector projects, such as social and regional development funding. However, this wasn't the only money that flowed from the EU to the UK: of the £350 million that the UK sent to the EU each week, about £100 million came straight back in the form of a rebate that had been established in the 1980s. In total, Stronger In reported that the UK's annual net contribution to the EU had been £5.7 billion in 2014. If we divide this by the number of days in a year, and the number of people in the UK, we end up with a number that's not too far away from the 30p mentioned above. Net spending on the EU from the UK, which adjusts for the money going in the other direction, was a lot less than gross spending.

Is this a lot? It's unclear whether a bus claiming the UK spends £136.5 million a week on the EU would have been much less effective than a bus with a £350 million figure instead. It's just really hard to get our heads round numbers this big. Either way, though, while Vote Leave's figures might have been misleading, it's difficult to argue that they were flat wrong. The campaign was able to make use of big numbers to make it sound as if huge amounts of money were going in a particular direction.

Anyway, gross and net figures come up all the time, and people don't always use those specific terms:

- In a business context, the distinction is often made between revenue and profit. A restaurant that sells $100,000's worth of meals in a year might sound like it's doing brilliantly (in terms of revenue), but if it's spending $50,000 on rent and $60,000 on paying staff its profit is negative, at −$10,000, and it's probably not going to stay open for very long if that continues.
- People's wages or salaries are generally advertised or described in terms of **gross pay**, which is usually the employer's contribution. **Net pay**, on the other hand, is what the employee ends up with, which is usually smaller because of tax deductions, retirement contributions and potentially many other things as well, depending on what jurisdiction the people are in.

2.7 IS THAT A LOT FOR EVERYONE?

In the examples we've looked at so far, everyone's treated equally. The adjusted figure of £350 million a week is 30p per person per day: that is, 30p for each and every person in the UK. And £13,000's worth of taxis consists of many £76 taxi rides. People either have rat infestations at home or they don't. In some instances, this is totally appropriate and gives us a good sense of whether numbers are big or small. In other instances, this kind of summary actually masks important variations within the numbers we're looking at.

Let's revisit the BBC's taxi bill over Christmas: £13,000 was paid for 171 fares, which gives us an **average** of £76 per taxi ride. But it's almost vanishingly unlikely that each and every taxi ride cost £76; what's far more likely is that there were several taxi rides that cost around £20–£30 to get people from their homes in London to BBC studios also in London, and then a small handful of far more expensive taxi journeys further afield (remember that it's Christmas, so these journeys would have been more expensive than journeys of the same distance at other times of the year).

So we need to think about **distributions**: not just how much there is in total, but how much there is for each person, state or species. An easy way to start thinking about this is to refer to two different types of average: *means* and *medians*, which you've probably heard about before. We're going to use the example of house prices; if you live in the UK, Canada, the United States, Australia, or one of the other countries in the world with an obsession about house prices, this will probably sound familiar.

In the year ending September 2017, the **median** selling price for residential properties (houses and flats) in England and Wales was £225,000 (ONS, 2018). That means half of the houses in England and Wales in that period sold for less than (or dead on) £225,000; the other half sold for more than (or dead on) £225,000. It doesn't matter whether the more expensive half of houses were sold for £225,001 or £20 million – the median will be the same.

In that same year, the **mean** selling price for houses in England and Wales was £290,347. When you add up the total amount spent on all houses in England and Wales in that year, and divide it by the number of houses that were sold, you end up with £290,347. Obviously, £290,347 is a lot more than £225,000. (How much more? We'll look into that in a few sections' time.) And there are some areas where the differences are even more stark: in Kensington and Chelsea, in London, the median selling price for houses was £1,300,000, while the mean selling price was £2,073,530. By contrast, in Luton the median selling price was £240,000 and the mean selling price was £240,350, meaning there was almost no difference at all. (There was only one area where the mean selling price was lower than the median selling price, namely Barking &

Dagenham, as a handful of properties sold for drastically lower sums of money than the median house price.)

Knowing how the mean and median house prices vary across different parts of the country might give you a flavour for how some areas are more expensive than others. But it won't tell you the cheapest place to live in the country. It also matters how much house prices differ in each area. In some places, there is a lot of **variance** (with some very cheap properties and some very expensive ones), but in others, house prices don't vary so much. While the median house price in Middlesbrough was £125,000, the **lower quartile** – the house price where a quarter of houses are cheaper and three-quarters are more expensive, unlike with medians where it's half-and-half – was just £70,000. The equivalent figures in Stevenage were £264,000 and £237,000.

Distinguishing between means and medians is important; means are often distorted by the very expensive (or very cheap), whereas medians are not. The difference between the means and medians in this case arises because of a few expensive houses that drag the mean up but do not affect the median. While this could be offset by very cheap houses, they can only be so cheap because no house costs less than £0! Because of this, it's important to know both the measure of central tendency (the mean or the median) and the measure of spread, or variance (see Box 2.2)

2.2 Central Tendency and Spread

We have discussed above measures of central tendency – means and medians being the most obvious. These give an idea of what our best guess for something is – that is, if we know nothing else, what's our best guess for how much a house costs, or how much someone earns? But we also need to think about how much variation there is around that best guess, so we can think about how sure we are.

We can measure this in a number of ways. For instance, the **range** measures the gap between the highest and lowest measure (e.g. the lowest and highest priced house). The problem with this is that if there is a really unusually expensive (or unusually cheap) house, it can distort our results and give a misleading impression of how house prices vary. An alternative might be to look at the **upper** and **lower quartile** – that is, the range within which half of all property prices lie.

Another option is the **standard deviation**: this is how far away house prices are from the mean, on average. So if we work out the distance of each house

(Continued)

> price from the mean, and take the average, it will give us the standard deviation; a big standard deviation implies more variation. Another measure you might see in the literature is variance – this is the standard deviation squared.
>
> There is another way of showing the distribution of something, and that is to draw a graph to display it. There are some examples of this in Figure 2.1 below.

But knowing about these **summary statistics** masks other important differences. Let's look at it from another recent angle. In October 2017, the White House Press Secretary, Sarah Sanders, tweeted:

> The average American family would get a $4,000 raise under the President's tax cut plan. So how could any member of Congress be against it?

At the time, the US government was indeed passing legislation to lower income taxes. Let's assume that Sanders' statement was true: that the average American family would take home $4,000 more in the year following the introduction of the legislation. Is that a lot?

Incomes are **right-skewed**, with median incomes across the world lower than mean incomes. Very few households earns less income than $0 a year; plenty of households earn incomes between $30,000 and $70,000 a year; a small handful of households earn incomes in the millions of dollars. While the numbers differ, this pattern is repeated all over the world. You can see the difference between left-skewed, so called Normally distributed and right-skewed distributions in Figure 2.1.

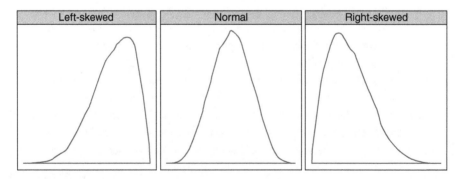

Figure 2.1   Some different distributions

So while the average (or mean) American family might take home $4,000 more in a year, it doesn't follow that half or more of the families in America will take home that much more money. What happened was that a small fraction of house-holds took home a lot more than $4,000 more each year, while most households took home a lot less. In practice, Sanders' figures might not have been inaccurate, but they were certainly misleading.

But maybe this is an issue that the Republican Party was aware of. We need to know how tax cuts affect poorer people's incomes, and not just take the average of all American families. In this context, a few months later, Paul Ryan – who was, at the time, the Speaker of the House of Representatives – tweeted:

> A secretary at a public high school in Lancaster, PA, said she was pleasantly surprised her pay went up $1:50 per week … she said [that] will more than cover her Costco membership for the year. (Stewart, 2018)

Analysis from the Tax Policy Center indicated that the top 1% of earners in the United States would take home an additional $51,000 a year. This contrast between the top 1% and a school secretary (divide $51,000 by 52 to get a direct comparison) might help to illuminate why just looking at average figures can conceal important differences. Don't just take the average, whether mean, median or **mode** (the most common number), at face value – it might mask important nuances.

On the other hand, though, we shouldn't just dismiss all summary statistics. Looking at a spreadsheet of the sales price of every single house isn't very useful if you want to get a sense of which areas are more expensive than others: knowing median house prices is more practical. Similarly, looking at a spreadsheet of every single person's income over 10 years isn't helpful if you want to get a sense of whether incomes have gone up or down over the period; again, median incomes are more helpful. Just remember that they're not telling you the whole story.

2.8 IS THAT A LOT OF *STUFF*?

Up to a point, money seems to make sense to us: 30p doesn't sound like a lot, while £350 million does. But people aren't always very good at translating amounts of money into something else.

Sometimes, however, we are. You might be pretty good at estimating how much of different foodstuffs $10 (US) could buy. In 2017, you could get about 66 eggs, 22 pounds (about 10 kg) of flour or about 8 avocados. (Grocery costs are often volatile; it's partly for this reason that the question 'How much is a pint of milk?' has caught out so many politicians when they're being interviewed.)

But sometimes we're not. On 30 January 2018, the British *Independent* (along with several other media organisations) reported that police had seized the equivalent of £50 million of cocaine from a flight to a small Hampshire airport (Wilcock, 2018). Questions had been raised about why a small jet had flown from Bogotá to Farnborough, which is an airport limited to a maximum of 49,000 flights a year, all of which are private. When people saw the news story, they generally weren't surprised to learn that a private jet flying from Bogotá to Farnborough had £50 million's worth of cocaine on it.

But is £50 million's worth of cocaine a lot? It certainly sounds like a lot. To make sense of the number, we need to understand several other things. Let's look at this list as a starting point:

- First, how expensive is cocaine? If cocaine is incredibly expensive, then £50 million's worth might not actually be that much.
- Second, how many people use cocaine in the UK? Is £50 million's worth a large fraction of the UK supply, or a drop in the ocean?
- Third, how much cocaine gets used in a single sitting? Or, to put it another way, how much is a normal amount of cocaine for a cocaine user to use?

(There are all sorts of other things we could ask: How pure is the cocaine that people tend to buy? It's likely that £50 million's worth of cocaine ends up being a much larger volume of product on the street than it is in Farnborough Airport because it'll be cut with something else. What's the markup on cocaine for dealers, and how does this compare with the markup for importers? It might be that we're looking at total retail sales of £50 million, of which the importers receive a relatively small fraction. Let's stick with these first three questions for the moment.)

In order to answer 'how expensive is cocaine?', then assuming we trust the media report that the amount seized corresponded to £50 million's worth, we can simply divide that amount of money by the amount of cocaine. It turns out that £50 million's worth of cocaine corresponds to 500 kg, or half a metric tonne. This, it turns out, is the amount of cocaine that you can squeeze into 15 large suitcases: they each contained somewhere between 34 and 37 tape-wrapped packages, on average a bit less than a kilogram of cocaine each.

So we can simply divide 50 million by 500,000 to find out how much a gram of cocaine costs: a neat, round £100.

OK, so how much cocaine gets used in the UK in general? We can refer to the Crime Survey of England and Wales (CSEW) for this (Scotland's a bit different).

The CSEW suggests that in 2016–17, around 2.3% of the population aged between 16 and 59 had used powder cocaine (as opposed to crack); the figure for people aged 16–24 was just under 5%. However, of that 2.3%, 61% of them had only used it once or twice in the preceding year (Broadfield, 2017).

Finally, how much cocaine do people take when they're taking cocaine? With alcohol, people in countries with drinking cultures often have an intuitive grasp of what's a lot: you might think six pints of beer is a lot, or a bottle and a half of wine, or six double whiskies. But how much is a lot of cocaine?

According to Drugwise, which is a charity promoting evidence-based information on a range of drugs, a 'weekend user' might use a quarter of a gram of cocaine in a session, while a heavier user might use between one and two grams a day (Drugwise, 2019). So, for the 62% of our cocaine users who use cocaine only once or twice a year, a reasonable amount of cocaine might be a quarter of a gram. This means that our 500 kg of cocaine actually corresponds to 2 million doses of cocaine (divide 500,000 by ¼). Given that 2.3% of 16–59 year olds in England and Wales have used cocaine, 500 kg is more than enough for a dose for each of them, which for many of them will be the only time they use cocaine.

So, is £50 million's worth of cocaine a lot of cocaine? Yes.

2.3 The Purity of Drugs and Why it Matters

There's more to interpreting numbers around drug use than this. In this example, we took the estimate of the value of cocaine as being £50 million at face value, but is this true? Again returning to Drugwise, it estimates that the average gram of cocaine in the UK costs £40, which is far below the £100 that you'd expect given the police estimates.

The issue here is around purity. A £40 gram of cocaine might be something that's around 40% cocaine, while an £80 gram of cocaine might be something that's around 70% cocaine. If the cocaine that was brought over from Bogotá was 100% pure, then the £50 million estimate might be about right; if it was lower than this, it might have been an exaggeration by the police.

The difficulty, of course, is that if you're buying cocaine it's almost impossible to know how pure the cocaine you're buying actually is. The effects of 40% cocaine and 100% cocaine are hugely different from one another, particularly for risks on heart damage and overdose, and this is often what puts people in danger.

You can read more about the effects of 100% cocaine in an interview with the UK government's former chief drugs advisor, David Nutt, in Usher (2017).

2.9 IS THAT A LOT *MORE* (OR LESS)?

When we're looking at whether numbers are big or not, there are different ways to express how much bigger or smaller one number is than another. Whether they're all mathematically equivalent or not, they can sound very different from one another depending on how they're reported.

We discussed the fact that healthcare is expensive. Another thing that's expensive, and that takes up a huge amount of government spending in several different countries, is defence: members of the military won't work for free, weapons are expensive, and so on.

NATO (the North Atlantic Treaty Organization, which is a military alliance), sets its member states the target of spending 2% of its GDP on defence (GDP is Gross Domestic Product – the value of goods and services produced by the country). This 2% figure might not sound like a lot, but, again, in order to make sense of whether or not 2% constitutes a lot we need to think about what GDP is in the first place: it's not 2% of overall tax revenue, or of overall government spending, it's 2% of a bigger number than that.

As it happens, NATO member states don't consistently spend 2% of GDP on defence; some spend less, some spend more. But there was a discussion on this in the UK during the financial year 2014–15; in this year, the UK spent 2.2% of its GDP on defence, but it was projected that in June 2015 this fraction would fall to 1.87% of GDP by the following year (to find out more about the UK's defence spending, see Dempsey, 2018).

Is that a big decrease? Let's start by looking at it in two different ways, which, although they sound like they might be similar, are actually very different.

As a **percentage change**, this represents a 15% drop between the two years. You can get the percentage change by *dividing* the second number by the first number: if you divide 1.87 by 2.2, you end up with 0.85. So the percentage change is −15%.

As a **percentage point change**, this represents a 0.33% change. You can get the percentage point change by *subtracting* the second number from the first number: if you subtract 1.87 from 2.2, you end up with 0.33. So the percentage point change is –0.33%. The main distinction is that a percentage change is a relative comparison, while a percentage point change is an absolute change.

There are a couple of other things to flag up here as well, though. The first is that GDP varies a great deal year-on-year across countries. So if a country's productivity shoots up over a 12-month period, it's likely that its GDP in that year will be a great deal more than it was in the previous year. Given this, if the amount spent on defence stays the same across both years (or, indeed, only slightly increases), it'll mean that the percentage of GDP spent on defence will actually fall. So a decline in defence spending from 2.2% of GDP to 1.87% of GDP doesn't necessarily mean that any less money is being spent on defence; it could be that even more money is being spent on defence, in the context of an economic boom.

So in this example, was it a lot less? You could express the change in defence spending as a 15% decrease if you were talking about a percentage change, or a 0.33% decrease if you were talking about a percentage point change. You could also look at what actually happened, and note that the UK ended up spending half a billion pounds *more* on defence in 2015–16 than it did in 2014–15, even adjusting for inflation, which ended up as a percentage increase of 1.5%! To be clear, that's a percentage increase of the number of pounds spent, not the fraction of GDP; when you look at it in terms of fraction of GDP it was negative, but if you look at it in terms of money it was positive.

So was there a big decrease in military spending? Let's run through it again:

- The percentage change in military spending as a percentage of GDP was −15%.
- The percentage point change in military spending as a percentage of GDP was −0.33%.
- The percentage change in military spending in pounds was +1.5%.
- The percentage point change in military spending in pounds … doesn't exist (because there's no GDP percentage to compare it to; the comparisons we could draw, if we wanted, are with previous years, and with other countries).

Whether you think any of these numbers is big or small, it's clear that they're all very different from one another. If you're dealing with small changes in small numbers, looking purely at percentage change can be misleading, particularly when there's a denominator involved.

Let's look at another example, where small numbers can make relative changes seem dramatically different from one another. In order to do so, we can go back to health data. If you refer back to front covers of tabloid newspapers with numbers on them, you'll see a lot of discussion of foods, pills, treatments and exercises that might either cure or cause cancer (and in some cases do both!). See Battley (2018) for a rather extensive list.

In 2012, one example that was widely reported in the global news was on computerised tomography (CT) scans. CT scans are a particular kind of x-ray to identify what's going on inside the body, and after a paper was published in *The Lancet* (Pearce et al., 2012), CNN ran with the headline 'CT scans for children linked to increased cancer risk' (Bonifield, 2012), while the BBC ran with 'CT scans on children "could triple brain cancer risk"' (Dreaper, 2012). Both stories explained that brain tumours were three times more common among people who'd had at least two CT scans in childhood, while leukaemia was three times more common among people who'd had five to ten CT scans in childhood.

If we're thinking in the language of percentage changes, then 'triple' means an increase of 200%. This sounds huge. However, in order to understand the denominator, it's important to know how many people develop brain tumours and how many people develop leukaemia. In fact, the chances of developing these cancers are very small: 0.4 children out of every 10,000 children develop brain tumours, and 0.6 children out of every 10,000 develop leukaemia.

In order to reframe these as percentages, this means that 0.004% of children develop brain tumours, and 0.006% of children develop leukaemia. Triple these numbers and, among children who've had multiple CT scans, we're looking at 0.012% of children developing brain tumours, and 0.018% of children developing leukaemia. To put it another way, the percentage point difference of developing brain tumours between those children who've had multiple CT scans and those who haven't is 0.008%; the corresponding difference for developing leukaemia is 0.012%.

Among medical professionals, **relative risk** – the difference in risk between different groups – is often described in terms of additional cases in a given-sized population. Here, this increased risk can alternatively be reported as one additional case of brain cancer and one additional case of leukaemia for every 10,000.

What should we learn from this? Describing how the frequency of rare events increases purely in terms of percentage can be irresponsible: a tiny number multiplied by three is still a tiny number. And, to be fair, this story was largely reported very responsibly in the media, which effectively balanced the fact that CT scans are associated with increased risk, and tests should only be conducted when there's an appropriate clinical justification for doing so. In these cases, the benefits generally outweigh the risks (Cancer Research UK, 2012).

2.10 IS THAT A LITTLE?

Most of the numbers that we see in the media are big numbers, and we should be sceptical about whether they really are big numbers or not.

But this doesn't just include news media. If you watch TV news (and it's not on the BBC), read any news sources online (and you don't have an ad-blocker activated), or ever read a newspaper, you'll be exposed to advertising. It's easy to forget how central advertising is to the media.

When a product's being advertised, it makes sense to make it look as cheap as possible. Not in the sense of 'low quality', but in the sense of making the price look like a small number. If the price is small, then buying whatever it is isn't a big deal, right? This applies whether it's a big-ticket item or not: whether it's a toothbrush, a weekly shop, a holiday, a phone, a car or any other kind of miscellaneous widget.

It's hard to manipulate the presentation of the cost of a toothbrush. But it's common to manipulate the presentation of the costs of other items. This partly involves using some techniques we've seen before, but there are other things which can be brought in as well; if an advertiser combines lots of different approaches, that's one way to make numbers seem smaller.

The most vivid example of this is in car sales. Cars are advertised very differently in different countries; in the UK, it's most common to see what's referred to as a sticker price in car advertising. A sticker price is the amount of cash you need to take the car away that day – no finance, no complications. (Of course, sticker prices generally increase quickly once people start adding customisations and so on. The advertised price is often the most basic version of the car it's possible to get.)

In the United States, the way in which prices of cars are advertised is very different. We recently looked at a car commercial during a fairly ordinary break on a major news station there. In this commercial, the most prominent figure was $659: the voice-over, and a very visible number on the screen, explained that the cost of the car was just $659 per month.

Sure, $659 per month doesn't sound as much money as a car could be otherwise. But in order to make sense of whether $659 a month is a lot of money or not, the first key thing to identify is how many months you'd have to pay: $659 a month for six months is clearly a lot less money than $659 for six years.

In this case, the commitment was for $659 per month for a period of three years, hence a total of $23,724.

But that's not all: in the small print were the words 'with total due at lease signing of $4,954'. This means we're ending up looking at $4,954 + $23,724, which is $28,678.

Is that a lot? Maybe, maybe not, but it's certainly a lot more than $659. Dividing up a total cost so that you're looking only at the spend per month makes numbers look smaller; playing down the initial total that you have to spend means you're emphasising net figures rather than gross figures. In this case, the gross figures are the most important ones, as you're still having to pay them.

This is echoed in all sorts of different ways in other examples. It's easy to make numbers look smaller by dividing them by number of months – and it's even easier if you divide them by numbers of days: one health insurance supplier in the UK refers to its prices as 'from £1.15 per day'. It's easy to make numbers look smaller by leaving out the expensive parts.

2.11 CONCLUSIONS

Lots of big-sounding numbers aren't that big when you put them in context; lots of small-sounding numbers end up pretty big when you take the rest of the context into account. In this chapter, we've aimed to give you some of the tools to use when you're presented with a big- or small-sounding number, in order to provide the necessary context to make sense of them. This involves working with a few fairly straightforward statistical concepts, such as outliers, gross and net figures, different kinds of change, and absolute and relative risk.

The next thing to think about is whether these numbers are meaningful in the first place. Sometimes we're spooked by numbers because they seem suspiciously big or small, and the way to understand what's going on is to interrogate the numbers themselves a bit more, and that's what we've been addressing here. At other times, though, the sizes of the numbers themselves aren't the problem: just because something's numeric doesn't mean it's correct. There are plenty of techniques to generate dodgy statistics, and these often happen before the numbers even appear; under those circumstances, the techniques we've discussed in this chapter aren't as relevant as they might sound.

The truth is that often numbers aren't definitely big, or definitely small, and they depend on our own beliefs and political inclinations. For some people, £10 billion extra to spend on the NHS might be far too much. For others, it might be not nearly enough. The point is that it is easy to manipulate numbers so they sound extra-big or extra-small. Hopefully, this chapter will help you spot when this has happened, so you can make up your own mind.

2.12 CONCEPTS LEARNED IN THIS CHAPTER

An **outlier** is a case that's wildly different from the others in a dataset. Examples include: someone who's 2.5 metres tall in a group of people who are close to average height; someone earning millions of dollars per year from their main job in a group of people who are paid close to the median; and a country with a GDP of more than $100,000 per head.

A **gross figure** is a figure that doesn't include any deductions. For example, gross pay is the amount paid to an employee by an employer and doesn't adjust for tax.

A **net figure** is a figure that includes deductions. For example, someone's net pay is the amount of money that they actually receive once they've been paid and tax has been deducted.

The **mean** of a set of numbers is what you end up with when you add them all up, and divide by the number of them that there are. For example, the mean salary in a country is what you end up with if you add up everyone's salaries, and divide by the number of people earning salaries. It's often referred to as the **average**.

The **median** is another type of average. The median of a set of numbers is the number in the middle when they're ranked. For example, the median salary is the salary that's more than what half the salary earners are paid, and less than what the other half of the salary earners are paid.

The **mode** (also a type of average) is the most common number in a set of numbers. For example, the modal hourly wage is the hourly wage that the largest number of people are paid, which is often the minimum wage.

A **distribution** is set of the values in a given dataset. Some distributions include the following:

- A Normal distribution is often referred to as a bell curve, with lots of observations distributed evenly around the mean with the same number above it as below. Examples include adult women's heights. In a perfectly Normal distribution, the mean will equal the median. Note that, despite its name, a Normal distribution isn't 'normal' and often we'd expect data to be distributed in other ways.
- A skewed distribution has more values at one end, with some outliers at the other end. Examples include the income distribution: this is a right-skewed distribution, with outliers on the right-hand side.
- A bimodal distribution is like a normal distribution, but with two peaks rather than one. Examples include the number of cars on the road throughout the day: peaks tend to come as people are travelling both to and from work.
- A uniform distribution is flat, with equal numbers of observations all the way along the distribution. Examples include how frequently different numbers are in winning lottery numbers.

Summary statistics is a generic term for some of the statistics that describe a distribution. The summary statistics for a continuous variable might be the mean, median, mode, minimum (smallest value) and maximum (largest value).

A **percentage** reports a number out of 100. For example, 59.5% of Germans report being Christian.

A **percentage change** reports how much a number has increased or decreased on a previous observation in relative terms. For example, if the UK changes its spending on defence from 2.2% of GDP to 1.87% of GDP, the percentage change is a decrease of 15%.

A **percentage point change** reports how much a number has increased or decreased on a previous observation in absolute terms. For example, if the UK changes its spending on defence from 2.2% of GDP to 1.87% of GDP, the percentage change is a decrease of 0.33%.

Absolute risk is the fraction of a group in which a given event occurs, and it's a term commonly associated with medicine and comparing different groups. For example, the risk of getting lung cancer is greater among smokers than it is among non-smokers. The difference in absolute risk between the two groups is the fraction of smokers who get lung cancer, minus the fraction of non-smokers who get lung cancer.

Relative risk involves dividing the absolute risk of a given outcome for one group by the absolute risk of that same outcome for a second group. So the relative risk of getting lung cancer for smokers, compared with non-smokers, is the fraction of smokers who get lung cancer divided by the fraction of non-smokers who get lung cancer.

Quartile are the values at a quarter, half and three-quarters of the way through a distribution. So, the lower quartile is the value for which a quarter of the distribution lies below it and three-quarters above it. The upper quartile is the value for which three-quarters lie below it, and a quarter above it. The middle quartile is another word for the median value. The interquartile range is the gap between the upper and lower quartile.

The **standard deviation** is the average amount that a measure is away from its mean.

The **variance** is the square of the standard deviation.

2.13 QUESTIONS FOR CLASS DISCUSSION

1   Pick one of the headlines from the *Daily Express* listed at the start of the chapter, and search for the original story online. If you're able to find it (and if you're not, try a different one), read the original story. Having done so, is the number in the headline a big number? Why, or why not? Have any of the techniques in this chapter been used to make the number look unusually big?

2   Find a news story that's been published online today where the headline features a number, and read the story in full, also making a note of any numbers the story might include. First, rewrite the headline so that the number sounds as dramatic as possible, using as many techniques from this chapter as you can. Second, rewrite the headline again so that the number sounds as unremarkable as possible, again using as many techniques from this chapter as you can. How different do the three headlines (including the original one) look?

FURTHER READING

Dilnot, A. and Blastland, M. (2008) *The Tiger That Isn't: Seeing Through a World of Numbers*. London: Profile.

Greenhalgh, T. (2010) *How to Read a Paper: The Basics of Evidence-Based Medicine*. Oxford: Wiley-Blackwell.

Spiegelhalter, D. and Blastland, M. (2014) *The Norm Chronicles: Stories and Numbers about Danger*. London: Profile.

REFERENCES

Battley, P. (2018) Kill or cure? Available at http://kill-or-cure.herokuapp.com/a-z/a

Bonifield, J. (2012) CT scans for children linked to increased cancer risk. CNN, 6 June. Available at http://thechart.blogs.cnn.com/2012/06/06/ct-scans-for-children-linked-to-increased-cancer-risk/comment-page-1/

Broadfield, D. (2017) Drug misuse: findings from the 2016/17 Crime Survey for England and Wales. Home Office. Available at https://assets.publishing.service.gov.uk/gov ernment/uploads/system/uploads/attachment_data/file/642738/drug-misuse-2017-hosb1117.pdf

Cancer Research UK (2012) Repeated childhood CT scans increase risk of cancer in adulthood. News report, 7 June. Available at www.cancerresearchuk.org/about-us/cancer-news/news-report/2012-06-07-repeated-childhood-ct-scans-increase-risk-of-cancer-in-adulthood

Dempsey, N. (2018) UK Defence Expenditure. House of Commons Library Briefing Paper. Available at http://researchbriefings.files.parliament.uk/documents/CBP-8175/CBP-8175.pdf

Dreaper, J. (2012) CT scans on children 'could triple brain cancer risk'. BBC News, 7 June. Available at https://www.bbc.co.uk/news/health-18342867

Drugwise (2019) Cocaine and crack. Available at https://www.drugwise.org.uk/cocaine-and-crack/

Full Fact (2018) Spending on the NHS in England. Full Fact. Available at https://fullfact.org/health/spending-english-nhs/

Hunt, E. (2017) Trump's inauguration crowd: Sean Spicer's claims versus the evidence. *The Guardian*, 22 January. Available at https://www.theguardian.com/us-news/2017/jan/22/trump-inauguration-crowd-sean-spicers-claims-versus-the-evidence

Joseph, A. (2017) BBC racked up nearly £13,000 on taxis for workers in just three days last Christmas. Mail Online, 10 December. Available at https://www.dailymail.co.uk/news/article-5164611/BBC-racked-13-000-taxis-workers-Christmas.html

McGuinness, F., Powell, A. and Brown, J. (2017) People claiming unemployment benefits by constituency, July 2017. House of Commons Library Briefing Paper. Available at https://researchbriefings.parliament.uk/ResearchBriefing/Summary/CBP-8075

ONS (Office for National Statistics) (2018) House price statistics for small areas in England and Wales: year ending September 2017. Available at https://www.ons.gov.uk/peoplepopulationandcommunity/housing/bulletins/housepricestatisticsforsmallareas/yearendingseptember2017

Pearce, M. S., Salotti, J. A., Little, M. P., McHugh, K., Lee, C., Kim, K. P., Howe, N. L., Ronckers, C. M., Rajaraman, P., Craft, A. W., Parker, L. and Berrington de González, A. (2012) Radiation exposure from CT scans in childhood and subsequent risk of leukaemia and brain tumours: a retrospective cohort study. *The Lancet*, 380(9840), 499–505. Retrieved from http://dx.doi.org/10.1016/S0140-6736(12)60815-0

Pleasance, C. and Rahman, K. (2015) Revealed: Britain's capitals of vermin – Birmingham is worst for rats but Southwark has the most mice, roaches and bed bugs. *Daily Mail*, 24 April. Available at https://www.dailymail.co.uk/news/article-3053576/Newcastle-pest-infested-place-UK-living-Tyneside-likely-call-exterminator-bug-numbers-reach-record-levels.html

Politico (2017) Transcript of White House press secretary statement to the media. Politico, 21 January. Available at https://www.politico.com/story/2017/01/transcript-press-secretary-sean-spicer-media-233979

Reynolds, M. (2017) REVEALED: The benefits capital of Britain, according to these new figures. *Daily Express*, 13 April. Available at https://www.express.co.uk/news/uk/791651/Benefits-capital-of-UK-Britain-Birmingham-unemployment-handouts-ONS-figures

Stewart, E. (2018) Paul Ryan tweets – then deletes – brag about public school worker who saw $1.50 pay raise. *Vox*. Available at https://www.vox.com/policy-and-politics/2018/2/3/16968502/paul-ryan-costco-tax-bill-tweet-twitter

Usher, T. (2017) What 100 percent pure cocaine actually does to you. Vice, 23 May. Available at https://www.vice.com/en_uk/article/zmbkay/what-100-percent-pure-cocaine-actually-does-to-you

Wallace, T. and Parlapiano, A. (2017) Crowd scientists say women's march in Washington had 3 times as many people as Trump's inauguration. *The New York Times*, 22 January. Available at https://www.nytimes.com/interactive/2017/01/22/us/politics/womens-march-trump-crowd-estimates.html

Wilcock, D. (2018) UK Border Forces find £50 million-worth of cocaine at small Hampshire airport on private jet from Colombia. *The Independent*. Available at https://www.independent.co.uk/news/uk/crime/cocaine-smuggling-arrests-50-million-private-jet-uk-border-force-drugs-farnborough-airport-bogota-a8185366.html

3 Recognising which numbers you should trust: 'Where is data from?'

Key concepts

population, administrative data, study units, sample, survey respondents, sampling frame

3.1 INTRODUCTION

How do you know when to trust data presented in the media? Whether we're talking about the written press (remember that?), radio talk shows with experts, or even social media like Twitter or Facebook, many people are sceptical of what's presented by the news media. In a 2016 *Eurobarometer* survey measuring public opinion across Europe, the country whose population most distrusted the written press was the UK, with 72% saying that they tend not to trust it, followed by residents of Russia and Greece, with 64% and 63% remaining sceptical, respectively. Overall, across Europe, the most trusted news medium is radio with almost 60% across all countries saying they trust it. The least trusted source of news is social media: almost 60% claim that they tend not to trust them.

We live in a digital society. Every day 2.5 quintillion bytes of data are created (which is 10 to 18th power), 90% of it in just the last two years. This also means that there's more and more numerical data out there. But having lots of data is not helpful when you don't know where that data is from. And if you don't know your data source and how it was created, it's impossible to assess the quality of data you are dealing with.

In this chapter readers will learn how to recognise a high-quality dataset, and how to know who is being asked questions in a survey. The chapter will start with the importance of looking at the source of the data first. We'll follow this up with a critical examination of related concepts, such as a population, a sample and a survey. We'll then reflect at more length on how to conduct a survey properly. Once we know where data comes from and what the 'sample' of the study is, we'll be able to reflect on the limitations of different data sources – such as censuses, administrative data and so-called 'Big Data' – in terms of who is included in the data and how those people were measured.

3.2 DON'T TRUST THIS NUMBER, IF …

Imagine you're walking down the street, and you notice a piece of paper on the pavement. For whatever reason, you decide to pick it up and find that it describes something rather interesting: it reveals what appears to be inside information that – if true – could make you a lot money. Unfortunately, the paper is torn, so you can't identify the source of the information. Would you trust it? How much of your own money would you be willing to gamble on this partial information? We suspect that you'd need to verify the source because there's no way to be sure that it contains real and reliable information. But how many times in TV or print news have you encountered such information, such as percentages, without any mention of a data source? You'd probably hesitate to believe information found on the street, yet a lot of people believe data reported online or in print media without knowing where it came from.

When thinking about whether data is worth your attention, the *first* rule of thumb is don't trust any numbers that don't reveal the source of the data. The source of the data tells you plenty of things about the numbers you look at, and will help you to make an informed decision about whether the way data is used to support an argument in a news story makes sense and is likely correct.

Reputable data sources generally include public institutions (though it depends on the country) such as a governmental agency or statistical authority. Of course, we might not always trust a governmental agency (again it depends on the government and how independent the agency is), but in general, in most developed countries, 'official' sources tend to be reliable. We'd probably also trust data reported by a respectable research company (some examples of reputable organisations are Gallup, Ipsos MORI, YouGov and the Pew Research Center). Such companies have well-developed data quality procedures applied to all data collection and reporting (although that doesn't mean they get it right all the time!). But we should be sceptical if a data source is an unknown institution, generated via social media, or created by a source with a dubious reputation (perhaps an organisation with particular political leanings). We might also be sceptical of some government sources that are known to use state-run news to influence the opinions of people both inside and outside their country.

At its most extreme, information published by satirical newspapers is sometimes picked up by the mainstream media and reported as if it was real. This was the case with a satirical piece in *The Onion* in September 2012 (just before the US presidential election), where the paper made up a poll by Gallup showing American voters were more favourable towards Iranian president Mahmoud Ahmadinejad than Barack Obama. Despite the dubiousness of the source, Iran's state-run news agency Fars News reported this poll as real! If anything shows the importance of checking the source of your data before using it, this does (*The Onion*, 2012).

The *second* rule of thumb is: don't trust data if you don't know when it was conducted. Data is dynamic – measurements at different points in time are likely to produce different results. So knowing when your data is collected is essential if you want to know what the data really means.

People's opinions and attitudes change over time, so whenever data is reported it's necessary to check whether or not the information is up to date. For example, when measuring voting intentions before elections, research companies often get volatile results when asking people who they plan to vote for early in the campaign. It's often only in the few days before an election that results become more precise, as people form their final opinions. As such, it's important to monitor voting intentions in the last few days before the election, and even then some portion of voters might change their mind at the last minute. In some countries, such as France and Italy, polling is banned in the last few days before an election. This is an attempt to reduce the influence that polling can have on the way people vote.

Let's look at the UK General Election in June 2017. According to the BBC poll tracker, the advantage of the Conservative Party was very large at the beginning of May and polling companies estimated that the party would get 46 to 49% of the votes while Labour would receive 29 to 32%. From mid-May – as the BBC reported – the race tightened, and on 7 June, a day before the election, the estimates were between 41 to 46% and 33 to 40%, respectively. The final outcome had the Conservatives winning 43% of votes, while Labour won 41%. The initial results weren't wrong, necessarily. But they were out of date by the time the actual election came around.

It's worth reiterating that even if the source of the data is trustworthy, and timely, we still shouldn't trust everything that is said about it. Surveys can still be misinterpreted and presented in misleading ways. So perhaps the *third* rule of thumb is: don't trust data if you don't know how it was constructed and then interpreted. What we mean here is that you should look into the original research report and often also check the original wording used. The same data tables might be interpreted very differently by different journalists and, when some results are taken out of context from the whole study, what is reported might be misleading. Any information, even when based on numerical data, might be framed very differently in different media reports. For example, in February 2017 the *Daily Mail* reported the results of a study of people who are single in America, and claimed that 'Android users are 15 times more likely to judge someone negatively for having an iPhone, while Apple users are 21 times more likely to turn their noses up at an Android user' (Roundtree, 2017). This headline isn't wrong, and the data is from a well-constructed survey. But the interpretation is somewhat misleading because the vast majority of both Android and iPhone users didn't care what phone their partner used! (See Chapter 2 for more on absolute and relative risk, and how easily such statistics can be summoned up.)

So even results coming from a reputable source can be interpreted in a way that is unintentionally deceptive. Without knowing how the opinion was measured in the source, and in this case the large numbers of apathetic participants ignored by the *Daily Mail* headline, we can't make this judgement ourselves – we need to dig deeper into the results themselves.

3.3 TYPES OF NUMERICAL DATA

The next step in deciding whether to trust data or not is checking what type of data it is. Different data types will cover different populations, so the information they represent might not be relevant for all people in a country or a city, but only for some of them. You have already seen in this book some examples of different kinds of data. We discuss some of these now.

3.3.1 Survey

Having already used words like 'surveys' and 'respondents', we should be clear about what the words mean. A **survey** is a way of collecting information from people, about them, their families, or the organisations they work in. You can ask questions about people's lives, who they are, what they do, or what their preferences are. More importantly, you can ask people about things that are generally unobservable, like how they feel about a particular political issue, how worried they are about crime in their neighbourhood, or whether they feel their country is moving in the right direction. People can be interviewed face to face, over the telephone, or answer questions on their own – online or on paper (we'll talk more about these issues in Chapter 4). We call people who are interviewed **respondents**.

Information is collected using a predetermined questionnaire – if the survey is conducted well, respondents are usually asked questions in the same way, using the same wording, to try to make sure they think about the same experiences or behaviours while answering the questions. In most surveys people are presented with a number of options in response to each question, meaning that respondents are offered the same set of responses to choose from. Occasionally, open-ended questions are asked and participants are invited to write a response in a text box. This standardisation of questions and answers is necessary to make it more likely that the responses from different people measure the same thing. Finally, survey responses are converted into numbers which can be summarised, compared and statistically analysed.

3.3.2 Census and Other Official Statistics

A census is another way of collecting information about a population – it is a survey that contains all members of the population of interest. A census can get responses from nearly all residents of a region (e.g. a nation), or across all units of an institution (e.g. all schools). Because censuses measure everyone, we know that the sample matches the target population, because it is the target population, at least in theory. Just as in a survey, a census asks questions in a standardised way, translates them into numerical data, and provides data about the population.

Many countries have a regular population census, where every five (e.g. Australia) or 10 years (e.g. in many European countries and the United States) all residents are asked the same questions at around the same time: about their housing conditions, health, what they do, what their ethnic identity is, what languages they speak at home, and so on. This information is then recorded as geographic information so it can later be mapped, aggregated by neighbourhoods, cities, regions, and for the whole country.

Population censuses in Europe started in the eighteenth century, but some forms of censuses were present in Pharaonic Egypt, ancient Rome, and China during the Han Dynasty (Andres, 2012). Nowadays most European countries record very similar information in population and housing censuses, and you can access the data via the 'CensusHub' Eurostat webpage (see: https://ec.europa.eu/CensusHub2/). In the UK the most recent census, at the time of writing this book, took place in 2011, and before that every 10 years since 1801, except for 1941, which was cancelled due to the Second World War. In the United States censuses are also conducted every 10 years, and the last census was in 2010. The first American census took place in 1790 in some states. The population was classified into several categories: free white males of 16 years old and over, free white males under 16 years old, free white females, all other free persons, and slaves (go and explore it online yourself: https://www.census.gov/history/www/through_the_decades/overview/1790.html). The US census is mandated by the Constitution, as population size is used to determine the members allocated to each state in the US House of Representatives.

This is not to say that censuses don't sometimes miss some groups of people in practice. It is very difficult for census organisers to track down people without a permanent address, like those in nomadic communities, or the homeless. Usually there are special procedures developed to count people in shelters and rough sleepers, but some are likely to be missed. Other groups might not want to, or won't be able to, complete a census – for example, undocumented immigrants, or people who cannot read. If all addresses are included in the sample, the census is likely to be incomplete. Despite the gaps in the census being usually small groups (and tiny numbers compared with gaps in other types of surveys), they are usually groups that are in some way marginalised, so it is a problem if they are not counted (both literally and figuratively). Censuses provide very high-quality information, but it would be foolhardy to suggest it is perfect. Think about that US census in 1790. Classifying individuals as either free or slaves is of course highly problematic by today's standards. Who knows what those conducting a census in the year 2200 will think looking back at today's census?!

3.3.3 Administrative Registers

Administrative data is collected not for the purpose of research itself, but for keeping records by governmental departments and agencies. This involves educational registers, health and patient registers, business registers, court records, tax records, vehicle registrations, bankruptcy records, and so on. Like census data, administrative datasets cover entire populations (in fact they are often used as sampling frames for surveys). The way they differ from censuses and surveys is that they're not purposely collected to understand the population, but to keep records of some events happening, often related to some citizens' responsibilities, like paying taxes or registering a car. The data is usually quite accurate – for the most part it's in the government's interests for the data to be correct! But it won't necessarily tell you everything you want to know.

For example, the UK's Department of Work and Pensions (DWP), for example, collects information on individuals claiming some form of benefits (such as Housing Benefit and Jobseeker's Allowance). This is not, however, the same thing as unemployment, so the number of people claiming benefits for being out of work will be different from measures of unemployment estimated using a survey. Those claiming benefits are not all seeking work, so may not classify themselves as unemployed (as it is often defined) in a survey, while not all those who are unemployed claim benefits. Indeed, the DWP's administrative data shows that 1.4% claim Jobseeker's Allowance, while the UK's Labour Force Survey finds 4.3% to be unemployed (in August 2017). The two figures are measuring slightly different things, and should not be used interchangeably. If a journalist wants to write about people claiming benefits, the 1.4% might be a more useful figure. If they want to write about the state of the economy, 4.3% is probably a more useful figure.

3.3.4 Big Data

Online data and transactional data, which are generated digitally, have recently risen to prominence under the broad umbrella of 'Big Data'. It constitutes data of huge volume, high velocity (created in near real time) and great diversity (Kitchin, 2014). Like administrative data, Big Data is not generated by asking people questions, but by recording people's actions, which are automatically saved as digital traces, like clicks, shares or likes on social media, purchases online or in shops, geographic location (recorded with a phone's GPS), or urban traffic data collected by monitoring devices. Big data can come from many very different sources and be used in a range of different ways (making it a somewhat questionable term – everyone has a different idea of what makes data big!). Some of such data is open and free to use by anyone, such as Google Trends data (what people search) or tweets from public accounts, but some is not free to use (e.g. Facebook data).

Big Data is often seen as an alternative to surveys – and it has many advantages. It's very cheap to collect (you don't need to hire an interviewer) and provides an often massive sample size. It's used heavily by commercial companies that want to know about customers' shopping patterns. Big Data is sometimes used to find things out about society as well. For example, trends in what people search for on Google have been used as a measure of how important certain political issues are. That is, if individuals are searching for certain words (say, 'Jobseeker's Allowance') it can tell us something about society (e.g. that there are lots of unemployed people, or the economy is performing poorly) (Mellon, 2013). It has also been used to track trends in the flu, by following when people are searching for particular search terms related to symptoms of the flu. This is great, and particularly impressive given that such data is completely free to use, publicly available and immediate, making it potentially more useful than official sources of data that take a long time to be processed and published.

But despite its size, there are things that Big Data will never be able to do as well as a good old-fashioned survey. When using Big Data, the **target population** is unknown and cannot be easily controlled. Not everyone uses Google; not everyone uses loyalty cards; not everyone is on Twitter. So if we want to know the state of play among everyone in a country or in the world, Big Data will not be able to tell us, even with the increasingly complex algorithms that are used by data analysts to correct for such things. Often it would be used as a last resort, when surveys were simply too expensive to run. In that case, an appropriate amount of scepticism should be given to such results.

For instance, if you want to predict the result of an election, it is unlikely that Big Data will provide an accurate answer – a carefully conducted poll is more likely to be effective. However, if you are interested in the results of hundreds of separate elections (e.g. Congressional races in the United States), it would not be practical to conduct separate surveys for each one, and it might be that Big Data is the best option available to you. But its being the best option doesn't mean the results it produces will be correct!

Big Data also opens up new questions about the ethics of holding data and using it for ways that it was not originally intended. With surveys, participants should be made aware of what the data will be used for. But when someone searches for something on Google, they do not intend for it to be used by governments, political parties or commercial companies. Despite the limits of Big Data, it has the potential to be very powerful, and that's a problem if that power is used unfairly, or against certain groups. These are issues that are still being grappled with and will continue to be thought about over the coming years as Big Data is used more and more.

3.4 POPULATIONS AND SAMPLES

At this point, we are going to focus on survey data. Survey results are notoriously misreported in media reports. Often, this is caused by a misconnection between what population the news story talks about and what population the survey refers to.

In January 2016 *The Independent*, a British daily newspaper, published an article entitled 'Over a third of students "no longer wish to study medicine" amid the junior doctors' contract row, says poll'. The article read:

> The Student Room – which houses the largest online community of medical students in the UK – recently surveyed almost 1,550 students to find 37 per cent who had once hoped to study medicine have now said they no longer wish to do so as a result of health secretary Jeremy Hunt's proposed contract changes and the industrial action being taken by dissatisfied staff.

This all sounds very serious – 37% of students that originally wanted to study medicine have changed their minds after some proposed changes to doctors' contracts. Should we be worried that in future there won't be enough medical staff in the NHS in the UK? If fewer young people are interested in studying medicine – as this poll would suggest – the NHS might face staff shortages when those students would have graduated.

You might already have guessed that there's something wrong with the way the poll is presented. Respondents were recruited via an online community of medical students. Not all students (nor students interested in studying medicine) are registered on the site: from the webpage of the Student Room we find out that around 70% of students use the site every year (The Student Room, 2017), meaning at least 30% are excluded straight away, and that's if we believe the website's description of its users (which we arguably shouldn't). It might be that this 30% have very different views than those interviewed and active on the portal. We also don't know the proportion of current or future medical students (how could we know that?) that use the portal.

Most tellingly, *The Independent* refers to students who 'had once hoped to study medicine', while the interviews were actually conducted with those who were *registered on the Student Room*. These are very different populations; although those registered on the portal might also be potential medical students, their characteristics and opinions are probably different from those of prospective medical students who have never been on the site. Not only that, but many in the sample might never have chosen to study medicine, regardless of the contracts that would end up on as doctors if they did. If we wanted to research medical students in general we would have to first establish who we are talking about. That is, the target population or the people we intend to study.

We know that 1,550 people were interviewed. This is the number of people who agreed to take a part in a study, known as **respondents**. Those who were invited to the study form a sample. A **sample** is a fraction of the population you intend to study, a smaller set of people who are invited to a survey. Your *achieved* sample is the respondents you ended up with (confusingly, this group is also sometimes called a 'sample'). The proportion of those who were invited to the study who actually agree to take part is the **response rate**. In the case of prospective medical students surveyed via the Student Room we don't know how many were invited to fill out the survey. We also don't know how many refused or ignored the invitation. And we don't know if those who refused are different from the survey respondents. If only 1% of medical students filled out the survey, the chance that those 1% are unusual in some way is quite high. For example, people who use the website heavily might have been more likely to respond, and it might be that those people are, for example, richer than those who use the website less often. Students with a more negative opinion about the proposed reforms, or students less likely to study medicine anyway, in the media might have been more likely to take part in the survey. We really don't know, and that's a problem if we want to know what the survey results really mean.

So what should The Student Room have done to make its survey more useful? Before conducting any survey, it should have clearly defined the target population of students.

Specifically:

- Who they are: what are their characteristics? (In this case, the survey is aiming to survey prospective medical students, but that is a difficult group to define, and doesn't match The Student Room users.)
- Where they live or are based, which could be a country, a region or a group of specific neighbourhoods (The Student Room is mainly used by UK students, so foreign students might be missed).
- What time period the survey covers (e.g. The Student Room survey gave a single snapshot of time).

The problem with The Student Room Survey is that it didn't consider that the website does not reach the population it wants to: namely, aspiring medical students.

Once a population has been identified, researchers will use this to draw a sample from that population. These individuals are selected from a list, known as **a sampling frame**, of the whole population. This list is never perfect: it might be a list of addresses, or registered voters, or employees. Some examples can be found in Box 3.1.

3.1 Some Examples of Surveys

Table 3.1 provides details on three different surveys, where **study units** are individuals, households or companies. The American Community Survey is an ongoing survey that has been conducted since January 2005 to provide up-to-date estimates of the population across the entire United States. It's used by government to distribute funds depending on people's needs, such as planning labour market policies and building new schools or hospitals. The General Lifestyle Survey in Great Britain is smaller in size and collects information on the lifestyle and behaviour of the adult population: smoking, drinking, access to vehicles, or general health. Finally, the European Company Survey is conducted by one of the EU agencies, Eurofound, but fieldwork is carried out by a range of agencies in Europe. Study units are companies across the 28 EU countries (including the UK) as well as Iceland, the Former Yugoslav Republic of Macedonia, Montenegro and Turkey.

Table 3.1   Examples of sample designs

	American Community Survey 2016	General Lifestyle Survey 2011	European Company Survey 2013
Who conducted the survey	US Census Bureau	Office for National Statistics in the UK	Eurofound, European Foundation for the Improvement of Living and Working Conditions
Target population	All ages, regardless of legal status or citizenship, living in US and Puerto Rico at a given address for at least two months	People and households in the UK, defined as adults aged 16+ living in private households and students in halls of residence	Businesses and other organisations – including the public sector – with 10 or more employees, in 32 countries covered by the survey
Sampling frame(s)	The Master Address File, Census Bureau's official inventory of known housing units, group quarters, and selected non-residential units in the US and Puerto Rico	Postcode sectors are drawn first and then addresses within sectors	National business registers of companies or establishments
Drawn sample or response rate	3,527,047 housing units and 206,415 group quarters were selected	11,381 addresses were selected	Response rate 34%, from 18 to 71% per country
Achieved sample	2,229,872 housing units and 160,572 group quarters	7,960 households and about 15,000 individuals	300–1,650 per country, 30,113 interviews with management and 9,094 with employee representatives

Sources: Gallup (2013); ONS (2013); US Census Bureau (2014).

The aim of the sampling frame is to provide the best possible coverage of the target population. This was badly achieved in the medical students example discussed above. The Student Room membership list was chosen as a sampling frame, and many prospective medical students were not included in it, whilst many who might never have studied medicine were included. But no sampling frame is perfect – they all exclude some in the target population. The dashed line in Figure 3.1 represents a sampling frame which misses many members of the target population, but also contains many people who are not of interest to the study, so doesn't cover the population well (Sampling frame 2). Yet, even a fairly good sampling frame might miss some important groups (Sampling frame 1), and whether or not it will represent the population well, depends greatly on how the sample is constructed.

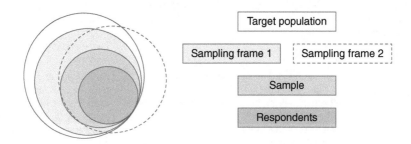

Figure 3.1   Diagram showing how respondents end up being only a proportion of the target population

In the case of students who wish to study medicine, the sampling frame providing the best coverage could be a list of all A-level students who are eligible to apply (maybe those studying biology, chemistry, etc.) who have stated a desire to apply for medicine. Such a list does not exist and creating it would be a lot of work. Hence, it is much easier to send a poll to an online community containing many types of students, hoping that some members of the population of interest will be there too. But, in the end, the results are quite useless, because we cannot know who is in the final sample.

3.5 GOOD SURVEYS, BAD SURVEYS AND EVERYTHING IN BETWEEN

A lot of data-driven stories reported in the media use some survey research as supporting evidence, yet many surveys are done rather badly. This section will consider some types of survey that are less powerful, or in some cases can produce results that are misleading or even downright dangerous.

3.5.1 A Poll vs a Survey

You're probably familiar with the terms 'opinion poll' and 'polling company' – perhaps they were for an election prediction, or to see how people liked a product.

A poll is a quick method of finding out what people think about one narrowly defined topic. A poll asks only a handful of questions – it doesn't collect comprehensive information about participants. By comparison, a survey asks a range of questions to analyse data in more depth, such as the underlying causes and factors that shape the attitudes or behaviours of respondents. You may have seen polls as single questions popping up on the Web, or you might have been invited to answer questions by commercial polling companies.

Polls can provide useful information, especially when effort is made to make them representative (see Chapter 4). However, they rarely provide the level of detail that a full survey can. A poll might be able to tell us, for example, who is likely to win an upcoming election, but it will struggle to find out about the motives of why people voted for whom they did.

3.5.2 Push Polling

Both surveys and opinion polls are useful to find out things about people and to measure preferences, such as attitudes towards climate change or recent political debates. They shouldn't be used to influence respondents into holding a particular political or commercial view. A push poll is something that looks like a real survey aiming to measure opinions or behaviours, but in fact it is a marketing tool used to propagate ideas and change the minds of its respondents. An example is the 2016 Mainstream Media Accountability Survey, which was issued by the Trump/Pence election campaign team in the aftermath of the 2016 US presidential election. The questions encouraged respondents to provide answers in line with the campaign agenda, for example asking how enthusiastically respondents agreed with the statement 'The mainstream media takes Donald Trump's statements out of context, but bends over backwards to defend Hillary's statements.' Polls like this are worded both to direct the respondent to a particular answer and to potentially change the respondent's mind as well. Push polling breaches the principle of integrity in survey research (or any other social science research), which is the commitment to conduct the research according to the highest quality standards and measure rather than generate public opinion. It is also against research ethics to use the results in a different way than was communicated to respondents. As such, we should be wary of the conclusions drawn from push polls: they are likely to show what the survey distributor wanted to find, and not, in all likelihood, the truth.

3.5.3 Surveys Supporting Adverts

Many companies use consumer surveys to show that people really like their product. Sometimes these are conducted by reputable companies, and the results are trustworthy. However, it is also often the case that these surveys are done in such a way as to show what the company wants: their shampoo makes your hair extra shiny, or their washing machine is the most reliable.

How do they do this? In general, they do it by asking only a small sample of people what they think. Would you trust 30 people if they all recommended a product, like a face cream or a shampoo? Perhaps 30 might sound like a lot, especially if they were 30 friends you knew well. But if you ask only a small number of people something, there is more chance that you will find something that isn't actually there. Commercial companies love these aberrations, even though they don't really mean very much, because statistics can give an air of objectivity to what they are saying. Such companies use these sorts of statistics in TV adverts ('90% would recommend this pogo stick!'), with small print below, stating that only a small number of people (say, 30) were asked for their opinion. If the sample is very small like this, you should be sceptical about what it's saying. In contrast, good-quality surveys rely on a large number of participants (we'll answer the question 'how many?' in Chapter 8).

3.5.4 Audience Surveys

Often media organisations do their own polls or surveys, after embedding them on their webpages or social media pages. The result of this is that the people who reply to those surveys are people who go to a particular webpage, or follow certain sorts of people on Twitter. It will exclude people who don't happen to go on those websites. Using this procedure means your sample will not be representative of the population at large (see Chapter 4 for more on this), effectively excluding people who aren't a member of this audience, such as those people who don't read a particular news website. In the UK, a survey embedded in the *Daily Mail*'s website (a right-leaning paper) will have a different group of people answering it than one in the *Daily Mirror*'s website (a left-leaning paper). Those who like one paper likely wouldn't want to read the other, so wouldn't see the survey on the webpage! Again, we should be sceptical of these surveys, as these questions will only be answered by online readers of the news organisation. This type of selection process produces biased and unreliable results, if you wanted to generalise them for a wider population – see Box 3.1 for an example. Yet, in some other cases, if the group of people you are interested in are the readers of a particular newspaper or online media only, an audience survey might be the preferred method (see Box 3.2 for an example).

3.2 A Twitter Poll That Went Viral

On 15 May 2017, weeks before the general election in the UK, Shehab Khan – a journalist working for *The Independent* newspaper in the UK – tweeted 'Who are you going to vote for in the general election? Vote + RT to increase sample size', and linked to a poll about the upcoming election. Shehab Khan explained that his intention was not to measure electoral preferences, but to get people to talk about politics and be more politically engaged. The poll went viral. It was picked up by a few polling experts and survey enthusiasts and retweeted over 2,500 times.

Out of 22,154 people who voted in the Twitter poll, 64% said they would vote for the Labour Party, 12% for the Conservatives, 15% for the Scottish National Party (SNP) and 9% for another party. But the result of the election on 8 June was very different: the Conservatives got 42% of votes, Labour got 40% and the SNP got 3%. As people connected in social media networks tend to have more similar opinions (you're more likely to follow people who support the same party), the poll caught on among similar people: in this case Labour and SNP supporters. So the Labour and SNP supporters forwarded it to their followers, who were quite likely to be also Labour and SNP supporters, and so on.

Source: Khan S. (2017) Tweet: https://twitter.com/ShehabKhan/status/8641678752 12447746

3.6 CONCLUSIONS

One of the United Nations' Fundamental Principles of Official Statistics is proper reporting of statistical data:

> To facilitate a correct interpretation of the data, the statistical agencies are to present information according to scientific standards on the sources, methods and procedures of the statistics. (United Nations, 2013: 2)

We can see from the above examples how going back to the source allows us to find important contextual information about who commissioned the data, when the data source was created, and whether or not reported statistics are sensibly presented. Often this kind of information is missing in the media or too briefly presented to make a judgement. Once you know where the data comes from, you can explore it yourself.

The key message from this chapter is that to recognise a good-quality dataset you need to identify first where the data comes from. So next time you find a piece of paper with some data on it, ask plenty of questions first:

1   **Who commissioned and conducted the study?** This might shed light on who was behind the design of the study and what the purpose was: whether it's an independent academic institution or well-known market research company, or if it's a political party or campaign, who might want to use data as a political marketing tool.

2   **When was the data collected?** If it's old data, the findings might not be particularly relevant to the news currently taking place.

3   **What kind of data is it based on?** A sample survey, census, administrative register or a Big Data source, or some sort of small-scale poll, conducted with a handful of readers of a local newspaper? If it's the latter, you can forget about the results being representative.

4   **Who is the target population in the media report?** And is it the same as the target population of the reported study? Who was excluded? If the population doesn't fully overlap, are claims made in the media report justified?

Perhaps the key message is that these questions are not always clear cut. One person's reliable data might be entirely untrustworthy to another. And even if data is from a trustworthy source, it can still be manipulated and twisted to fit certain agendas. But knowing where the data comes from is an important step in knowing whether something you read can be trusted.

3.7 CONCEPTS LEARNED IN THIS CHAPTER

Study unit: this is the basic unit of your study, the one you are interested in finding things about; it could be individuals, groups of people (like households) or institutions (such as schools, companies or organisations).

Administrative data is collected by organisations primarily for record keeping (not research purposes).

The (target) population: this comprises units of your study – individuals, groups or organisations. You need to define it in terms of space and time: their demographic characteristics, where they live/are located and when.

Sampling frame: this is the source you use to draw a sample, such as a postcode list, a list of addresses, a company register, an electoral register, or anything else which allows you to identify your study units.

Survey: this is a study which collects information, usually by asking a series of questions, about some members of the target population. The fraction of this target population that is asked these questions is called a sample. People who are interviewed – the respondents – are asked questions in the same way and their answers are converted into numbers, so they can be statistically described and analysed.

3.8 QUESTIONS FOR CLASS DISCUSSION

1   Go to the webpages of the surveys listed below. Define the following aspects of the surveys: study units, target population, sampling frame, sample size and response rate.

- European Quality of Life Survey: https://www.eurofound.europa.eu/surveys/european-quality-of-life-surveys
- The Australian Survey of Social Attitudes: http://aussa.anu.edu.au/
- Annual Survey of Entrepreneurs: https://bhs.econ.census.gov/bhs/ase
- Millennium Cohort Study: www.cls.ioe.ac.uk/page.aspx?sitesectionid=851

2   Select a question from the latest wave of The European Social Survey (ESS, www.europeansocialsurvey.org/) and create a social media poll (e.g. embedded in Twitter). Ask your networks to forward your poll. Compare your results of the ESS results for your country or the whole of Europe. What have the results revealed about your survey sample representativeness?

FURTHER READING

Blair, J., Czaja, R. F. and Blair E. A. (2013) *Designing Surveys: A Guide to Decisions and Procedures*. London: Sage.
Fowler, Jr, F. J. (2013) *Survey Research Methods*. London: Sage.

REFERENCES

Andres, L. (2012) *Designing and Doing Survey Research*. London: Sage.
Gallup (2013) 3rd European Company Survey: Technical Report. Working document for The European Foundation for the Improvement of Living and Working Conditions prepared by Gallup Europe. Available at https://www.eurofound.europa.eu/sites/default/files/ef_files/surveys/ecs/2013/documents/ecs2013docs/3rdECS2013Technical Report.pdf
Kitchin, R. (2014) Big Data, new epistemologies and paradigm shifts. Big Data & Society, 1(1), doi: 2053951714528481.

Mellon, J. (2013) Where and when can we use Google Trends to measure issue salience? *PS: Political Science & Politics*, 46(2), 280–90.

ONS (2013) General Lifestyle Survey, 2011. Sample Design and Response. Appendix B. London: Office for National Statistics.

Roundtree C. (2017) Sex before first date is okay but don't have an Android or cracked phone screen – annual singles in America survey reveals dos and don'ts of dating. *Daily Mail*, 7 February.

The Onion (2012) Gallup Poll: Rural whites prefer Ahmadinejad to Obama. *The Onion*. https://politics.theonion.com/gallup-poll-rural-whites-prefer-ahmadinejad-to-obama-1819573947 (accessed 23 November 2017).

The Student Room (2017) About The Student Room: https://www.thestudentroom.co.uk/content.php?r=127-about-the-student-room-where-students-connect (accessed 23 November 2017).

United Nations (2013) Resolution adopted by the Economic and Social Council on 24 July 2013, 2013/21. Fundamental Principles of Official Statistics.

US Census Bureau (2014) American Community Survey Design and Methodology (January 2014). Version 2.0.

4 Making surveys representative: 'Who you gonna call?'

Key concepts

representativeness, survey mode effect, probability sampling, coverage error, sampling bias, non-response bias, data weighting

4.1 INTRODUCTION

In 'what's the matter with polling?' Professor Cliff Zukin, former president of the American Association for Pubic Opinion Research, painted a bleak picture of the polling industry. He reflected over a few recent 'disasters': election polls which failed to accurately predict the results of the 2014 mid-term elections in the United States, the 2014 presidential elections in Israel and parliamentary elections in 2015 in the UK. He asked rhetorically, 'how much can we trust the polls as we head toward the 2016 elections?', foreshadowing that the crisis over the polling industry was far from over. A year later, in June 2016, the referendum on whether or not to leave the EU revealed that the majority of people in the UK had voted in favour of leaving, which wasn't what the polls had predicted, and in October 2016, Donald Trump was elected as President of the United States, again not an outcome the pollsters had anticipated.

In each case, the failure to predict the election was a result of polls that were not representative of the population they were aiming to tell us things about. Although social scientists know quite a lot about how to draw a representative sample, in practice it is very difficult to achieve.

In this chapter we will explain what **sample representativeness** means, discuss how to manage it using different ways of interviewing people – paper, telephone, face-to-face and online – and what their limitations are. We will also learn how to improve sample representativeness after the poll is done, using a procedure called **weighting**. This chapter will obviously help you in running a survey, but also in interpreting surveys both in academic studies and in the news. It will help you judge whether the survey is really representing the group of people it claims to be representing. Throughout we will be using the example of political opinion polling and surveys – however, the lessons learned will be applicable to a range of surveys on other topics.

4.2 THE CONCEPT OF SAMPLE REPRESENTATIVENESS

Surveys are conducted to find out things about larger populations by looking at characteristics and opinions of respondents from a sample. Interviewing every-one might be impossible, or at least too time consuming and expensive. Instead, survey designers usually take a sample from that population. Social scientists had already experimented with sampling methods in the late nineteenth cen-tury, but a breakthrough study was a work by a Norwegian statistician entitled 'Representative Method' (cited in Bethlehem, 2009), which demonstrated how a randomly selected sample could be used to estimate statistics about the whole Norwegian population, without a need to count it all. The discovery that by talking to a fraction of a population, randomly selected, you can make esti-mates about the entire population has been crucial to social statistics. Surveys became more commonly used in some European countries in the 1940s and 1950s (Bethlehem, 2009). At the same time, the Statistical Office of the United Nations – which sets international criteria for statistics and demography – recognised 'sampling surveys' as reliable sources of statistical estimates. In 1950 the UN issued guidelines on how to report surveys properly, including the sampling frame and sampling method (UN, 1950). Life was made so much easier for anyone who wanted to use official statistics.

4.2.1 What Representativeness Means

In the procedure of drawing a sample your aim should be to guarantee that the sample represents the target population well, so the sample's opinions and characteristics reflect those of the population. How is it possible for just a small fraction of a population to represent a much larger group? One of the examples often given when we talk about sample representativeness is a blood test – you don't need to take all the blood from a person to find out whether they are healthy or ill. Another example comes from cooking – while preparing a pot of soup, to see whether it is tasty or not, you don't need to eat the whole pot; a spoonful would be enough. Surveys work in the same way: talking to some members of your target population can be enough to find out what the population as a whole thinks, detect common patterns in behaviour, or what people's life conditions are. By eating a spoonful of a soup you can infer that the rest of the soup will taste the same.

Often, when people hear poll results they disagree with, they say 'well, no one asked me!' Taking a sample doesn't deny the existence of different views of individuals within that sample. Although one individual may not have been surveyed, someone a bit like the individual, with similar views, probably has. Similarly, when you taste leek and potato soup, you will taste some leek and some potato. But you won't have tasted all the leek plants in the pot!

The good news about all of this is that, if we were to take a group of people chosen at random as the sample, then that sample would be representative of the overall population (so long as the sample is big enough to be able to include all the subgroups that we are interested in, see Chapter 8). That is the magic of statistics, and it allows us to infer things about the wider population from our sample. The bad news is that collecting a truly random sample is a very difficult thing to do because some groups of people are more likely to respond to survey invitations than others. Using the soup analogy above, we can't just stir the pot! It's even difficult to include everyone in your sampling frame. If you use people's addresses, for example, you exclude homeless people. If you use phone numbers, you exclude people who don't have phones, or who don't answer their phones.

Not only that, but getting people to respond to surveys at all has become harder over recent decades. In the two decades between 1997 and 2016, the response rate – the proportion of people agreeing to be interviewed by polling companies when contacted – in telephone surveys in the United States decreased from 36 to 9% (Kennedy et al., 2017). There are a few reasons for the drop in the response rates:

- many people no longer have a landline phone – a main source of quick telephone polls in the late twentieth century – and only have a mobile phone;
- more research is now being conducted, meaning that people get approached to participate in scientific studies far more than they used to;
- there is now more public awareness on how to avoid being interviewed by a research agency.

So, not only are we unable to target all the people we would like to while conducting a survey, but also a lot of people say no – more than a few decades ago.

At the same time, it's become far more expensive to conduct a survey both face to face and over the phone. If you want to interview 1,000 people over the phone, on average you have to call 11,112 numbers! On average an interviewer has to call 10 people without a response before someone agrees to take part. One solution to this problem is switching into web/online interviewing. However, this brings back the question of representation: that is, whether the opinions of people who are present online, and agree to answer questions via either their computer or phone, will reflect the opinions of the wider, target population.

Sample representativeness depends on what behaviours or opinions a researcher wants to measure (you want to capture a variety of those). The aim is to obtain a sample which is representative in terms of both socio-demographic characteristics and opinions you intend to study because, usually, people of different ages, classes or ethnicities will have different kinds of life experiences, and their opinions are likely to vary. It's not merely that proportions of particular groups need to be the same in the sample and in the population, such as 50–50 men and women, or 40–60 without/with university degree. If you want to make claims about your population as a whole you need to have a sample which is diverse not only across but also within particular groups.

Let's say you would like to measure voting intentions separately for men and women and for voters of different levels of education. You manage to obtain a sample reflecting your population by gender and education level. Your estimates might be still biased, as it could be that all the people you recruited with degrees were women, and men with degrees hold different political opinions from those of women with degrees. Sample representativeness could be seen as an ideal that researchers chase. Yet, it's very difficult to obtain this perfect mix and your sample will never perfectly reflect your target population. Indeed, apparently innocuous things, like how the data was collected, can change how representative the sample ends up being, as we'll see now.

4.3 A POLL VS A POLL: SURVEY MODES

A month before the EU referendum in the UK, in May 2016, *The Independent* reported that there was an 'industry-wide row' about the accuracy of polls (Stone, 2016). There were clear differences between the results found by phone polling and Internet polling, with each side arguing that their method of contacting participants produced better results. The BBC's EU referendum poll tracker shows that the Remain side had a clear lead for most of the campaign according to phone polls (BBC, 2016), with the highest difference of 58% for Remain and 38% for Leave (ORB poll for the BBC, 22 May). The race was much closer according to online polls, with some giving a lead to the Leave side.

Why were online and telephone polling so different during the EU referendum campaign? One answer is that the populations answering the questions put by each method were made up of different sorts of people. But another answer is that the ways in which people respond to various '**survey modes**' can be different. People might be embarrassed to say things in person or on the phone, but will admit to them on an impersonal computer screen. To discuss this further we need to dig deeper into how both types of polls are conducted and how respondents are selected. There are two elements which distinguish modes from each other: (i) the kind of device used to record answers; and (ii) whether an interviewer is present. Both these modes are discussed in Box 4.1.

4.1 A Brief History of Survey Modes

In early survey research, during the 'era of invention' of 1930–60 (Groves, 2011), the two dominant methods of interviewing were face-to-face personal interviewing and mail/postal interviewing. In both cases pen and paper were used to record answers. Given the small numbers of survey companies and the novelty of the method, the response rate was as high as 90% around that time. In the next survey era, the 'expansion era' (1960–90), thanks to post-war technological advancement and the spread of landline telephones, Computer-Assisted Telephone Interviewing became the new standard (see Table 4.1). In this method, an interviewer would call a randomly selected number, conduct the interview, and record answers on a computer. Interviews without an interviewer were possible too, where respondents would listen to a voice recording and use the numbers on their phone's keypad to respond. While this made data collection much easier, it also had its downsides. The introduction of telephones led to the first hiccups in response rates, as it's easier to stop an interview by hanging up the phone than to walk out of a room.

Since 1990, new technological developments have changed the rules of the survey game once again. In 1998 only 9% of households in the UK had Internet access; in 2017, it was 90% (ONS, 2018). Over the same period, mobile phone use similarly grew, being available to 16% of households in 1997, and 95% in 2017, while landline use has declined. The share of mobile-only households

(Continued)

has been estimated to be around 18% in the UK (Ofcom, 2017). In the United States, the number is even bigger: roughly 50% of adults use only mobile phones (Blumberg and Luke, 2017).

Table 4.1   Survey modes

Recording device	Interviewer presence	Survey mode name	Survey mode acronym
Pen and paper	No interviewer	Self-administered questionnaire	SAQ
	With interviewer	Pen and paper personal interview	PAPI
Telephone	No interviewer	Interactive voice response	IVR
	With interviewer	Computer-Assisted Telephone Interviewing	CATI
Computer	No interviewer	Audio Computer-Assisted Self-Interviewing	ACASI
	With interviewer	Computer/Tablet-Assisted Personal Interviewing	CAPI, TAPI
Internet browser	No interviewer	Web/online interviewing	CAWI
	With interviewer	–	–
Mobile text or app	No interviewer	Mobile interviewing	–
	With interviewer	–	–

With these changes in technology, the devices used for interviewing have changed too. During face-to-face interviews, answers are now recorded either using laptops or other portable devices such as tablets. 'Traditional' telephone interviewing still happens, but the shift towards mobile phones opened new possibilities. Respondents are invited to participate in polls via text and online interviews. Survey design software makes it easy to adapt a questionnaire for a phone screen. Finally, there are a few phone apps which offer users small monetary rewards or vouchers in exchange for completing surveys.

In sum, the family of survey modes has been growing and becoming more flexible in response to changes in communication practices and lifestyle, and in response to changes in people's willingness to be interviewed. The image of an interviewer going from house to house with hard copies of a questionnaire is being replaced by a person filling in a quick poll on their phone while they're on the bus. Yet, the shift towards new technologies – online and mobile interviewing – and self-administered interviewing has not fixed the problem of low response rate, and has produced differences in results based around the type of survey.

Survey mode effects are the influences that a method used to collect answers might have on the answers themselves. In other words, the same person might give different responses according to whether interviewed face to face or online. This is partly due to whether the interviewer is physically present, but also because we process information differently when we see questions and when we hear them. Not only do people spend different amounts of time interpreting the question – with an interviewer, you've got to listen to the question being read out – but also answers can vary based on whether you get all the questions together, or one by one. Respondents interviewed over the phone may not be paying attention because of what's going on around them; they'll also lack visual stimulus from an interviewer for more complex questions. Respondents to a self-administered web interview can answer questions at their own pace at a time that is convenient for them – and can take breaks whenever they want to. This can affect the answers they give as well.

An experimental study carried out into this 'mode effect' by the Pew Research Center (PRC) demonstrated that the largest differences in what people said between telephone and Internet surveys were related to questions on life satisfaction, prejudice and political attitudes (PRC, 2015). Questions that asked respondents to evaluate themselves and other people, or that asked about 'social taboos' (e.g. behaviours that are generally condemned by society, such as some sexual practices or drug use), were found to be more sensitive to the 'mode effect'. People asked by telephone, in the presence of an interviewer at the other end of the phone, tend to present themselves as both happier and more concerned about discrimination against minority groups (such as people from minority ethnic groups or LGBT people), and less critical about the performance of political leaders. For example, while 27% stated a very unfavourable opinion about Hillary Clinton in a 2016 online survey, the equivalent number for people interviewed over the phone was only 19%.

So what caused the 2016 EU Referendum differences between Internet and phone polls? There might have been a survey mode effect at play: perhaps Leave voters were more likely to be honest in an Internet poll than a telephone one. An inquiry into the 2015 elections in the UK suggested, however, that the difference in predictions wasn't due to mode effects (Sturgis et al., 2016). Instead, it may have been representativeness: that the two methods were sampling different populations, or perhaps certain groups didn't want to talk on the phone but were more willing to talk online (i.e. self-selection of some unique respondents into each survey mode).

4.4 IMPERFECTION IS INEVITABLE

In 2016, pretty much every polling company predicted that the UK's EU referendum would be won, narrowly, by Remain. While they were wrong, it wasn't the polling industry's worst 'goof' (see next section). Inaccuracies in electoral polling happen from time to time, but research looking at how accurate polls have been over the period 1942–2017, from a total of 30,000 polls about 351 general elections in 41 countries, demonstrated that the accuracy of polls has actually been quite stable over decades (Jennings and Wlezien, 2018). Although the polling errors – how much electoral polls differ from the actual vote shares – haven't changed much, they have more of an impact when the final result was close, like in the US presidential elections in 2016 and the 2016 EU Referendum in the UK.

Survey companies learn from imperfections in polling of previous elections, and sampling procedures are improved with time. In general, people who are more interested in politics are more likely to agree to participate in surveys, so pollsters aim to oversample those who are not very engaged in politics. However, the rules of the game are constantly changing as well, and pollsters often can't know how much they've changed until after an election has already happened! During the 2015 General Election campaign in the UK, young people were oversampled by survey companies, because they're less likely to agree to be surveyed in the first place. But as it turned out, young people didn't show up at the polling station as much as they were expected to, and much less than older people. Because older people tend to be more likely to vote Conservative, this meant that the Conservative vote was underreported (Wells, 2017).

Sometimes polls aren't as useful as we'd like because the interviews were not conducted with representative samples due to imperfect sampling frames. Surveys rely on sampling frames with some **coverage error**, which is the proportion of the target population not covered by the sampling frame, and the difference between the covered and non-covered population. For example, a sampling frame of landline numbers will not capture people who use only mobile phones, while a sampling frame of web users will exclude people without Internet access. After a campaign in which polls which had incorrectly predicted a 'hung' parliament in the 2015 UK General Election, an investigation concluded that the polling miss was mostly caused by relying on web surveys with so called opt-in panels, where people self-select into a study (see Box 4.2), which did not have representative coverage of voters (Sturgis et al., 2016). Online surveys had disproportionately large proportions of Labour supporters and disproportionately small proportions of Conservative supporters.

While some error in survey estimations will always occur, it can be lowered by improving the sampling procedure, using sampling frames with better coverage, and larger sample size. But, as we will see in the next example, a big sample size is actually much less important than the representativeness of the sample.

4.2 Online Surveys

Online interviewing has become increasingly popular. Most survey polling companies have their own Internet panels, which are samples of respondents invited to take part in various quick polls or longer surveys. Panel members are recruited offline and online (through pop-up windows and ads) to ensure that groups who are often underrepresented are present, but people also opt in to become panel members in exchange for rewards and vouchers or just because they're keen to express their opinions, making the panel-sample likely to be unrepresentative. From this unrepresentative sample a (possibly) representative sample is drawn, but this process is not simple random sampling from members of the target population (that would simply reproduce the non-representativeness of the original sample). As socio-demographic traits of the population of interest are often known, some companies apply more advanced methods, like 'matched random sampling' (HuffPost/YouGov, 2017). Knowing the socio-demographic makeup of the US population by age, gender, ethnicity, etc., from the Census Bureau's American Community Survey data, email invitations are sent to panelists whose characteristics match those of the US adult population. As such, a company draws a purposeful sample from its panel which is not a random sample of the panel population, in order to make the sample more representative than it originally was.

Some Internet panels are fully selected and recruited offline. GfK KnowledgePanel in the United States is selected from a random sample of addresses; LISS Netherlands is created by sampling from a population register. Some probability-based panels, as they're called, recruit members via telephone by dialling random telephone numbers, such as EKOS Probit Canada. As such, unlike opt-in panels, every member of the target population (assuming they have a phone or an address) has a chance of selection into a panel, and of subsequently being invited to do a survey. In some samples, people who do not have a computer or access to the Internet are allowed to be included, by providing them with equipment and training, as in the German Internet Panel. People who would not normally take part in online studies therefore have a chance to be a respondent, lowering sampling bias.

Online surveys are done in very different ways. Some are quite unreliable and rely on a sample of self-selected respondents, with a poll embedded

(Continued)

in a webpage, unlikely to produce good-quality results. Others come from well-managed Internet panels or probability-based panels, with an army of survey statisticians working on sampling procedures. When considering data it is always important to understand the process that led to people being chosen for the sample, and what it means for the analysis that follows.

4.5 WHEN POLLS GO *REALLY* WRONG

In 1936, US magazine *The Literary Digest* (LD) made one of the worst polling blunders in history. The magazine had conducted successful polls since 1920 (being at worst 1 percentage point out), but the context of the 1936 elections turned out to be different. LD used the same method as in previous years, which was to send out questionnaires to a sample created on the basis of a few sources: telephone directories, lists of automobile owners, LD's own subscribers, and registers of various clubs and professional associations. At the end of August 1936, 10 million voting ballots were sent out; 2.38 million were returned. With such a massive sample, it is unsurprising that LD was confident.

In earlier political polling, respondents were haphazardly approached in the street. This procedure is known as **non-probability sampling,** where respondents are recruited through self-selection or deliberate identification of participants, meaning some people can't be selected. This 'old-school' intercept interviewing – when passers-by are invited to answer a few questions – does not give all eligible voters in a given city or country an opportunity to take part in the study. Most people will never walk down that street, and those that do might have very different voting intentions to those that don't. Instead, LD pollsters gave a chance to express voting intentions to all of those who were listed in a huge, 10 million sampling frame, mostly a mix of automobile registrations and telephone numbers.

Unfortunately, having such an enormous sample did not help LD in 1936. Its poll predicted that 57% of voters would vote for the Republican candidate, Alfred Landon, and 43% for the Democratic candidate, the incumbent president Franklin D. Roosevelt. On 3 November the reality proved to be very different, with Roosevelt winning in 46 out of 48 states and taking 61% of the popular vote. This polling mistake cost LD a lot – the magazine was closed down in 1938.

Let's unpack exactly what problems caused the LD poll fiasco. For a *representative* survey of 2 million, from a population of 128 million, the sampling error (see Chapter 8) would be tiny: 0.06%. Yet, this was not really a probability sample; although all people on the 10 million sampling frame were selected, the chance was not given to many more who were not included in the frame. This seminal polling failure demonstrates that having a large sample size doesn't necessarily mean your survey is any good. You can still be very wrong if you miss an important section of a population from your sampling frame. A truly representative sample of 1,000 people is likely to be much more informative than an unrepresentative sample of 2 million. This systematic error in sampling is called **sampling bias**. In the case of the LD poll, the negative effects of the Great Depression played a crucial role in shaping people's political attitudes, which were very different for richer and poorer people, and President Roosevelt's supporters were underrepresented in the eventual sample, as they were less likely to have a car, or a telephone, or be a subscriber to LD. A later (survey) study found that among those without an automobile and a phone, 79% would vote for Roosevelt and only 19% for Landon (Squire, 1988).

Sampling bias can even happen when your sampling frame has ideal coverage, but some groups of respondents have much higher or lower response rates, due to their being too busy or reluctant to participate. Later studies examining what when wrong with the LD poll in 1936 showed that even if all 10 million of the people sampled had replied, the prediction still would have been inaccurate, but at least the poll would have correctly foreseen Roosevelt's win (Squire, 1988). The sample was biased, but even more bias was introduced by the non-response, as supporters of the Republican candidate were more likely to return the ballot.

Probability sampling is a 'gold standard' for scientific social surveys and polling by large companies because each member of the population has a known and (ideally) equal chance of selection. If the sample is big enough, and the data is randomly selected from the population, the data will tend to have very similar characteristics. In the above example, this would mean selecting people from across the whole of the American population, rather than just LD readers. The problem is that it's very difficult to get a true probability sample where everyone has the same chance of being sampled, and of responding.

Unfortunately, many surveys, like the LD poll above, are done using **convenience sampling** – that is, surveying people who are easiest to get to fill in the survey. Because this approach does not select participants from the entire population, it means samples are highly likely to be unrepresentative.

4.6 MATCH THE SAMPLING PROCEDURE TO WHAT WE WANT TO KNOW

Sometimes, drawing one sample is not appropriate for some research situations, so it's important to be sure the right process has been used for the research questions being asked. Let's go back to the study which investigated the accuracy of election polls from 1942 to 2017. The authors also found that errors tend to be lower in systems with proportional representation (Jennings and Wlezien, 2018). In such systems the number of votes each party receives corresponds directly to the number of seats they take in Parliament – MPs, senators, and so on. In other electoral systems people vote directly for a representative of their geographical area. This means, in theory, that a party could come a close second in every constituency and, despite a large number of votes, would get no representatives in government. In other words, the number of votes each party receives overall doesn't always correspond to the number of seats it receives. Hence, conducting one, large poll of voting intentions among UK voters would not work very well as an indicator of the final election result. Instead, for some electoral systems, ideally, we would randomly select a representative sample in each constituency. Alternatively, some pollsters will assume that a change in the national results from a previous election can be applied equally to the results at the state/constituency level – but this will also miss local circumstances that go against that trend (or 'swing').

Similarly, for US presidential elections, a national sample isn't so useful because the contest is decided by the electoral college: votes for the presidency are allocated based upon elections within each state (usually in a winner take all system). On a number of occasions (as in the 2000 and 2016 elections), the winner of the nationwide popular vote has not won the presidential election. And if we were interested in US Congressional elections, we'd need to divide this even further, since House of Representatives' votes are based on Congressional districts (see Chapter 6 for more on how different this result can be from general patterns). However, this is an increasingly expensive enterprise, and is often unreliable because knowing how representative samples are to lots of different and very local areas is very difficult to do. In reality, only districts that are believed to be close to the margin might be polled more often (and often have very small sample sizes and poor sampling strategies), so unexpected swings in preferences in some districts might remain undetected.

4.7 IMPROVE SAMPLING OR IMPROVE WEIGHTING?

The most famous photo of the 1948 US presidential election was a smiling President Harry S. Truman holding a copy of the *Chicago Daily Tribune* with the headline: 'Dewey defeats Truman', the morning after Truman had won the election.

What went wrong? Some pollsters argue that, in fact, the polls were correct in thinking that public opinion was in favour of Dewey. What they missed was that Dewey supporters were less likely to vote than Truman supporters. If true, the polls had been right in measuring the national sentiment, but wrong in predicting the election – or, thinking another way, the population being measured by the polls was the whole US population, and not the smaller population of people who actually voted.

Since that election, the measurement of voting intentions has been improved to correct estimates by who is actually likely to vote. Post-fieldwork data adjustment – weighting – in survey research has come onto the scene.

Weighting is a procedure used to adjust an unrepresentative sample and make it act like a representative sample. Once an organisation stops collecting data for a given poll, the profile of the sample that ended up participating is validated against external data describing the profile of the population of interest in the study. For example, if in your sample the proportion of men to women is 40/60, while it's 50/50 in the target population, you'll more heavily weight responses from the group that's underrepresented to balance it out. In this case, if only 40% of your sample are men, you'll more heavily weight men's responses. Basically, a weight is a new variable in your dataset which you apply when computing statistics, like finding out how many people support a candidate, or are unemployed, or intend to move house next year. (In practice, normally statistical software does the calculation for you, so we won't go into the details of that. But if you want to know more about weighting in practice, see Box 4.3!)

Weighting is usually applied when any of the probability sampling techniques are used, because we know the probabilities of selection and data adjustment has to have good foundations. Meanwhile, if convenience sampling is used, the proportions of some groups could be too far away from those in the actual population or some groups not included at all, hence weighting would be very difficult, if not impossible, to do. Even with probability sampling there are still risks if we accidentally weight unusual individuals or groups too heavily. Sometimes, if they get weighed too heavily, just one person can distort the results from the entire sample. In one example, a USC/Los Angeles Times Daybreak tracking poll in 2016 – based on an online panel of around 3,000 respondents, with a daily sample of approximately 400 people – the opinions of one 19-year-old black man from Illinois were given 30 times more weight than the opinions of an average respondent (Cohn, 2016). How could this have happened?

The answer lies in the categories that were used to assign weights. If you weight based on one variable (like gender), there are rarely big problems,

4.3 How Weighting Works in Practice

Weights are really useful to surveys – but how are they created in practice? Let's unpack a few key aspects of the weighting procedure first to see how it works:

- **Calculate base/design weight** – depending on the sampling procedure, some people in your sample could have been given more chances of being selected. So the first step in weighting is to compensate for unequal probabilities of selection. For example, in the case of landline telephone surveys you call households, which will have a varying number of members. People living in larger households will have a lower probability of being selected, so you have to correct it.
- **Adjust for non-response** – not all people will respond to your survey invitation and response rates might vary across subpopulations, resulting in overrepresentation of people being more willing to answer. In the second step we would look at the response rate by regions or other grouping variables used to stratify the sample.
- **Post-stratification weight/calibration** – you also explore the distribution of key socio-demographic variables, like gender, age group, ethnicity or education levels, in your sample (after applying both previous weights) and 'calibrate' against reliable auxiliary data for your population (e.g. the most recent census data for residents). Usually you cross-tabulate the variables with each other, so you would look for the proportions of men and women separately across different age groups, selected ethnicities and qualifications. For instance, you would have a different weighting variable for 25–34-year-old men, who are white and highly educated, and a different weight for 55–64-year-old women, of minority origin, with secondary education.
- **Weight trimming** – as you do not want to manipulate the proportions of the sample more than appropriate, it is good practice to decide on minimum and maximum cut-off points of the weight. Usually weights 4–5 times larger or smaller than the mean weight or values outside the 95 percentile distribution are trimmed. This stops very small and potentially unusual groups from being overcompensated.

because the groups are big, meaning there are lots of people in each. However, if you weight based on too many variables, those groups become small, and so are more at risk of being unrepresentative for that group. With the USC/LA Times poll, the survey was weighted based on three-year age groups, race and gender. Crucially, those age categories were very narrow, and after creating categories for all combinations of age, race and gender, there was only one person in the black, male, aged 18–21 category. The young man was also unusual, because he reported support for Donald Trump. In general, black Americans were far more likely to support Hillary Clinton. According to this poll, only 4.4% of black people supported Trump. As such, although this voter single-handedly represented an entire group of young black men, his opinions were not representative of the group at all. If the weight had been composed differently, allowing for wider age bands and trimming excessively small or high weights (see Box 4.3), this would not have happened.

While weighting helps to improve proportions in the sample across categories (i.e. compensate for under/overrepresentation of defined age groups), weighting will not help much if the sample is not representative within categories (e.g. within an age group). For instance, if young men who are 18–25 years old are underrepresented, we might correct their proportion by weighting. However, if we've got plenty of men aged between 22 and 25, but hardly any between 18 and 21, then increasing the influence of those 22–25 year olds won't solve the problem; 18–21 year olds might have different opinions from 22–25 year olds, but weighting for an 18–25 age band won't correct for that. On the other hand, using demographic categories that are too narrow may have their own problems, as the USC/LA Times example shows – a few outliers, or even just one, might distort the results of an entire survey.

Weighting is even more complicated in polls that try to estimate how people will vote. Knowing which candidates people prefer isn't the same as knowing election results: some people won't show up on the day. Hence, polling companies develop **turnout weights**, which adjust for the probability that a person will vote. Usually, people are asked to assess how likely they are to vote in the forthcoming election, or, in general, how often they vote. For example, a survey might ask a question like 'Please rate your chance of voting in the forthcoming election on a scale of 1 to 10' (PRC, 2016). Following this, people who aren't as likely to vote are downweighted, and those more likely to vote are upweighted. People who respond 'Don't know' aren't excluded from calculations; instead, they're asked how they voted in previous elections, and their potential vote is incorporated (albeit with a lower weight) (Sturgis et al., 2016; 2017). Yet, this learning from the past can also be dangerous. Some companies in the UK used turnout levels from the 2015 election to estimate the results of the General Election in June 2017; this time, they underestimated the Labour vote because more people of certain age groups voted than they did in 2015.

In sum, while the poll results that you see in the media have almost always been the subject of weighting, you'll rarely see how the weights were calculated. Yet, it matters a lot. If you wanted to find out, you'd need to read the survey's technical report in order to judge whether or not the assumptions in the weighting procedure make sense.

4.8 CONCLUSIONS

In the aftermath of the 2016 US presidential election, one French newspaper, *Le Parisien*, decided to abandon commissioning polls on people's voting intentions until after the presidential elections in 2017 in the country. This was to move the discussion away from whether polls are right towards actual discussion of the candidates. The editor explained that polls 'don't do their job badly – they give a snapshot. The problem is the way the media uses them' (Chrisafis, 2017). We totally agree! The way the media present polls makes a difference. The 'bandwagon effect' – when people change their mind to jump onto the 'wagon' of the majority – occurs when the media use polls to predict election winners (Van der Meer et al., 2015).

Some people might think that all polls are the same, but there are plenty of differences from poll to poll. But apart from the measurement and the way we ask about opinions, even tiny differences in the sample composition, the survey mode used, or how data ends up being weighted will shape the result. Applying random sampling does not guarantee accurate survey estimates unless everyone approached agrees to participate. While it is easier to 'calibrate' a sample's socio-demographic profile with its target population, it's impossible to know people's opinions and attitudes *before* conducting the survey, so it's difficult to correct for unrepresentativeness in people preferences and opinions. Understanding these peculiarities is a step towards better reporting of data in the media.

4.9 CONCEPTS LEARNED IN THIS CHAPTER

Convenience sampling: an approach to sampling where individuals are selected because they are easy to get hold of, rather than because they have been selected randomly from a pre-defined population. In comparison with probability sampling, this is likely to lead to unrepresentative samples.

Coverage error: the error in survey estimates stemming from under-coverage of the sampling frame, meaning some members of the target population are not included in the frame. It could be seen as the difference between an ideal sampling frame covering all members of the target population and the actual, imperfect sampling frame you work with.

Data weighting: this is a data adjustment procedure you can apply after survey data has been collected, to make your unrepresentative sample behave as if it were representative of the target population. Data weighting corrects for different probabilities of selection between different groups of people, or different response rates across geographical regions. Weights are used to calibrate your sample to the socio-demographic profile of the target population.

Non-response bias: even if the sample you drew was perfectly representative, some people might be less likely to agree to take part in the survey, because they are busy, not interested in being a respondent, or approached in a way that put them off. This causes bias if their opinions are distinctive and leads to non-representative results.

Probability sampling: this is a sample selection method, in which every member of a given population has a chance of being selected to participate in a survey. This can be distinguished from sampling methods that use self-selection, convenience (first-comes, first-served basis) or accident to select study participants.

Sample representativeness: a concept driving survey research design, and the extent to which the mix of your sample characteristics and opinions reflects the mix of the target population. The ideal is for the sample and the population to be as similar to each other as possible.

Sampling bias: this occurs when statistics from the sample do not reflect true values of the statistics in the target population; it happens when there is a lower chance of selection to a particular subpopulation, which is distinct from the rest of your target population. Sampling bias is one source of inaccuracy in survey statistics.

Survey mode effect: this is the influence that the method used to conduct a survey – such as face-to-face, telephone, computer or mobile interviewing – has on the survey data. The mode influences measurement error (how accurately we measure opinions and facts) and non-response bias (who does the survey in the first place).

4.10 QUESTIONS FOR CLASS DISCUSSION

1   Investigate the coverage of the electoral register in the UK as a sampling frame for a survey of the general, adult population. Specifically reflect on the following:

    a   Who has a right to vote in the UK?
    b   How does it differ for different elections? Who, in terms of nationalities, is on the register?
    c   Is the register open?
    d   What sources of coverage error have you identified?

See this webpage for some useful information: www.electoralcommission.
org.uk/faq/voting-and-registration/who-is-eligible-to-vote-at-a-uk-general-
election

2   How would you construct a probability-based panel in a country which does
not have one? The aim is to give all members of the country's population the
same chance to be selected. First, look at the webpages of some of the panels
described in Box 4.2. Then, identify which sampling frame would give you
the most complete coverage in the relevant country. You might want to decide
to mix some sampling frames, but remember to control for duplicates (so you
don't give some people a higher probability of selection).

3   Is the elected body in your country (e.g. a parliament) representative in terms
of socio-demographic characteristics of the adult population in your country?
Compare proportions of populations by gender, age group, qualification levels, ethnic background, etc., in the elected body to proportions of these groups
in the adult population in your country. Do you think this matters?

FURTHER READING

Turner, A. G. (2003) *Sampling Strategies: Handbook on Designing of Household Sample
Surveys*. Geneva: United Nations Statistics Division. ESA/STAT/AC 93, 2.
United Nations Statistics Division (2008) *Designing Household Survey Samples: Practical
Guidelines (Vol. 98)*. New York: United Nations Publications.
Yansaneh, I. S. (2003) *Construction and Use of Sample Weights: Designing Household
Surveys Samples: Practical Guidelines*. Geneva: United Nations Statistics Division.
ESA/STAT/AC 93, 5.

REFERENCES

BBC (2016) EU referendum poll tracker. www.bbc.co.uk/news/uk-politics-eu-referen
dum-36271589
Bethlehem, J. (2009) The rise of survey sampling. Statistics Netherlands Discussion Paper
09015.
Blumberg, S. J. and Luke, J. V. (2017) Wireless substitution: early release of estimates
from the National Health Interview Survey, July–December 2016. National Center for
Health Statistics, 05/2017. Available at www.cdc.gov/nchs/nhis.htm
Chrisafis, A. (2017) French newspaper abandons opinion polls in run-up to election. *The
Guardian*, 13 January. https://www.theguardian.com/world/2017/jan/13/french-news-
paper-le-parisien-abandons-opinion-polls-french-presidential-election-vote
Cohn, N. (2016) How one 19-year-old Illinois man is distorting national polling
averages. The Upshot, *The New York Times*, 12 October. https://www.nytimes.com/2016/
10/13/upshot/how-one-19-year-old-illinois-man-is-distorting-national-polling-
averages.html

Groves, R. M. (2011) Three eras of survey research. *Public Opinion Quarterly*, 75(5), 861–871.

HuffPost/YouGov (2017) Methodology. http://data.huffingtonpost.com/yougov/methodology

Jennings, W. and Wlezien, C. (2018) Election polling errors across time and space. *Nature Human Behaviour*, 1.

Kennedy, C., Keeter, S., Mercer, A., Hatley, N., Bertoni, N. and Lau, A. (2017) Are telephone polls understating support for Trump? Pew Research Center, 31 March. www.pewresearch.org/2017/03/31/are-telephone-polls-understating-support-for-trump/

Ofcom (2017) Fast Facts. https://www.ofcom.org.uk/about-ofcom/latest/media/facts

ONS (2018) Internet access – households and individuals, Great Britain: 2017. Office for National Statistics in the UK. https://www.ons.gov.uk/peoplepopulationandcommunity/householdcharacteristics/homeinternetandsocialmediausage/bulletins/internetaccesshouseholdsandindividuals/2017

PRC (2015) From telephone to the web: The challenge of mode of interview effects in public opinion polls. Pew Research Center, 13 May. www.pewresearch.org/2015/05/13/from-telephone-to-the-web-the-challenge-of-mode-of-interview-effects-in-public-opinion-polls/

PRC (2016) Can likely voter models be improved? 2: Measuring the likelihood to vote. www.pewresearch.org/2016/01/07/measuring-the-likelihood-to-vote/

Squire, P. (1988) Why the 1936 Literary Digest Poll failed? *Public Opinion Quarterly*, 52(1): 125–33.

Stone, J. (2016) Pollsters are having an industry-wide row over EU referendum poll accuracy. *The Independent*, 20 May. https://www.independent.co.uk/news/uk/politics/eu-referendum-poll-phone-online-accuracy-yougov-comres-a7039351.html

Sturgis, P., Baker, N., Callegaro, M., Fisher, S., Green, J., Jennings, W., Kuha, J., Lauderdale, B. and Smith, P. (2016) *Report of the Inquiry into the 2015 British general election opinion polls*. London: Market Research Society and British Polling Council.

Sturgis, P., Kuha, J., Baker, N., Callegaro, M., Fisher, S., Green, J., Jennings, W., Lauderdale, B. and Smith, P. (2017) An assessment of the causes of the errors in the 2015 UK general election opinion polls. *Journal of the Royal Statistical Society: Series A (Statistics in Society)*, 18(3), 757–81.

UN (1950) The preparation of sampling survey reports. Statistical Papers Series C No. 1. Statistical Office of the United Nations. http://unstats.un.org/unsd/publication/SeriesC/SeriesC_1_revised.pdf

Van der Meer, T. W., Hakhverdian, A. and Aaldering, L. (2015) Off the fence, onto the bandwagon? A large-scale survey experiment on effect of real-life poll outcomes on subsequent vote intentions. *International Journal of Public Opinion Research*, 28(1), 46–72.

Wells, A. (2017) The pollsters' experimental election. YouGov blog, 1 June. https://yougov.co.uk/news/2017/06/01/pollsters-experimental-election/

Zukin, C. (2015) What's the matter with polling? *The New York Times*, 20 June. https://www.nytimes.com/2015/06/21/opinion/sunday/whats-the-matter-with-polling.html

5 Graphics in the media and how to read them: 'What does this mean?'

Key concepts

class intervals, correlation, quartiles, percentiles, categories, logarithmic scales, various graph types

5.1 INTRODUCTION

What's better than a number in the media? Lots of numbers in the media of course! You could put them in a list; you could put them in a table. But if you've got loads of numbers, it might be better to put them in a graph. If you are a journalist, this will make your article visually arresting, your readers will be amazed at how beautiful your news story looks, and everyone will be persuaded of the argument that you're making. Right?

There are lots of good reasons to use **graphs** in the media, rather than just reporting a list of numbers. If you've got a lot of numbers, it's much easier to communicate them all in a single graphic than as a table or a list, and it's much easier to detect patterns when you present data visually rather than as a list of numbers.

There are also lots of good reasons to use graphs in the media if you want to mislead people. Because graphics often tell such a compelling story, readers might miss details that could actually undermine the story you're trying to tell. But there's a number of techniques that journalists, government researchers, etc., can use to tell a particular kind of story using graphics. These techniques aren't wrong per se – the graphs are often still accurate – but can make the graph tell a completely different and often misleading story, using the same data. There's loads of different techniques for this – by the time you're reading this book, even more will probably have been invented – so we can't go through them all. You'll be alert to the sort of approaches that different people use, though, so when new misleading techniques are introduced, you'll be able to identify them, and see through them to the real story.

In this chapter, we'll first discuss why you might want to use graphs in the first place: what they can tell you that numbers as a series of digits can't. We'll then discuss some of the different graphs it's possible to draw, and some of the different graphs that we see in the media, in order to think about why different graphs are suitable for different tasks. Finally, we'll discuss some of the different ways in which graphs can be used to mislead people, and how a lot of the time these are based on bait-and-switch, where you'll expect one thing and end up with something else. By the end, you'll have a good sense of the different options that are available to people who make graphs for the media, and how to identify when they can mislead.

5.1 Terminology in Data Visualisation

You might be wondering why we're using the word 'graphs' so much and not using a phrase like 'data visualisation' (or 'data vis'), 'infographics' or even 'chart'. In this chapter, we're just using 'graph' to mean any kind of visual representation of data. As terms get more and more complicated and sound like they need more specialist knowledge, often they don't. If someone is using fancier language, they might be trying to show how smart they are and that you should just trust what they've said. This is not always wise!

5.2 WHAT'S THE POINT OF GRAPHS?

Imagine that you've found a piece of paper with numbers on (you'll remember stumbling on rogue pieces of paper with mysterious data in Chapter 3 too; truly, you're the luckiest person alive). It seems to report a relationship between moustaches and happiness. (What do these numbers mean? We don't know. This is why knowing where your data's come from is so important.) But what is it? You look through all the numbers individually; in the first row (first and second column), the moustaches score looks fairly low, and the happiness score looks really low compared with the others. In the second row, the moustaches score is a bit higher, and the happiness score is a lot higher. In the third, both scores are a lot higher again. But going through all these numbers takes ages, and you can't be sure what the relationship between these two sets of numbers (or two variables) really is.

The piece of paper includes a sentence at the top: 'People with big moustaches are happier than people with small moustaches.' But you're becoming sceptical of claims made without evidence. Is every single person with a big moustache happier than every single person with a small moustache? To answer this question, you need to compare each one of the observations that you're dealing with (Table 5.1).

Table 5.1   Relationship between moustaches and happiness

Moustaches	Happiness	Moustaches	Happiness
35.64	0.71	34.87	23.35
39.83	47.13	63.08	98.07
64.57	84.14	54.43	58.93
54.63	54.69	52.62	65.11
50.17	58.92	31.06	15.78
46.64	35.24	60.80	81.58
32.86	11.36	26.18	4.19
41.62	30.39	50.60	70.59
35.38	21.85	44.11	25.27
41.52	25.94	43.83	30.42
46.30	51.29	57.02	93.12
60.38	70.81	35.68	24.41
64.20	67.90	48.34	47.68
60.20	76.70	44.68	38.24
39.19	21.99	31.17	1.31
58.26	77.10	40.75	30.60
50.97	47.69	44.60	46.78
62.08	83.85	51.83	52.13
46.23	55.12	47.56	58.42
63.05	93.01	56.12	61.55
52.54	57.97	41.74	40.12
47.54	57.96	47.25	53.34

So what happens if we draw a graph instead (Figure 5.1)?

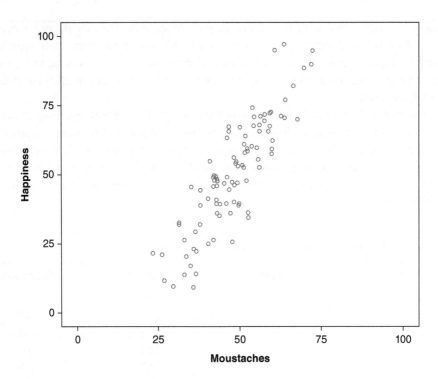

Figure 5.1   Relationship between moustaches and happiness

This is exactly the same information as was in the table. What we have here is the moustaches scores on the **x-axis** (going left to right) and the happiness scores on the **y-axis** (going bottom to top).

It's clear from this graph that in our mysterious, made-up data (remember Chapter 3 – check your sources!), that (broadly) as the moustaches scores go up a bit, the happiness scores go up sharply. This isn't always the case – there's a decent amount of variation – but this is easier to understand than the original table was.

But, hang on – you've just found some more mysterious data from the sky. This seems to show the relationship between *beards* and happiness (Table 5.2).

What do we think? If the last table was difficult to make sense of by eyeballing, this is even worse, though there are not as many numbers as last time. Sometimes 'beards' is high and 'happiness' is low, sometimes the opposite is true; and sometimes they're both low and sometimes both high.

Just like last time, this piece of paper includes a sentence at the top. You're told 'People with big beards are no happier than people with small beards.' But you could interpret this in several different ways. Is everyone equally happy? Is it that

Table 5.2   Relationship between beards and happiness

Beards	Happiness	Beards	Happiness
37.95	80.69	73.07	26.85
76.67	79.54	76.41	32.23
57.18	50.31	53.07	15.31
56.67	13.00	50.00	19.15
61.02	14.15	46.67	22.62
65.12	18.00	43.07	27.23
69.74	22.62	39.49	32.62

people with medium-sized beards are the happiest of all? We could imagine lots of different graphs leading to this same conclusion, so, once again, we'll need to interpret the full set of data.

Is the relationship between beards and happiness positive or negative? Let's try drawing it again (Figure 5.2).

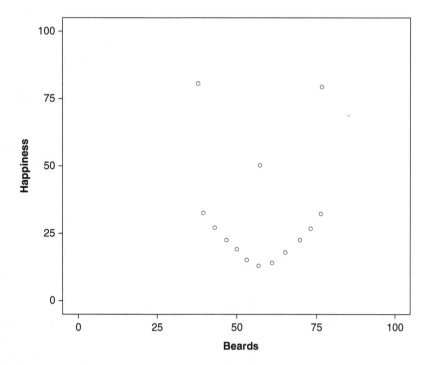

Figure 5.2   Relationships between beards and happiness

Brilliant, someone's helpfully drawn us a smiley face. Just what we wanted.

Anyway, what have these examples shown us? The crucial thing is that when there's a lot of data, if we want to make sense of it, it's often helpful to draw it. Similarly, in the media, if there's a story that involves a lot of data points – for example, not just observing the number of people who are living below the poverty line, but how this number is different in different years or different places – it generally makes sense to publish a graph rather than just a table.

5.2.1 What's the Point of Graphs rather than Statistics?

This is a bit unfair, though. The choices aren't just to put all the data in a table, or to draw a graph of them; you can also use summary statistics, as we discussed in Chapter 2. You don't need to include every data point to know how much crime decreased in England and Wales since 1997, nor do you need a table of every single house sale in every year since 1997 to know how much an average house sold for last year. Summary statistics, such as averages, can do some of the work for us without needing to draw a graph.

Equally, summary statistics are a radical simplification of the data (graphs are too, sometimes, but often a lesser simplification). By definition, if you're using summary statistics, you're not presenting all the data that's available to you. That's not a bad thing on its own, but if you use *only* summary statistics you might be missing something important.

In statistics, this was most famously illustrated in 1973 by the statistician Francis Anscombe. He generated four datasets, with 11 data points in each. They had almost identical summary statistics: the means of two variables, which he called x and y, the variance of x, the variance of y, and the correlation between x and y (some of these terms you'll recognise from Chapter 2, others you'll learn about in Chapter 10).

So, you might assume the datasets would be more or less identical. The summary statistics are the same, so the datasets are the same, right? Again, you can look at a table (Table 5.3).

But, again, this table doesn't help. There's a couple of odd things you might spot, but there's 88 numbers to look at here, so it's difficult to tell what the overall patterns are. So let's draw some graphs instead (Figure 5.3).

This is a bit more like it. To reiterate, the summary statistics for these datasets are identical. But by looking at all four datasets at once, we can see that – in spite of the fact that so many summary statistics are identical – these patterns are very different from one another. In the first case, it looks like we've got something that

Table 5.3   Anscombe's quartet

I		II		III		IV	
x	y	x	y	x	y	x	y
10	8.04	10	9.14	10	7.46	8	6.58
8	6.95	8	8.14	8	6.77	8	5.76
13	7.58	13	8.74	13	12.74	8	7.71
9	8.81	9	8.77	9	7.11	8	8.84
11	8.33	11	9.26	11	7.81	8	8.47
14	9.96	14	8.1	14	8.84	8	7.04
6	7.24	6	6.13	6	6.08	8	5.25
4	4.26	4	3.1	4	5.39	19	12.5
12	10.84	12	9.13	12	8.15	8	5.56
7	4.82	7	7.26	7	6.42	8	7.91
5	5.68	5	4.74	5	5.73	8	6.89

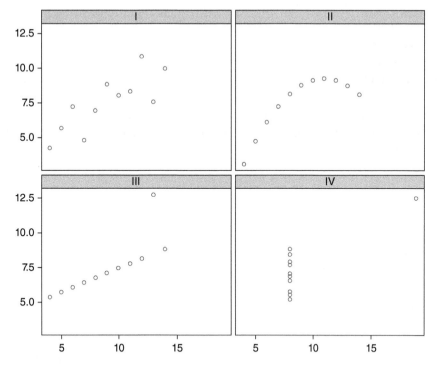

Figure 5.3   Anscombe's quartet

gradually increases. In the second, it looks like we've got a pretty close relationship, with numbers increasing as far as about 11, then decreasing. In the third and fourth, we've got some outliers.

So there's a lot of value in drawing graphs – they can reveal things that other forms of data presentation can't. It's often better to draw a graph than a table because it's easier to make sense of, and it's often better to draw a graph than use summary statistics as summary statistics leave a lot out.

But this is all rather abstract so far. What kinds of graphs do we see in the media? What kinds of stories do they tell? How can they be used to tell stories in particular ways?

5.3 WHAT KINDS OF GRAPHS DO WE SEE IN THE MEDIA?

Although graphs in the media can seem complicated, ultimately the huge majority of them are based on four basic graph types. These are:

- pie charts
- bar charts
- line charts
- scatterplots

Which graph type you use depends on what kind of story you're telling. Crucially, it also depends on what kind of *variables* you're working with, and how many of them you've got.

5.2 What Are Variables?

Throughout this chapter, we're talking about different kinds of variables – the relationship between two continuous variables, the way that you might draw a graph using one, two, three categorical variables, and so on. So let's talk a bit more about variables.

A **variable** is an attribute that can vary. Variables can differ between people, they can differ between cats, they can differ between countries, they can differ between planets. And so on. For example, height is a variable, because one person might be taller than another. Population is a variable, as countries have different numbers of people living in them, and individual countries have had different numbers of people at different points in history. Country name is a variable, as not every country is called France.

A **continuous variable** is a variable that can hold continuous, numeric values. So height is a continuous variable: some people are 159 cm tall, other people are 181 cm tall, and so on. Personal income is a continuous variable, as some people are paid $25,000 (US) a year, while others are paid $40,000 a year, and so on.

A **categorical variable** is a variable that can hold categorical, non-numeric values. So eye colour is a categorical variable: some people have blue eyes, some people have brown eyes, and so on. Vote choice is a categorical variable, as (in Germany) some people vote for the Greens, others vote for the CDU, and so on.

An important variety of categorical variables is **ordinal variables**. These are variables that consist of categorical values, but those values are in an order. For example, if I want to understand how people feel about snowball fights, I might give them the options 'Very enthusiastic', 'Fairly enthusiastic', 'Not very enthusiastic' and 'Not at all enthusiastic'. These categories clearly go from high to low, but they're still categories.

Confusingly, you'll often see people converting continuous variables into categorical variables. So while height is usually a continuous variable, with options like 180 cm and 175 cm, if the options are 'taller than 160 cm' and '160 cm or shorter', it's a categorical variable.

As with so many statistical terms, you'll pick it up as you see more examples. Luckily, we're about to run through loads of examples.

5.3.1 Pie Charts

If you've got a single categorical variable, and you want to show the relative sizes of the values of this categorical variable, you might want to use a **pie chart**. Pie charts are normally used to show the relative sizes of categories, so you might use a pie chart to show:

- proportions of people from different religious groups in a country;
- proportions of tax revenue in a country from different sources (income tax, sales tax, corporation tax, and so on);
- proportions of people who use each of the different mobile phone networks.

Here's an example. Figure 5.4 shows people's religious affiliations in Germany (using data from Evangelische Kirche in Deutschland, 2016).

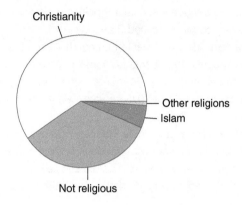

Figure 5.4   Religion in Germany

It's a no-frills example. We can see that the biggest category is Christianity, with more than half of the German population reporting that they're Christian. After this, we've got people who aren't religious, at around a third of the population. This leaves Islam, which is a much smaller slice of the pie, and other religions, much smaller again.

More generally, in looking at this, you're likely to have thought the pie consists of an entire population, and the slices consist of the fractions in each category. Here, you'd have been right. But this isn't always the case.

Pie charts aren't that versatile, and lots of people who work in graphics hate them. There's nothing you can use a pie chart for that you can't use a **bar chart** for, although pie charts are particularly good for identifying whether one category forms the majority of all responses: for example, Figure 5.4 shows clearly that most Germans are Christian. The one thing you should never do is make three-dimensional (3D) pie charts, because they are difficult to interpret and look awful.

5.3.2 Bar Charts

If you've got a single categorical variable, you might want to use a bar chart instead of a pie chart. Let's start by showing exactly the same data as last time (Figure 5.5).

As before, this reports the fraction of the German population who have different religious affiliations, and the numbers sum to 100. Any pie chart can be converted to a bar chart in this way – all you have to do is unroll it.

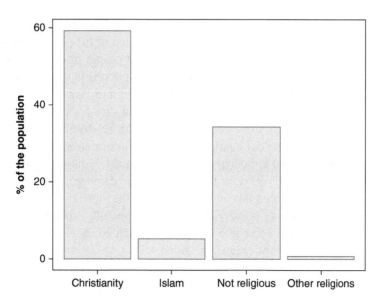

Figure 5.5 Religion in Germany

Alternatively, we could have drawn this bar chart as in Figure 5.6.

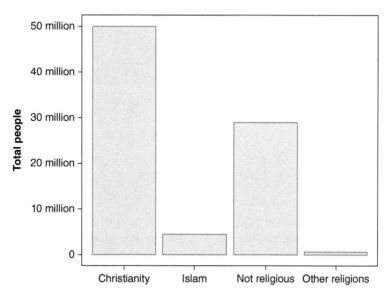

Figure 5.6 Religion in Germany

This looks almost identical to the last one, but there's a crucial difference. In the last bar chart, the bars corresponded to the fraction of the population in each group; here, the bars correspond to the number of people in each group. This might sound petty, but it's a crucial way in which pie charts and bar charts are different from one another: bar charts don't always sum to 100%.

These are two ways to visualise single categorical variables, using bar charts. However, bar charts can show more than just the relative size of different groups. It's possible to use bar charts to summarise information about more than one variable (which we'd almost always advise against doing with pie charts).

For example, imagine you want to understand the demographics of countries in South America. You could take a dataset that has the number of people in each country, but it's unlikely to be very illuminating (hopefully, nobody will be surprised that there are lots of people in Brazil). Which country has the youngest population? Let's take a look (Figure 5.7).

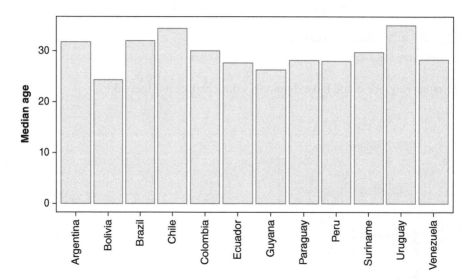

Figure 5.7   Median ages in South American countries

This graph shows the median (see Chapter 2) ages of people in each of the countries in South America. We can see that, by this measure, Bolivia has the youngest population in South America, and Uruguay has the oldest. We also could have used bar charts to show the percentages of people under 18, the mean age, or anything else.

It's worth mentioning that we have to think about this graph for a bit longer than we did for the last few graphs. We might think, for example, that Chile has a larger population of old people than Brazil. But Brazil's population is over 10 times the size of Chile's, meaning that although its median age is smaller, we would expect the number of old people to be larger. This graph doesn't include any information about how many people there are in each country, but it can mislead us into thinking things that are not true. Relying on misunderstandings like this is crucial to how graphs can be used to mislead people in the media. We'll be back to that later.

5.3.3 Line Charts

What do you do if you've got two continuous variables and one of them's time? You probably use a line chart.

Line charts are pretty common throughout the media, but they're especially common in the financial media: you can see line charts denoting how different stock market indexes are doing, how exchange rates between different currencies are changing, how rates of inflation have gone up and down, and so on.

Line charts aren't only used to denote change over time, but that's the main context in which you'll see them in the media. Let's start with a simple example: the population of the UK at each census since 1851 (Figure 5.8).

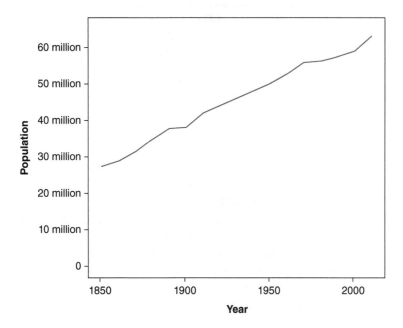

Figure 5.8   UK population since 1851

This is easy to interpret. The population of the UK more than doubled between 1851 and 2011, and the rate of change was pretty consistent.

We can compare this with a second graph, which shows the populations of the UK and the United States over the same period (Figure 5.9a).

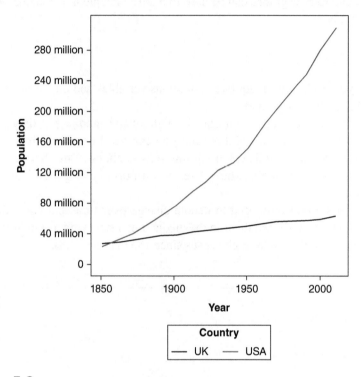

Figure 5.9a   UK and US populations since 1850

This, again, is easy to interpret. We've got a *legend*, which tells us that the UK is shown in black, while the USA is in blue, and both lines increase over the period. It's possible to have line charts with huge numbers of different lines on them – you could imagine a graph that looks like this with a separate line for each of the countries in the EU, for example – and as long as it's clear what variables we're looking at, it's easy enough to figure out what's going on.

So, what we've got here is two time series showing how two statistics (the total population in each country) have changed over time. These statistics don't have to be counts, as here – we could have looked at the median ages in each country, for example – but the crucial thing is that there's only one observation at each time point: the line never goes back on itself. Line charts usually imply change from left to right, so the x-axis variable should be time, otherwise a bar chart would be more appropriate. For example, if we redraw Figure 5.7 as a line chart, we end up with what we see in Figure 5.9b.

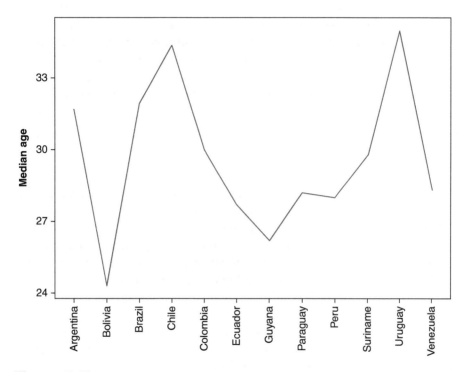

Figure 5.9b   Median ages in South American countries

This figure conveys exactly the same information as Figure 5.7, but it now looks very different. We're so used to reading line charts as conveying change over time that we might initially think that the median age in South America has changed hugely; in fact, it's just that it's not a good choice of graph to use. (Also a line chart implies linearity – that we go from Argentina to Bolivia, from Bolivia to Brazil, and so on – but, really, we're comparing all the countries.)

Anyway, what do you do if you've got two continuous variables, but neither of them is time?

5.3.4 Scatterplots

5.3 The Gapminder Foundation

The example of the relationship between GDP and life expectancy comes from Hans Rosling, who was a Swedish statistician. Hans Rosling founded the Gapminder Foundation, which aims to improve global development through the effective and responsible use of statistics. They argue that one of the key ways to improve human development is to improve the lives of the world's poorest, showing that, as income increases, quality of life and life expectancy improve dramatically. You can explore this relationship further at gapminder.org

In the media, when a story's being told about the relationship between two continuous variables, you'll probably see a **scatterplot**.

In a scatterplot, there is usually a single point for each observation. So, if you're drawing a graph that shows the relationship between weight and height for 500 adults, you'll have a graph with 500 points on it; if you're drawing a graph that shows GDP per person and life expectancy for every country in the world, you'll have a graph with 195 points on it. And it'll look a bit like the one in Figure 5.10.

(In practice, scatterplots that show relationships about the world very rarely have all 195 countries of the world in them. It's not easy to get reliable data on what GDP per head is in North Korea, for example.)

Part of the reason why you see scatterplots so frequently in the media is that they often tell a fairly straightforward story. We can see here that there's a wide range of life expectancies in countries with very low incomes, but more generally it appears that, as GDP increases, life expectancy also increases.

Although the main setting in which scatterplots are used is in reporting the relationship between two continuous variables, it's possible to include more information. For example, you might want to understand the relationship between GDP per head and life expectancy in the context of the population of each country, and where it is. Maybe the graph in Figure 5.10 exaggerates this relationship, because most countries in the world have below-average populations (there's that difference between mean and median again – see Chapter 2).

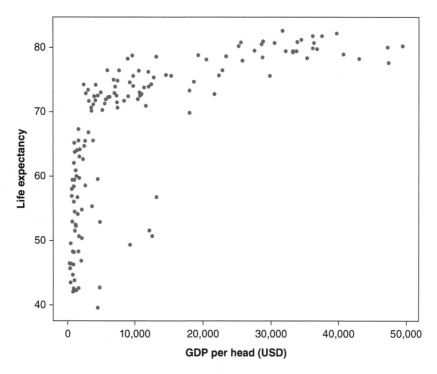

Figure 5.10   GDP and life expectancy across the world

Figure 5.11 adapts the graph a bit. We can now see that the majority of countries that are in the bottom left – with low GDP per head and low life expectancy – are in Africa. We can also see that this relationship doesn't seem to be affected by out-liers: we can see China and India, the two countries in the world with the largest populations, towards the top left of the graph. If they were way off the overall trend in the graph, that would be one thing, but this relationship looks like it's solid.

One last thing to look at with scatterplots is the introduction of the **log scale**. The graphs we've seen so far that included continuous variables – line charts and scatterplots – both used **linear scales** on the x- and y-axes. But there were a lot of observations on the left-hand side of the graph – countries where GDP per head was low – which makes it difficult to make out what the relationship between GDP per head and life expectancy is among poorer countries. We can use a log scale to try to find out what's going on here, as in Figure 5.12.

This data in this figure is exactly the same as in the last one. The only difference is that the x-axis, which reports GDP per head, is now on a log scale rather than a linear scale. This means it's easier to find out what's going on in the countries where GDP per head is lower than $5,000.

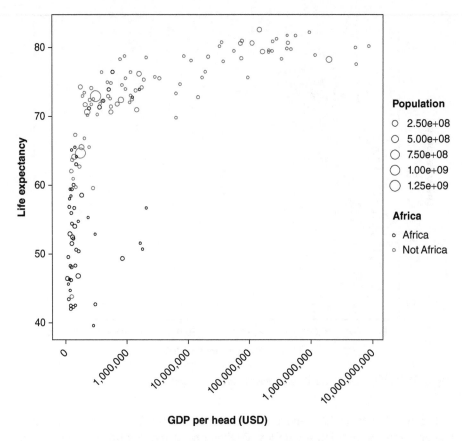

Figure 5.11   GDP and life expectancy across the world

This shows clearly that the positive relationship we can see in the top right of the graph isn't quite as strong in the bottom left, but that there's still a positive relationship. It really shows that the biggest differences in life expectancy are between very poor and fairly poor countries. A country that goes from a GDP per head of $800 to $1,600 is likely to vastly increase its life expectancy; a country that goes from a GDP per head of $40,000 to $40,800 (an increase of the same number of dollars) isn't likely to see a big difference (although, see Chapter 10, we can't assume this causal relationship based on this data alone).

That said, you don't see log scales in the media very often. If you'd seen this graph in the media, you might have inferred that the relationship between GDP per head is fairly linear, so for human development to improve, the

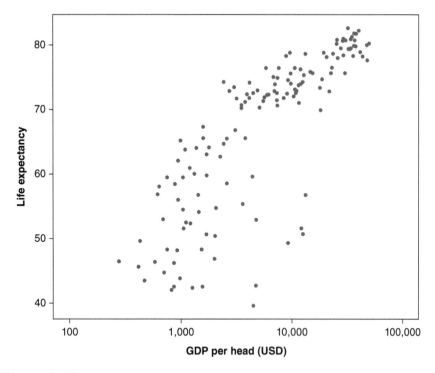

Figure 5.12   GDP and life expectancy across the world

most important thing is to improve GDP everywhere. Actually, this graph shows that the most important thing is to improve GDP in the world's poorest countries. It's misunderstandings like this that people working in the media can take advantage of, by presenting graphs that are technically accurate but misleading.

So, what are some of the ways that the media can mislead us with graphics?

5.4 WAYS THE MEDIA CAN MISLEAD US WITH GRAPHICS

Here, we're going to focus on two broad categories of misleading with graphics, focusing on the y-axis and on the x-axis. You'll see that these both present a range of opportunities for disinformation, but there are plenty more options available. This will give you a sense of what's most common, and should make you more alert to techniques for misleading people that we don't cover in this section.

5.4 Truncated Axes

While truncated y-axes are often used to mislead people, this doesn't mean that every single graph that has a continuous y-axis should start at zero. For example, let's say you wanted to draw a graph of the average temperature in every country in Europe in July. Do you have to start each bar at zero? If so, zero what: Fahrenheit? Celsius? Kelvin? If we start our graph at 'true zero', that is zero Kelvin, the graph would be all but useless.

It also often doesn't make sense for line graphs to start at zero. If you're drawing a graph of how GDP has changed over time, all it takes for a recession is for one quarter's growth to be negative. But you probably can't detect a quarter's growth being negative if it only falls by 0.25%. In this case, it makes sense for the lower bound of the y-axis to be near the lowest value that it ever takes, so it's easier to get a sense of variation over time.

But how do you decide where to start or finish the graph? We'll talk about that next.

In all electoral systems, political parties use a range of different techniques to persuade people to vote for them. In the UK, which has a first-past-the-post system (i.e. the party with the most votes in a local area wins the seats for that area), one technique is to try to persuade people to vote tactically. If you support the Conservative Party, you're most likely to want a Conservative MP, but if you're in a constituency where you think the Conservative candidate has no chance of winning, you might be persuaded to vote for the Liberal Democrats to keep Labour from winning.

One way of persuading people that their preferred candidate has no chance of winning is to truncate the y-axis. In bar charts, the convention is to go from zero to the maximum number, so if there are two bars, and one number is twice the other, the corresponding bar is twice as tall as the other. But it's possible to present bar charts where this isn't the case.

In the UK, the Liberal Democrats are notorious for truncating the y-axis, to persuade people to vote for them. As an example, in the lead-up to the 2010 General Election in the UK, some Lib Dem campaign material included a graph that looked a great deal like the one in Figure 5.13. (We've stripped out annotations like 'It's a two-horse race!', and so on, that emphasised the Lib Dems' position that they were the only party that could realistically beat Labour.)

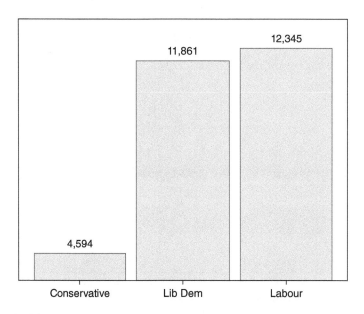

Figure 5.13   The result of the 2005 General Election in Islington South & Finsbury

If you saw this graph, you'd probably be persuaded that the Conservatives were no-hopers in this election. They're miles behind both the Lib Dems and Labour. So if you'd normally vote Conservative, you might draw the conclusion that your party had no chance, and if your priority was to keep Labour out, you might vote Lib Dem instead.

Except, of course, while the Conservatives were behind, they weren't as far behind as this graph implies. If we make the y-axis start at zero instead, Figure 5.14 shows what the graph looks like.

The Conservatives are still behind, but they're nowhere near as behind as they looked in the first graph. Given that the polls at the time were indicating that the Conservatives were likely to do a lot better in the 2010 election than they had in the 2005 election, this smaller-looking difference (which actually corresponds to identical numbers) might mean the Conservatives might still win.

(In the end, this strategy backfired for the Lib Dems. Having won 38% of the vote in this constituency in 2005, their vote share fell to 34% in 2010 – which, to be fair, was better than the 11% they got in 2015.)

So that's one way of misleading people with the y-axis: acting as if it starts at zero, when it doesn't, implies that differences are bigger than they actually are.

But what's better than misleading people with the y-axis? Misleading people with *two y-axes*. This involves, effectively, drawing two graphs on top of one another, with a consistent x-axis.

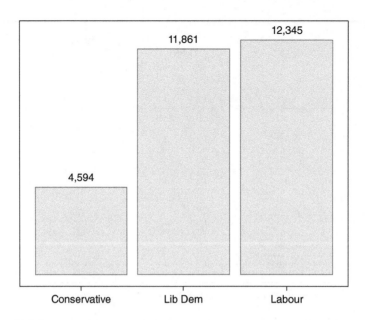

Figure 5.14   The result of the 2005 General Election in Islington South & Finsbury

On 22 April 2014, the *Daily Mail* asked, 'Has removing lead from paint and petrol reduced CRIME? Toxin linked to surges in crime and violent assault.' The story asked whether a rise and subsequent fall in crime could partly be linked to the change in the amount of lead that children were exposed to as they were growing up, and asked whether the importance of other social factors – 'poverty, drugs and alcohol' – may have been exaggerated.

The story was illustrated with a graph that looked a lot like Figure 5.15. There's a lot going on in this graph, so we'll go through the different elements one by one.

This graph shows how two different things varied over time. The first variable is preschool blood lead, which is a measure of how much lead people tended to have been exposed to as children. This measure is shown on the left-hand y-axis: it started at around 6 in 1950, rising as high as 17.5 in 1973, and eventually falling as low as about 4 in 1995. You can see the dates that this corresponds to on the higher line of the two numbers on the x-axis. The figures themselves are the black line.

The second variable is the British Index Crime trend, which is a measure of the crime rate in Great Britain. If you look at the right-hand side of the graph, you can see how this varied, from as high as about 11,250 crimes per 100,000 people in 1993 to as low as about 3,000 crimes per 100,000 people in 1969. (We'll discuss

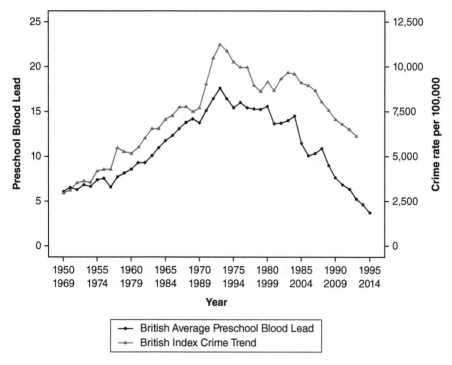

Figure 5.15   Relationship between British Average Preschool Blood Lead and British Index Crime Trend

how crime rates have changed, and how to measure them, later in the chapter.) This time series corresponds to the lower line of numbers on the x-axis. The figures themselves are the blue line.

What's the story here? It looks as if the conclusion is: if children are exposed to lead before they start school, they're more likely to commit crimes (see Chapter 10 to read about a related concept of spurious correlation). And they're not likely to commit crimes when they're in preschool, so we lag the time by 19 years: we're looking at the age at which the children who were (or who weren't) exposed to lead, and looking 19 years later, to see whether the amount of lead that children are exposed to predicts crime rates.

This looks very dramatic: the increases in both accompany each other, and the decreases in both accompany each other as well. Not only that, but they start almost identical, while the crime rate ends up outpacing the lead rate: as the amount of lead increases, the amount of crime increases even more 19 years later. You might well conclude that crime rates can be explained by lead exposure.

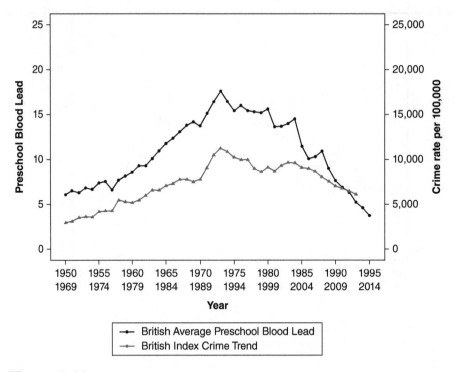

Figure 5.16   Relationship between British Average Preschool Blood Lead and British Index Crime Trend

But the graph could have been drawn like Figure 5.16 instead of Figure 5.15. How would our conclusions have been different if we'd seen Figure 5.16 instead of Figure 5.15?

The numbers in Figure 5.16 are exactly the same as the numbers in Figure 5.15. You can see why they look different by looking at the y-axis on the right-hand side: the canvas of the graph goes up to 25,000 crimes per 100,000 people. So the blue time series only goes up half as high as it used to.

This time, it looks like the numbers roughly accompany each other on the way up (i.e. an increase in lead seems to accompany an increase in crime) but they don't accompany each other on the way down, with blood rate collapsing from 1984, accompanied only by a relatively minor decrease in crime. Except, of course, the decrease in crime only looks minor because we've made it take up less space than we did before.

Finally, we can consider what the graph looks like if we play around with the numbers again, as in Figure 5.17.

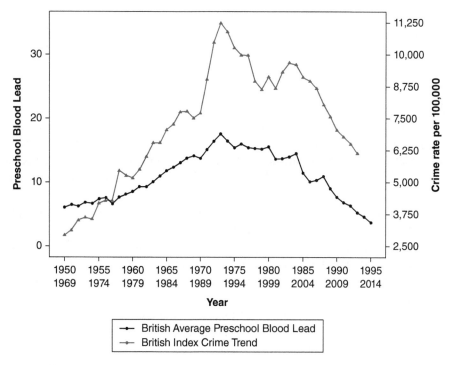

Figure 5.17   Relationship between British Average Preschool Blood Lead and British Index Crime Trend

This looks different again. It looks as if lead is actually pretty stable, starting at a higher rate than crime, although with crime overtaking it in the 1950s, and while it increases until the 1970s and falls again, it's nowhere near as volatile as crime. So this might lead you to conclude that there's not much of a relationship between crime and lead.

In fact, in this instance we started the preschool blood levels at 0, but started the crime rate per 100,000 at 2,500, rather than at 0 as in other graphs. Extending the range of the graph like this means that crime rates look volatile, because we're exaggerating differences as far as we can, while making differences in preschool blood lead look as small as possible.

It's not difficult to manipulate multiple time series like this. If you want to make the graphs look as dramatic as possible, you can use techniques like choosing different amounts of time to lag by (why does this graph use 19 years, rather than 17 or 22?), and making the range of values look as similar as possible. If you want to imply no relationship, you can play around with the scales to make one of your time series look dramatic and the other look inconsequential. And there's always a transformation you can use to get your lines to cross over at a relevant point in history, at which your audience thinks the country you're writing about went to the dogs.

5.4.2 Misleading with the x-axis

While changing y-axes can affect the conclusions a reader makes from a graph, so can adjusting the x-axis. This is particularly the case when using line graphs that plot time-series data. So how do you decide when to start and when to stop? (Essentially, what years to include in your graph.) Sometimes the decision feels like it's made for you; if you're showing data from a survey that's only been running since 2005, you can't show data from before 2005. But if you're showing something that goes further back – for example, if you're a financial journalist reporting on interest rates in the UK, you're probably not going to go as far back as 1694 – you have to make a decision based on something else. The fact that you can decide about how far back to go can make things a bit easier – if you've got to make a decision, why not choose one that makes the story you're writing as dramatic as possible?

Let's start with a story headlined 'Racism on the rise in Britain' (Taylor and Muir, 2014). This story, from *The Guardian* in 2014, described how the most recent wave of data from the British Social Attitudes Survey showed that the fraction of people who admitted to being prejudiced against people of other races had increased since the previous year. (We'll leave out any questions about whether people's understanding of 'prejudice' changed over time, and whether the size of the increase was large, or distinguishable from no change, given how people were recruited to the survey – we talked about that in Chapter 4.) The subheadline was 'British Social Attitudes survey finds proportion of people in the UK who say they are racially prejudiced has risen since 2001'.

The report, from the research institute NatCen (2014), included a graph that looked a bit like Figure 5.18.

There are a few things to note here. The first is that a lot of the movement seems to be random: between 2001 and 2013, the numbers of people admitting to being prejudiced against people from other races bounced up and down year-on-year. And the fraction of people admitting prejudice in 2012 was a lot lower than in 2011, so even though there was an increase in 2013, the fraction of people admitting prejudice against people from other races was a lot lower than it had been two years previously.

What does this have to do with the x-axis? Have a look at the left-hand side of the graph. It looks as if prejudice decreased fairly quickly between 1986 and 2000; in this part of the graph, the numbers are fairly consistently moving downwards.

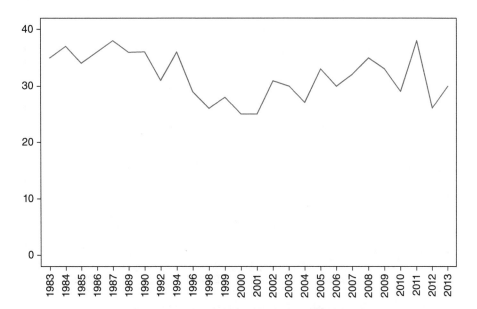

Figure 5.18   Self-reported racial prejudice in Britain, 1983–2013

But the numbers aren't evenly spaced. This survey hasn't been conducted every year – there was a period between 1987 and 1998 where several years were missed. This has exaggerated the rate of change in the graph, as a period of nine years here takes up as much space as six years elsewhere. An alternative way to draw the graph would be like that in Figure 5.18.

It's a bit less dramatic now, but this should also give you a sense of what's possible when you play around with the x-axis. Next, we'll show you how you can generate drama more spectacularly with the x-axis.

Crucially, that first graph wasn't incorrect. It reported each of the figures for each of the years, in order, and each of them was labelled. Most people aren't likely to read it like that, though. Normally, when you see a line graph, years are evenly spaced. So missing out individual years is an easy way to imply a story's more (or less) dramatic than the underlying data might suggest.

There's a more spectacular way to mislead with the x-axis, though. The above example may be misleading, but the worst thing you're likely to take away is that prejudice decreased in the 1990s more quickly than it actually did. And the reason's fairly innocent: they've plotted all the available data, with each of the waves of the survey that were available in order.

Another recent story in *The Guardian* had the headline 'Police data show crime rising at increasing rate in England and Wales' (Travis, 2017). In a long

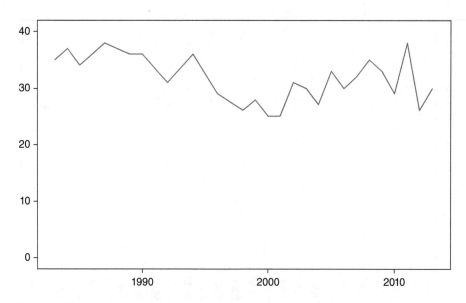

Figure 5.19   Self-reported racial prejudice in Britain, 1983–2013

list of types of offence, one of the details was that the number of thefts that had been reported to the police in the last year was 11% more than it had been in the previous year. This was in the context of a 13% rise in reported crimes in general, including an 8% rise in reported murders and a 27% rise in reported knife crime.

This was accompanied by a graph of violent crime, showing a gradual uptick from 2002, a gradual decrease a few years later, then a huge spike after 2013.

But let's stick with theft for the moment. The data was derived from the Office for National Statistics (ONS, 2017), and from there it was possible to get the data to generate different graphs. Using this data, the graph in Figure 5.20 shows how the number of reported thefts changed between 2009 and 2017 in England and Wales.

This looks fairly ominous. It looks as if the rate of theft decreased a great deal between 2010 and 2015, but then spiked dramatically between 2016 and 2017. This might make us suspect that the number of thefts is likely to increase even further in the coming years. (Although you might be wondering about the y-axis again here: why is the bottom around 1,700, rather than 0?)

The data that's available for reported crime goes back further than this, though. We've chosen 2010 because it looks extremely dramatic: it means we

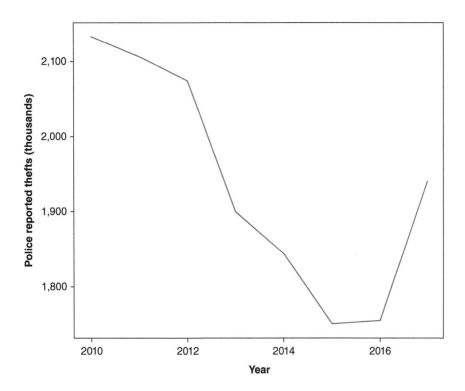

Figure 5.20   Thefts reported to the police in England and Wales, 2010–17

can see a large increase in the number of thefts, seeming to undo all the positive developments that took place between mid-2012 and 2015, in just one year. If you wanted to tell a story that this wasn't a big deal – that the increase in 2017 was a blip, rather than an indication that the number of thefts is just going to continue to increase – you might include the graph in Figure 5.21 instead.

The section of the graph from 2010 onwards is exactly the same. It just looks less dramatic now that it's been put into the context of the previous 30 years: the number of thefts reported to the police in 2003 was far higher than in any other year since. So it's easy to play around with the x-axis to tell the story you want; if you want to make it look like an increase is huge, you could leave out any years that contradict the story you're telling.

This has implications for readers of the news and media too. You should be asking what's being left out of graphs that you can see. If you see a graph that covers 2003 to 2015, what happened in 2002? What happened in 2016? There's often an innocent explanation – maybe the data wasn't collected, and you have to start and stop somewhere – but there's often a nefarious explanation, too.

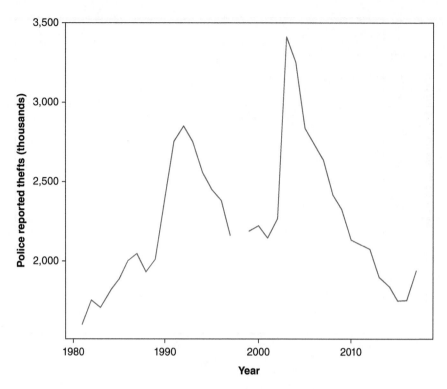

Figure 5.21   Thefts reported to the police in England and Wales, 1982–2017

5.5 Measuring Crime

Aside from any issues with when you start and stop measuring crime data, it's worth mentioning that the number of crimes reported to the police isn't a very good measure of the amount of actual crime taking place in a country. Some varieties of crimes are only rarely reported to the police, while some groups are unlikely to report crimes to the police – for example, undocumented migrants who are attacked might not report this to the police because they're worried about their immigration status. Indeed, an increase in reported crime could indicate that it has become easier for such marginal groups to report crime, which is a good thing! Survey data is much more reliable as long as its sample is representative (see Chapter 4), because it includes questions about whether people are victims of crime and whether they're reported to the police. This gives us a better sense of who are not reporting being victims of crime, and what kinds of crimes are unlikely to be reported to the police.

Figure 5.22 shows how these numbers compare with data from the British Crime Survey.

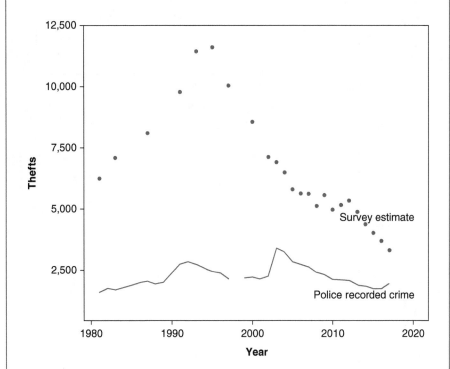

Figure 5.22   Thefts in England and Wales, 1982–2017

Now, not only does the increase in 2017 in the police recorded crime data look like a blip, but the increase in 2003 does as well.

5.4.3 Reflecting on This

Is there a neutral, unbiased way to present data graphically? We could make sure that we include as much data as possible. We could make everything we're doing explicit, so that someone who's checking carefully knows exactly what we've

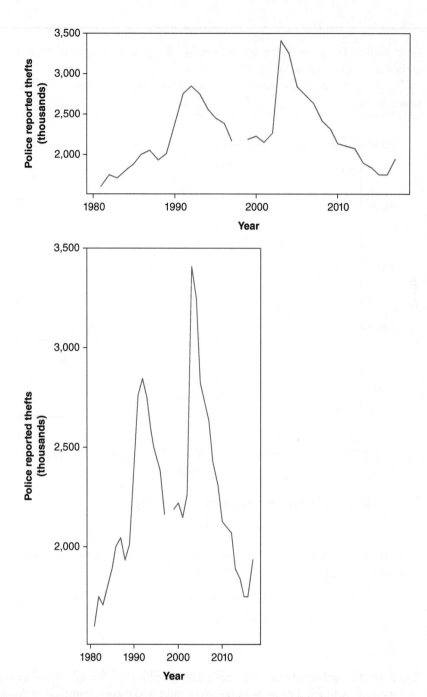

Figure 5.23   Thefts reported to the police in England and Wales, 1982–2017

done. We can adhere to conventions, so that people who don't have time to check everything carefully can intuitively understand our work without being misled.

But even if you do that, different presentations can be interpreted in different ways. Consider the two graphs in Figure 5.23, based on the example above about reported thefts.

Which one looks most dramatic? Probably the second one – the steep slope up to 2003 makes it look like there was a huge increase in crime in that year.

But they all contain exactly the same data (which is exactly the same data as you saw before). The only difference is the shape: if you've got something tall and thin, changes year-on-year tend to look more dramatic than something short and fat, which might be better at highlighting small differences between years when you've got a long series that you're looking at.

So there's no one best thing to do. Remember that graphs on TV are likely to be the shape of a TV, and that graphs in a newspaper are likely to fit into whatever space is available. Making a graph tall and thin isn't purely for exaggeration, and making it a landscaped rectangle isn't purely to hide important changes: it's likely to be because that's what the canvas available to the broadcaster is.

The fact is that all the ways of presenting data, whether graphs, summary statistics or whatever else, are only ever partial representations of the truth, and cannot tell the whole truth. As such, graphs will often present one side or the other of a story, either accidentally or deliberately.

5.6 It's Not All Bad!

While there are all sorts of different ways that the media can use graphics to mislead us, there are also loads of brilliant examples of the visualisation of data. We've avoided presenting a list of things to look out for that indicate that graphics are trustworthy, because it's always possible to put a graph together that fulfils certain criteria for trustworthiness while misleading you in a brand-new way. However, you might want to have a look at some examples of really effective data visualisation that have successfully brought stories to life. For some examples that we particularly like, why not Google some of the following?

- 'Design secrets behind the FT's best charts of the year'. In this page, you can see some of the graphs published in the *Financial Times* that it was particularly proud of – covering a range of topics from how new iPhones

(Continued)

affected Apple's share price in each year from 2007 to 2017, to how life expectancy has changed in different parts of the UK, to the ages of pandas living in captivity in different parts of the world. The graphs are all different from one another, but they all tell interesting stories.

- You can compare this with FiveThirtyEight's 'The 52 Best – And Weirdest – Graphics We Made In 2016'. This is a very different article, with much less explanation about each graph; in exchange, there are more graphs themselves. These cover all sorts of different issues, from how common it is for married couples at different ages to support different political parties, to the ages of people competing in equestrian events at the Olympics, to the fraction of medals won by the United States that were awarded to women. Again, the graphs are all very different from each other, and you can judge for yourself which are most effective.

- 'America is a Violent Country' is a graphic put together by Kieran Healy, which shows the differences in assault death rates between the United States and the rest of the OECD, which was subsequently adapted for the *The Washington Post*. It's a striking image that demonstrates huge differences between the United States and the other nations, and also demonstrates that assault death rates in the United States per 100,000 people have actually been declining since the 1970s. It doesn't include all the countries in the OECD; most significantly, it excludes Estonia and Mexico, both of which have relatively high assault death rates. You can decide for yourself whether, and how far, this makes the graphic misleading or not. The author posted a follow-up piece on his website with some discussion of this, and other issues.

5.5 CONCLUSIONS

So what have we learned? This might all feel fairly negative. While the value in graphics in the media often lies in an ability to convey a lot of information in a relatively small space, this value can be exploited. As we're fairly used to interpreting visual data, we don't normally critically assess what's included in graphics in the media – we assume the graphics we see follow conventions. And if these conventions are violated, that doesn't mean the graphics are wrong, but it does mean that we're likely to be misled.

It's not all bad, though. Applying a critical eye to the presentation of graphics means it's often fairly straightforward to see what's wrong with them: whether something's been left out, or whether something's been constructed in such a way to exaggerate or hide differences. This means we can identify the ways in which media are pushing a particular angle on a story.

More than this, graphs in the media often do more good than harm. Even a lot of the bad examples here aren't bad in and of themselves: they often contain more information, providing helpful insight, than any other way to present data. And if we can apply our critical perspective, we can figure out what's going on, and what we think the real story is, even with other people's presentation. When this isn't possible – for example, because the only years that have been included are the ones where something got worse, and the story ignores the many years of things getting better beforehand – we often know where to look to see if the data's been presented in misleading ways. We're in a position to identify when media are trying to mislead us with graphics, and we've got techniques to stop this from happening.

The next stage is to think about a type of graphic that we haven't talked about here. We've discussed how things vary across different variables, and across time: what about over space? Time to draw some maps.

5.6 CONCEPTS LEARNED IN THIS CHAPTER

A **graph** is any visual representation of quantitative data. It shows information about at least one variable. There are several different varieties of graph. In addition to the following, examples include a histogram, a density curve, a violin plot, a Sankey diagram and innumerably more.

A **pie chart** is a circular graph that shows the fractions of a whole, where each 'slice' of the pie takes up as much area as the fraction does of the whole. For example, a pie chart might report the fractions of people of different religions in a country. If the fraction of people reporting no religion were 28%, the slice of the pie representing people of no religion would take up 28% of the overall pie.

A **bar chart** is a graph consisting of vertical columns of different heights, with heights corresponding to some numerical measure. Most commonly, a bar chart shows the number of cases that fall into values of a categorical variable, but they can also show fractions, or statistics associated with values of a categorical variable. A bar chart might therefore show the numbers of people who live in each South American country, or it might show the median ages of people who live in each South American country.

A **scatterplot** is a graph that shows the relationship between two continuous variables, like height and weight of people, or average life satisfaction and unemployment rate per country. It consists of a single point for each case in the dataset, with information about two variables for those cases. The combination of all the points reveals patterns (or otherwise) in the data.

A **line chart** is a scatterplot in which the points are connected to one another, and there is at most one observation for each value on the x-axis. Most commonly, line charts are used to show how something has changed over time: an example line chart might show the median house price in each year since 1995 in England and Wales.

On a graph, the **x-axis** goes left to right. A variable associated with the x-axis will have its values spread across this. For example, a bar chart usually has its bars going from left to right, while in a scatterplot that has GDP on the x-axis and life expectancy on the y-axis, poor countries will be on the left and rich countries will be on the right.

On a graph, the **y-axis** goes bottom to top. In a scatterplot that has GDP on the x-axis and life expectancy on the y-axis, countries with low life expectancy will be towards the bottom, while countries with high life expectancy will be towards the top.

A **linear scale**, when applied to an axis of a graph, is a scale in which numbers increase through addition. For example, a linear scale might start at 0, and then increase in regular intervals of 10, with tick marks of 0, 10, 20, 30, 40 and 50.

A **logarithmic scale**, or **log scale**, when applied to an axis of a graph, is a scale in which numbers increase through addition. For example, a logarithmic scale might start at 1, and then increase at regular multiples of 10, with tick marks of 1, 10, 100, 1,000 and 10,000.

5.7 QUESTIONS FOR CLASS DISCUSSION

1   Find a news source close at hand – it could be a physical newspaper or maga-zine, it could be an online news source, it could be a broadcaster (except this won't work if it's radio). Starting at the top, keep skimming through until you find a graph; on most days of the year, it shouldn't take more than a minute or two until you find one. Having done so, answer the following questions:

    a   What kind of graph is it you're looking at?
    b   What are the variables that are involved?
    c   Does it include any of the techniques in Section 5.4 to potentially mislead its audience?
    d   How do you feel about it in general?
    e   Could it be drawn differently? If so, how? Is your proposed alternative better, worse or just different?

2   Return to your news source close at hand. This time, find a story that includes numbers but *doesn't* include a graph. Think about how this might be addressed. What kinds of graphs might be included in this story? Would they help under-standing, or would they just make the story more confusing?

FURTHER READING

D'Efillippo, V. and Ball, J. (2016) *The Infographic History of the World*. London: Firefly.

Heller, S. and Landers, R. (2014) *Raw Data: Infographic Designers' Sketchbooks*. London: Thames & Hudson.

Kirk, A. (2016) *Data Visualisation: A Handbook for Data-Driven Design*. London: Sage.

Povasec, S. and Lupi, G. (2016) *Dear Data*. London: Particular.

Tufte, E. R. (1983) *The Visual Display of Quantitative Information*. Cheshire, CT: Graphics Press.

REFERENCES

Center for American Progress (2009). *Health Care in Crisis*. Washington, DC: CAP.

Evangelische Kirche in Deutschland (2016). *Zahlen und Fakten zum kirchlichen Leben*. Hanover: EKD.

NatCen (2014) 30 years of British Social Attitudes self-reported racial prejudice data. London.

ONS (Office for National Statistics) (2017) *Crime in England and Wales: Year ending June 2017*. Newport: ONS.

Taylor, M. and Muir, H. (2014) Racism on the rise in Britain. *The Guardian*, 27 May.

Travis, A. (2017) Police data shows crime rising at increasing rate in England and Wales. *The Guardian*, 19 October.

6 Maps in the media: 'Where is this happening?'

Key concepts

map projections, gerrymandering, data classification for maps, coastline paradox, generalisation, normalisation

6.1 INTRODUCTION

You can't really avoid maps in the media, but sometimes you might want to. For example, an electoral map showing the dominance of the candidate you didn't vote for might make you feel queasy, or a map showing the spread of a particularly nasty disease may make uncomfortable viewing. Either way, both examples help us understand the *where* element of a story, which is often critically important. In the past few years political maps in particular have, it seems, been everywhere. Examples include maps of the 2016 US presidential election and the 2016 Brexit vote going viral on social media. These two examples also serve to highlight the potentials and pitfalls of using maps, which we discuss in this chapter. More broadly, the proliferation of open data and new mapping technologies means that maps are now a regular feature of the media landscape. That's why we think it's so important that they are well made and well understood.

Depending upon what we want to show, maps can be manipulated and designed to tell a story from a particular perspective, as Mark Monmonier explains in *How to Lie with Maps* (1991). This is because maps don't present simple truths, but instead reflect a particular view of the world, or serve the agenda of the mapmaker. This is not always true, or at least it is not always the case that people making maps have particular agendas, but maps are never value-neutral representations of the world. Therefore, this chapter is all about the kinds of maps we see in the media and the kinds of issues you need to be aware of when interpreting or making them. Towards the end of the chapter we also cover principles for effective mapping.

Now, if some of this sounds pretty negative, let us be clear that we think maps are wonderful, versatile visual representations of our world that can enlighten, inform and inspire. That's why they're so popular and why it's so important that we do our best to understand them and make good maps.

In the next section of the chapter we look at the question of when it might be a good idea, or a bad idea, to make a map, and the related question: 'does it make sense to map this?'. After looking at this question, we then consider the issue of maps that lie. In doing so, we borrow the idea from Mark Monmonier and explain that deception and sleight-of-hand have always been part of the cartographic tradition. Just enter 'maps propaganda' into the Internet search engine of your choice and you'll quickly understand what we mean.

Sometimes bad maps are caused by a combination of a lack of skills and knowledge. This is probably the most common explanation for bad mapping, but there is a darker side here. This then leads neatly on to the topic of '**gerrymandering**', which many people think of as the most devious of map-making practices. Indeed, gerrymandering can have very significant real-world impacts and can help tip the balance of power in national elections. Gerrymandering is the practice whereby political parties alter voting boundaries so that it increases the possibility that their representatives will be elected, and minimises the chances of their opponents getting into power. Given the tradition of skulduggery in certain areas of mapping, we end the chapter by reflecting upon best practices for mapping in the media, and beyond. The reason we include gerrymandering as a feature of this chapter is that it provides an excellent example of how the kinds of maps we regularly see in the media are a reflection of the wider political forces that shape society at large and not, simply, just lines on a page.

6.2 SO YOU WANT TO MAKE A MAP?

Maps can help you make friends and influence people, but the reverse is also true. Make a bad map and you'll soon hear about it. One example of this comes from the Eurostat Statistical Compendium in 2004, when the front cover famously left Wales off the EU map. The rest of Great Britain was shown, but Wales was nowhere to be seen. The First Minister of Wales laughed it off as 'a computer-generated image that has clearly gone wrong', but others were less forgiving and it created a minor diplomatic incident. This tradition of error by omission is particularly common, and has led to the development of an Internet sub-genre, including the now-famous 'Maps Without New Zealand' meme. Therefore, discerning analysts will always think carefully before deciding how to visualise any kind of data *and* be sure to include all areas when they do. They will also understand that a map might be the right way to go, but sometimes it might not; see Chapter 5 for useful data visualisation alternatives.

In order to help you decide whether your data should be mapped, we recommend that you first think what kind of data you have. One excellent resource in this regard is an ingenious chart developed by 'Chart Doctor' Alan Smith and his colleagues at the *Financial Times* in the UK. Partly inspired by Jon Schwabish's 'Graphic Continuum', and a work of art in its own right, Visual Vocabulary is a kind of data visualisation ready-reckoner that helps demystify the graphical representation of data. In Smith et al.'s (2019) guide, it is recommended that maps are only used when specific locations or geographical patterns in data are more important to the reader than anything else. This is a principle we believe in. Examples of when this is true might include the following:

- When you want to show the location of *where something happened*, such as an earthquake at a specific point in a city, or the locations of vehicle collisions.
- When you want to show *how a value varies across geographic space*. A basic example of this might be when you want to compare the percentage of people voting for a candidate across all counties in a US presidential election.
- When you want to show the *connections between places*. This kind of map is useful when you want to show something like trade flows between nations and you can represent the volume of trade, and its direction, by using lines of different thickness.
- When you want to show *geographical densities* of something. A classic example here would be crime mapping, since crime is often geographically clustered in small areas.

Another very important consideration in deciding to make a map is whether geographical accuracy is necessary, or in fact even desirable. Electoral mapping is the classic example of this, since traditional mapping can lead to distorted views about election outcomes. In the UK, for example, political constituencies have a median electorate of around 72,000 people. Excluding a small number of island constituencies, the size of the electorate tends to vary between 50,000 and 80,000. Yet when election results are mapped, the maps often don't seem to reflect the results, from a visual point of view, owing to the much larger variations in the geographical areas covered by constituencies, relative to their populations.

A good example of this is from the General Election of 2015, shown in Figure 6.1. In this map we can see a lot of dark colours, for the Scottish National Party, and a lot of blue, for the Conservative Party. Proportionately, however, we don't see much grey for the Labour Party. There are 650 constituencies in the UK and in 2015 the Conservative Party won 51% of them, with 36.8% of the vote. The

Labour party won 40% of the seats, and 29.0% of the vote. The SNP won 8.6% of all seats and had a 1.7% vote share (though it only contests seats in Scotland).

Yet, in the map, the black of the SNP accounts for 28% of all the coloured area, Labour in grey gets a 6% colour share and 49% of the map is coloured blue for the Conservatives. This visual data mismatch is the main reason why, in recent years, many news organisations have moved to representing areas using cartograms, a kind of diagrammatic map which represents areas in proportion to some underlying variable – usually population – at the expense of some geographical accuracy. We can see the results of the 2015 General Election in this format in Figure 6.1, beside the original map. Neither are truly 'correct', but the cartogram is in our view a more meaningful representation of the underlying data and is very effective in electoral mapping.

Once you get to the stage where you're sure that making a map is the way to go, another consideration is the end use. In the past, map making was typically confined to static maps that would be printed on paper or, following the advent of geographic information systems (GIS) software, viewed and explored on screen. However, with the rise of new web technologies over the past two decades there has been a transformation of possibilities in cartography. Some would argue that this has led to a proliferation of 'bad' maps, but it has also allowed media organisations and others to push the boundaries of what's possible.

Maps are hugely powerful, but when mapping we would be wise to consider first what the end purpose is, what format we aim to publish in, and, of course, who the intended audience is. Unfortunately, some people who make maps are rather devious or, more charitably, are less concerned with issues of accuracy and perception than they should be, so before any further discussion we need to reflect upon 'maps that lie' and how to avoid being sucked in by what may appear to be plausible geographic representations of reality.

6.3 HOW MAPS LIE: SOME EXAMPLES

If you really want to understand what it means to 'lie with maps', then we recommend reading Mark Monmonier's classic book on the topic. Here we provide an overview of the kinds of 'lies' that maps can tell, and why it is sometimes necessary. In this sense, we agree with the opening line of *How to Lie with Maps*, where Monmonier says 'Not only is it easy to lie with maps, it's essential.' The basic reason for this is that in order to make sense of the world we're representing, we need to simplify, generalise and abstract from reality. Sometimes, these 'lies' can be underpinned by good intent, such as helping map readers understand an issue by making a map simpler and clearer. Sometimes, however, they can be underpinned by deceit, such as when maps are used for propaganda purposes. In this section we cover some of the most important examples of how maps lie, from **map projections** to mapping house prices. We think you'll agree that it's better to be aware of these issues.

The first and most obvious way in which maps lie is in representing a three-dimensional object (the earth) on a flat plane. Clearly, this doesn't apply to globes or 3D representations in a web browser, but most maps that we view are presented on a flat screen or piece of paper. There is no way to do this without distorting the shape or size of the original feature, such as a country. Many times, both size and shape are distorted, but this kind of compromise typically has a higher purpose: to make a map easy to understand, or to aid navigation. The Mercator projection is a good example, since it was created in 1569 by Flemish navigator Gerardus Mercator for navigation at sea. Little did he know that close to 500 years later some people would be using this projection to project maps on the Internet! This is often a problem because the Mercator projection greatly distorts the size of areas the further away they are from the equator. This means that countries in Europe and North America appear much larger than they actually are relative to parts of the earth closer to the equator. You can see this in the example on the left of Figure 6.2, where we have displayed the earth using the Mercator projection alongside a more appropriate projection. We say 'more appropriate' because Arthur Robinson's 1963 projection provides a good balance between preserving the shape and size of countries.

Famously, in the Mercator projection, Greenland is similar in size to the entire content of Africa, when in fact Africa is around 14 times larger. Their relative sizes are not perfect in the Robinson projection example, but it is much closer to reality and, therefore, we would consider it an appropriate level of compromise. So, the first lesson here is that when making maps you must make sure you use an appropriate projection. Take a look at any world map in a print edition of a newspaper and you will quickly realise that not everyone understands this principle!

This first 'lie' is a necessary evil. We can never completely overcome the problem of representing a 3D object on a flat plane. This kind of compromise has a partner in crime in the world of mapping, by the name of **generalisation**. There are many ways in which maps can generalise, but an important one is in the representation of boundaries and coastlines. The example par excellence of this is the issue of mapping the coastline of Great Britain, which was popularised in 1967 by Polish-born, French and American mathematician Benoit Mandelbrot in his *Science* paper, entitled 'How Long Is the Coast of Britain? Statistical Self-Similarity and Fractional Dimension'. The paper includes some quite complex mathematical concepts, including fractals, but the basic answer to this question is that 'it depends upon how you measure it'. This is known as the 'coastline paradox' and was first

Conservative (330 seats)

Labour (232 seats)

SNP (56 seats)

Conservative (330 seats)

Labour (232 seats)

SNP (56 seats)

Figure 6.1   Map of UK 2015 General Election results

identified by Englishman Lewis Fry Richardson. Put simply, the length of a coast-line (or border) will *increase* as the unit of measurement *decreases*. Thus, if you were to measure the coastline of Great Britain using a matchstick you would get a much longer measurement than if you did it using a pole 100 metres long.

This issue means that we need to decide what level of generalisation is accept-able in maps, because coastlines, and all other line and polygon (i.e. enclosed shape) features, are represented in modern mapping software by a number of points (known as vertices) which are then connected to form lines and polygons. Using the most detailed map data available for Great Britain, via Ordnance Survey, we find that the coastline is about 11,000 miles (17,700 km) long. This can be seen in the top left of Figure 6.3. In the map on the top right, only 0.5% of the vertices have been retained and the coastline now measures around 5,300 miles (8,500 km). By removing 99.5% of the points which created the original Great Britain coastline we have *increased* the unit of measurement (i.e. the distance between vertices) and therefore *reduced* the overall coastline length. With only 0.005% of the original vertices retained (bottom left) we can see that the coastline becomes overly gen-eralised, though Great Britain is still recognisable. In the extreme example in the bottom right, only 0.0003% of the original vertices are retained and we just see a rough polygon shape. In this case, generalisation has clearly gone too far, since nobody would even be able to tell this started off as Great Britain!

There are two important reasons why we would prefer a greater level of gen-eralisation when making maps. First, it allows us to represent more clearly and simply the areas we are interested in. For maps in the media, there is often no need for the level of fine detail provided by the most accurate map data. The map of Great Britain on the top right is massively less detailed in terms of the number of points that go into defining the coastline, but it is very difficult to perceive at most scales. A second reason is that a more generalised coastline means working with smaller file sizes, which is often desirable when making maps in the media, where simplicity is often preferred.

The first two examples relate to how we represent the physical world and are fundamental to the discipline of cartography. Another category of 'lie' in map-ping is how we represent data on a map. A more in-depth exposition of this is given in Chapter 7, where we cover the 'modifiable area unit problem' identified by Stan Openshaw (1984), so here we simply wish to highlight the problem of choosing class breaks on a data-driven map. The term 'class breaks' refers to the way numeric data is divided into different groups (or classes) and then mapped using different colours (e.g. 0–5 could be blue, 6–10 could be yellow and 11–15 could be red). There are many different ways data can be grouped. To demon-strate this, and the way in which you can use different class breaks to 'lie', we will look at some maps of house prices in London. This is the kind of map we

Mercator

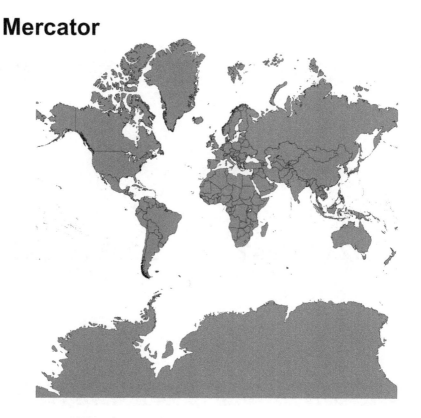

Robinson

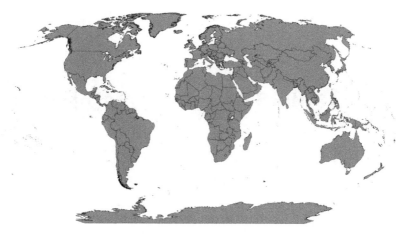

Figure 6.2   Comparison between Mercator and Robinson world map projections

Figure 6.3   The classic case of measuring the coastline of Great Britain

often see in the news, in print, online or on screen. If we take a dataset of small-area average house prices for London in 2015 and map them in our GIS software of choice, the chances are that, by default, a 'natural breaks' **data classification** will be used. However, this might not be the best choice of class break. In fact, depending upon the underlying structure of the data, it may be a very bad one.

What we've done in Figure 6.4 is to map this dataset using four different data classification ('class breaks' in technical terms) methods, in the form of a conventional *choropleth* map ('choro' from the Greek for *area* or *region*, plus multitude: the 'pleth' bit, as in plethora). If we wanted to give the impression that house prices in London were not that high – in contrast to popular opinion about their being 'out of control' – we might opt for the first map which uses an 'equal interval' classification where the range of values is divided by the number of classes (in this case, five) to determine the size of data groupings so that they are spaced using an equal interval from the lowest to highest value. On this evidence, most areas in London are in the lowest price band and house prices don't look that bad at all if you just glance at the map quickly. Look closely, however, and you can see that the lowest band goes from 0 to £1.8million, which is more than three times higher than the London average house from 2015. The numerical interval may be equal, but the number of areas in each class is certainly not.

The 'natural breaks' map shows a pattern determined by an algorithm which searches for natural 'breaks' in the data distribution and then creates different categories out of them. But as you can see, they vary in size and are not intuitive. In fact, from a human point of view, they are quite odd. The next option is 'quantile', where we have an equal quantity of areas in each category. With five classes, this means London is split into fifths in terms of price, and a clearer pattern begins to emerge, with central west London looking more expensive and the east generally less expensive. But the price ranges here are rather arbitrary and not the clean categories we generally use when thinking about real estate.

Therefore, we have also mapped prices using a manual classification where areas are grouped according to consistent £250,000 price bands, and the number of areas which fall into each category is shown in brackets. This is, we would argue, a more appropriate way of representing the underlying data. Rather than being 'right' it is, perhaps, the least wrong and the least likely to be classified as a 'lie'. You can think of this example as a kind of geographical alternative to the case of Anscombe's quartet described in Chapter 5. In that case, we showed how several datasets can have the same mean, median and standard deviation and therefore be interpreted as if they are similar, when in fact the opposite may be true. In the map case presented here we have the same dataset presented in four different ways, each of which might lead to a different interpretation of the same underlying data.

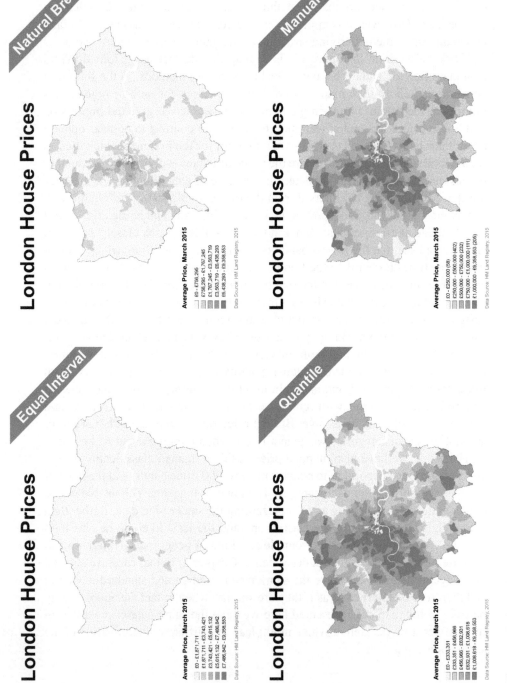

Figure 6.4 How different data classification leads to different maps

Another 'lie' we should mention occurs when map makers want to make sure their work isn't copied (an issue very much still relevant in today's media landscape!). In such cases, cartographers may insert fake places or features in order to catch out unsuspecting copyright infringers. This can also occur when a mapmaker wants to poke fun at sports rivals. One of the most famous examples of this is in the appearance of the towns of 'Beatosu' and 'Goblu' on the 1978–79 edition of the official state of Michigan map, which were supposedly added on the orders of Peter Fletcher, a University of Michigan alumnus and State Highway Commission chairman. The names of the towns come from 'beat OSU' and 'Go Blue', two common chants heard at American football games against rivals The Ohio State University, of which the author of this chapter, Alasdair Rae, is an alumnus. It is not known whether they were actually inserted as a 'copyright trap' to prevent unauthorised copying, but this example has entered map lore owing to its inclusion in *How to Lie with Maps*. Either way, it definitely counts as a lie.

Finally, as *The New York Times* revealed in 1988, almost every public map produced by the Soviet Union from 1938 to 1988 was 'deliberately falsified'. Apparently part of a scheme to frustrate foreign intelligence operations, the Soviet maps misplaced rivers, diverted streets, reshaped boundaries and left out key geographical features, on orders of the NKVD (the secret police). This is a particularly egregious example, but as you can see lying is very much part of the cartographic tradition.

6.4 'A NEW SPECIES OF MONSTER': FROM THE 'GERRY-MANDER' TO THE 'BROKEN-WINGED PTERODACTYL'

The cartographic deceptions of the Soviet state, cynical as they were, have some way to go before they match the ingenuity and opportunism of political gerrymandering. Named for Elbridge Gerry, the fifth Vice President of the United States and Governor of Massachusetts from 1810 to 1812, 'gerrymandering' is the process of redrawing electoral boundaries so that one political party has a numerical advantage in relation to the number of its voters within a given area, such as a Congressional District. A simplified example is shown in Figure 6.5. It is most famous in the United States but occurs all over the world. It is important to say here that although gerrymandering is typically thought of as an underhand practice, it doesn't have to be. It could be used, for example, to help ensure underrepresented minority groups have political representation. Yet this is very rare. What makes it bad is when, as typically happens, gerrymandering occurs in order to give the incumbent an advantage in any re-election battle and to increase the power of the already powerful.

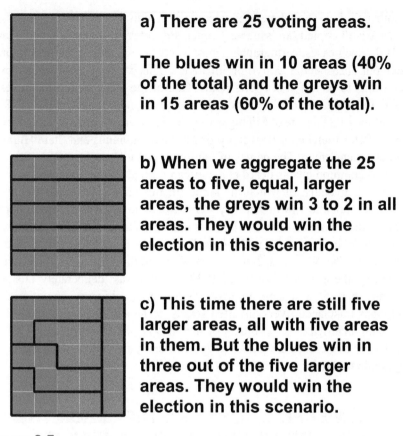

a) There are 25 voting areas.

The blues win in 10 areas (40% of the total) and the greys win in 15 areas (60% of the total).

b) When we aggregate the 25 areas to five, equal, larger areas, the greys win 3 to 2 in all areas. They would win the election in this scenario.

c) This time there are still five larger areas, all with five areas in them. But the blues win in three out of the five larger areas. They would win the election in this scenario.

Figure 6.5   A simplified example of gerrymandering in action

The term 'gerrymander' originally appeared as 'gerry-mander' in the short-lived *Boston Gazette* on 26 March 1812. Under the heading of 'THE GERRY-MANDER' was a subtitle which read 'A new species of Monster, which appeared in Essex South District in Jan. 1812', referring to the newly drawn electoral district in Essex County, Massachusetts. The shape of the district was, according to the *Gazette*, something like a salamander, and because Elbridge Gerry was the Governor under which this boundary was created, the portmanteau word 'gerry-mander' was coined and has been with us ever since. The original article on gerrymandering is written in a kind of spoof tone, and today seems rather quaint, but its real-world legacy certainly isn't.

The best way to understand present-day gerrymandering is to look at some examples, and the United States provides these. The graphic in Figure 6.6 shows some of the most famous gerrymandered districts, using Congressional District boundaries from the 114th US Congress. Here we can see six examples: Florida's

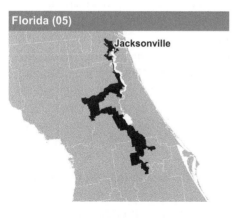
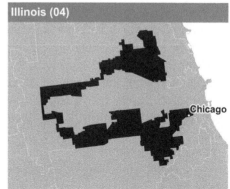
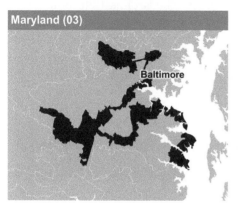
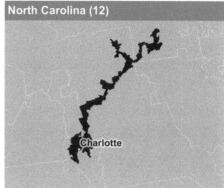
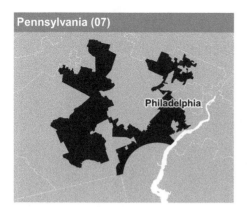
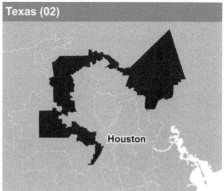

Figure 6.6   Some famous gerrymandered US congressional districts

5th Congressional District, Illinois' 4th, Maryland's 3rd, North Carolina's 12th, Pennsylvania's 7th and Texas's 2nd. The most obvious thing about these districts is their unusual shapes, with Illinois' 4th District being compared to earmuffs and Maryland's 3rd to a 'broken-winged pterodactyl'.

There is a large literature on the subject of gerrymandering, its origins and legality, so if you are interested we recommend that you read Anthony McGann's 'Gerrymandering in America' (2016) or, for a more blunt assessment of the topic, David Daley's *Ratf**ked: Why Your Vote Doesn't Count* (2016). The key point here is that simply by altering where we draw lines on maps, politicians can, in effect, select their voters, rather than the other way round, as it should be.

The examples below are among the most extreme, yet they do not actually look that bad when we compare them with some previous examples. North Carolina's 12th Congressional district provides a case in point. In Figure 6.7 we have shown six different iterations of the North Carolina 12th, from 1993 to 2017. The changing shapes are a reflection of significant legislative manoeuvring, and the most recent district looks much more coherent than its 1993 predecessor, yet it still looks very misshapen. There was a brief interlude during the period of the 106th Congress when the District looked more regular in shape, yet this didn't last long.

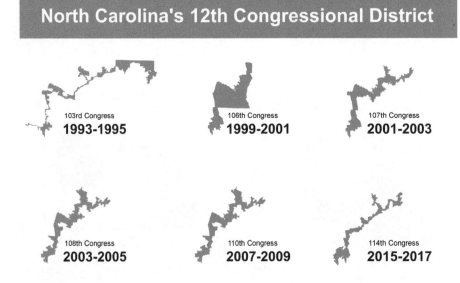

Figure 6.7   How North Carolina's 12th congressional district has changed over time

Given the present state, and recent history, of electoral geography in the United States, readers will not be surprised to hear that gerrymandering lawsuits are commonplace. At around the time of writing this chapter, in October 2017, the ongoing legal case centred on North Carolina's Congressional Districts was coming to a close and, as of 3 January 2018, the 12th District has a much less peculiar shape (Figure 6.8). We may not question the underlying logic of these shapes when we see them in the newspapers or on TV, but we believe it is important to understand how they came into being, and for that reason it's necessary to understand gerrymandering.

Although the shapes of the Districts we have presented here look particularly odd, visual interpretation alone is not the only way of spotting it. A pair of lawyers

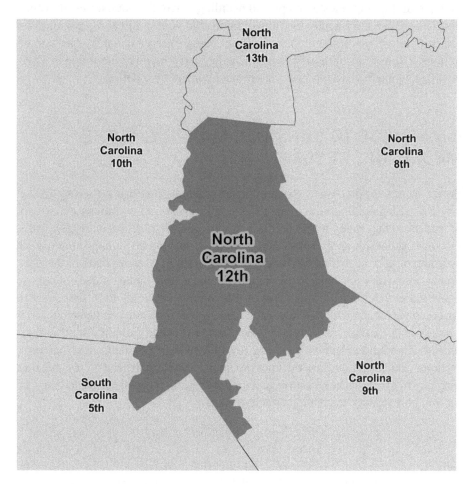

Figure 6.8   North Carolina's 12 Congressional District as of 2018

named Daniel D. Polsby and Robert Popper developed a formula which can be used to assess the extent to which individual areas are gerrymandered. The Polsby–Popper test is a measure of the compactness of a geographical area which produces a score ranging from 0 (not compact) to 1 (perfectly compact). More regularly shaped areas would be more compact and therefore achieve a score closer to 1 and thereby could be defended from accusations of gerrymandering. The opposite is true of the examples shown above.

We have focused here on the United States, since it provides the most famous examples of gerrymandering anywhere in the world, but other countries are not immune. Most democracies in the developed world have witnessed some form of gerrymandering. Therefore, one could argue, the seemingly rather dull practice of drawing lines on maps and deciding where the boundaries of voting districts are can have a massive impact upon who your political representatives are, who sits in government and – without being overly dramatic – the fate of nations. The species of monster known as the 'gerry-mander' identified in 1812 is still very much alive, and we recommend readers take notice.

6.5 A GUIDE TO SENSIBLE MAPPING IN THE MEDIA, AND BEYOND

So far in this chapter we've covered a lot of things that can go wrong in the world of mapping, and how to spot lies and problems. This is an essential part of understanding maps in the media and cartographic practice more generally. However, it doesn't really help when it comes to making good maps or avoiding common pitfalls, so that's what we cover in this section. You can think of this section as a kind of guide to sensible mapping in the media, though it does of course apply more widely. A full treatment of this topic is not possible in such a short space, so we recommend that interested readers seek out Gretchen Peterson's *GIS Cartography: A Guide to Effective Map Design* (Second Edition, 2009) if they wish to learn more. Here we focus on 10 of the most important basics: map projections, generalisation, line thickness, colours, labelling, legends, class breaks, mapping totals, scale and location, and map layout. If you get these right, you will be well on your way to creating effective maps.

6.5.1 Map Projections

Earlier in the chapter we discussed the importance of map projection and what happens when you choose the wrong one (i.e. Africa and Greenland can appear to be the same size). It is also important to understand what shape your readers

British   **WGS84**   **Europe Lambert**
National Grid   **Conformal Conic**

Figure 6.9   Great Britain illustrated using three different map projections

expect to see in a map, and in this regard projection can be critical. A good example of this is in Great Britain, where maps are most commonly shown using the British National Grid projection. If this projection is not used, Great Britain can end up looking 'short and stumpy', or otherwise misshapen. You can see this in Figure 6.9 where the leftmost map uses the British National Grid and the other two use inappropriate projections, leading to an odd-looking Great Britain which is likely to annoy and/or confuse many map readers. In this sense, map projections are like referees in a game of football: you only really notice them if they've done something wrong.

6.5.2 Generalisation

The level of generalisation in a map should vary depending upon the end use, format and scale at which the map will be presented to users. If we wish to publish a map of buildings in central London so that users can pick out the details of individual buildings then we might wish to use the example in the top left of Figure 6.10. The image in the top right has been generalised, so that individual buildings are often merged together and is less appropriate if we want users to be able to see the pattern of individual buildings. If, on the other hand, we just want

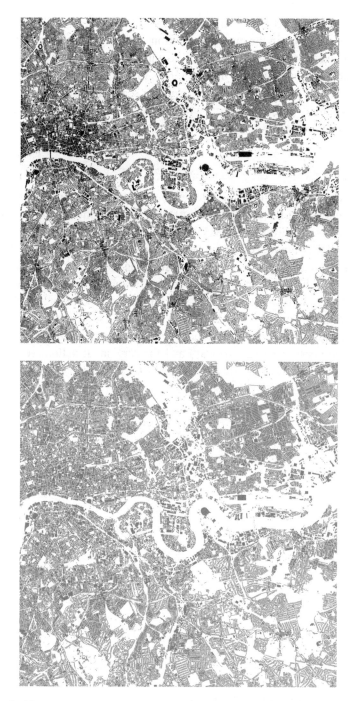

Figure 6.10   Map generalisation in focus (less generalised, right, vs more generalised)

to show the general pattern of the urban fabric, in a more zoomed-out map, the level of generalisation in the map in the bottom right may be perfectly acceptable, since the focus is not on individual map features but the overall pattern of urban development. A good general principle here is to aim for a level of generalisation appropriate to the purpose of the map, *and* the scale at which your map will be viewed. Most media graphics teams will understand these principles, yet they are sometimes overlooked.

6.5.3 Line Thickness

If you spend any time at all on the Internet looking at maps, you'll be familiar with this one. It may seem rather pedantic, but it can make all the difference! You see a map of a number of different areas coloured according to some variable, such as population, GDP or number of voters, yet the map is dominated by lots of thick black lines. What you really want to see is the underlying data, but it has been obscured owing to overly thick borders. We provide an example of this in Figure 6.11. The first map on the left has a line thickness of 1 mm, the second has a line thickness of 0.5 mm and the final one has a line thickness of 0.152 mm. In the examples with thicker line widths, the black can become overpowering, particularly in areas with long indented coastlines (e.g. Norway) and for very small nations (e.g. Andorra, between Spain and France, is not visible). A thinner line can make a big difference.

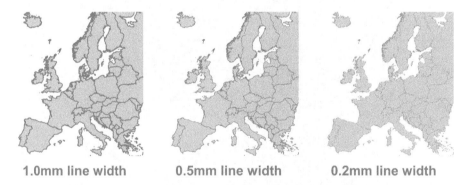

1.0mm line width   0.5mm line width   0.2mm line width

Figure 6.11   The impact of using different line thickness in map making

6.5.4 Colours

This is one of the most complex topics in cartography and graphic design, and one of the most difficult to get right. But if we stick to some simple rules, we can avoid basic errors. First of all, it's a good idea *not* to just accept the default colour scheme your mapping software might assign to your map. Furthermore, it's best to avoid red–green colour schemes because of the number of people with colour blindness for whom this would present a problem. Also, 100% black is best avoided because it can be overpowering and a very dark grey (e.g. 90% 'black') is a better alternative. It is also a very good idea to avoid using rainbow colour schemes of the kind commonly found on some weather maps. One of the big problems with rainbow colour schemes is the self-similarity of some of the colours, where readers just can't tell if a single colour represents blazing heat or freezing cold. In 2015, five leading scientists wrote a letter to *Nature* urging the scientific community to scrap rainbow colour schemes (Hawkins et al., 2015). So, if rainbows, black, and reds and greens aren't the way to go, what *should* you use? Well, read any GIS or cartographic design text or website and you'll be pointed towards Cynthia Brewer's ColorBrewer, a set of 35 colour schemes developed by Brewer and colleagues Mark Harrower, Ben Sheesley, Andy Woodruff and David Heyman. These colour sets are easily found online and will help you produce better maps. It is of course possible to use different colour schemes to create effective maps, but we recommend the ColorBrewer colour selection tool. It will also help to stop you making the mistake of including too many colours, which results in people not being able to differentiate between them, owing to a cognitive limit on human perceptions of colour.

6.5.5 Labelling

Map labelling, like colour selection, can be a minefield. Font choice, font masks, label placement, label hierarchy, label colour and the number of labels you use are some of the most important elements of labelling maps. Get it wrong and you will confuse your reader with unwanted map clutter and confusing visual messaging. To illustrate this, compare the map on the left to the map on the right in Figure 6.12. In the map on the left, four places are labelled. Three of them are labelled in capital letters using Arial bold font and one is capitalised in Arial bold, to indicate that it is a constituent part of the larger settlement of Milton Keynes, in England. The labels are just off-black, all have a slightly transparent white 'mask' or 'buffer' around them to help them stand out and a small black point to indicate where the central point of the place is. The sizes of the labels also vary according to the population and importance of the settlements, with the MILTON KEYNES label being largest and therefore most prominent. More labels could have been added, but here we have included just enough to give the map reader an idea of where the main settlements are and an indication of their relative importance in the settlement hierarchy. In the example on the right we have added many more labels, used the colour black

Figure 6.12   Labels really do matter!

with a white mask, and chosen a bold serif font (Bookman Old Style). This is an exaggerated bad example but we use it here to emphasise the importance of clarity and simplicity in labelling and the impact it can have when you get it badly wrong.

6.5.6 Legends (or Keys)

A map legend, or key, tells you what symbols or colours in a map represent. This is quite clearly missing in the example above, in order to demonstrate that although you can produce a clear map, it doesn't mean people will be able to understand it. In the Milton Keynes map example, a reader might be able to guess from the layout of the features what they are, but we should never assume this. A golden rule therefore is always to include a map legend and tell people what is in the map. Sometimes, it might even be possible to make the map legend do a little more work. One example of this, sometimes referred to as *a frequency histogram legend*, tells readers what the colours in the map represent but also displays the number of features within each category by re-sizing the colour patches relative to the number that appear in that category in the map. This can be seen in the two examples in Figure 6.13, where the first simply tells us which deprivation decile an area falls within, on a scale of 1 to 10. In the second example, the same legend is redesigned so that it tells us what proportion of areas in the map are in each category. Whether your map is a choropleth map, like the one below, or has symbols, lines or other kinds of features in it, you must explain what these features represent unless it is completely self-evident.

6.5.7 Class Breaks

Given their importance in map interpretation and the potential for misleading your audience, we covered class breaks above in the house prices in London example. If you're using a GIS to create maps it will automatically select class breaks when you attempt to symbolise your data, but most often you will need to alter this to make sure it is appropriate. The 'natural breaks' (or Jenks) classification was developed by cartographer George Frederick Jenks as a way to find natural groupings within a dataset that maximises the difference between classes. This can be a good choice if your data is unevenly distributed, but it is often not the best choice, as we saw above in the London house price maps. If you are creating a map showing the percentage of people in an area who voted a particular way, then an equal interval class-break system may be most appropriate, since you could specify 10 equally sized ranges, for example. If you just want to split your dataset into equally sized chunks so that the map has the same number

Indices of Deprivation 2015
Birmingham

Deprivation Decile

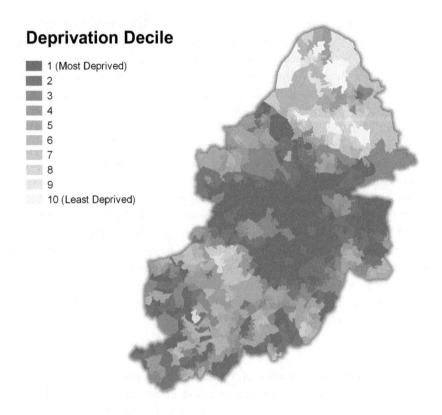

- 1 (Most Deprived)
- 2
- 3
- 4
- 5
- 6
- 7
- 8
- 9
- 10 (Least Deprived)

of features in each category, then a quantile classification should be used. As you saw in Figure 6.4, this puts the same number of map features in each category. In the London example we used five, but you could use any number (though a lower number tends to be better). In addition to manually classifying your data (as we did in the final house price map) you can also use more conventional statistical class breaks, such as geometric intervals or standard deviations. These may be appropriate but are often difficult to understand for a general audience.

Indices of Deprivation 2015
Birmingham

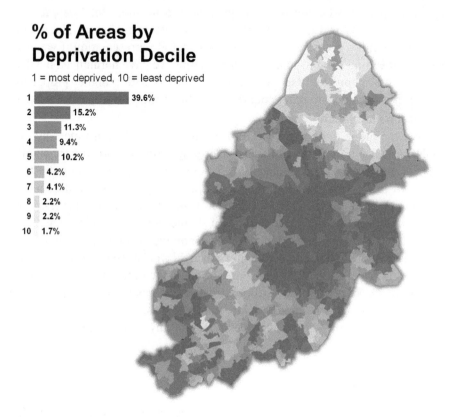

% of Areas by
Deprivation Decile

1 = most deprived, 10 = least deprived

1	39.6%
2	15.2%
3	11.3%
4	9.4%
5	10.2%
6	4.2%
7	4.1%
8	2.2%
9	2.2%
10	1.7%

Figure 6.13   Conveying more information in a map legend

6.5.8 Mapping Totals

Cartography is part science and part art, and the best maps strike a careful balance between the two. One area where this often gets a bit tricky is the **choropleth map**. A choropleth map is commonly used when showing the distribution of something (the 'pleth' bit) across geographic space (the 'choro' bit).

One very important thing you should almost always do when creating a choropleth map is to 'normalise' your data, so that instead of showing raw totals, it shows a proportion which can then be compared with other areas. A good example can be seen in Figure 6.14, where we have mapped the number of people aged five or under across counties in the lower 48 states of the United States for 2012. The first map shows the raw totals, but this just reflects the underlying population pattern whereby some counties have a lot more total *people* than others, particularly in California and along the eastern seaboard. The map is not *wrong*, but it's not very useful at all as a spatial representation if we want to extract meaning from it. In the second example we have normalised the data using the total population, so we can now see areas with a higher proportion of under fives, relative to other counties, and this is much more useful from an analytical point of view.

This example is quite a good one to use in order to demonstrate why you should normally normalise, since the underlying units (counties) vary significantly in population, from around 100 in Loving County, Texas to more than 10 million in Los Angeles County. If you are dealing with areas of equal, or roughly equal, populations then the impact of not normalising is far less. The other thing to be aware of is the figure you should use to normalise, which can be referred to as the reference population or denominator. In the under fives map we normalised using the total population, since this makes sense. Yet what if we are mapping street crime in urban centres? Should we normalise using resident population, workday population, footfall data? The answer is 'it depends'. In such cases it can become much trickier and, at times, this means not using a choropleth map at all – or perhaps even a map of any kind. But, as a rule, you should normally normalise.

6.5.9 Scale and Location

In the representation of geographic features, there are two related elements that we have not mentioned so far: scale and location. The first tells readers how big or small the features on the map are, with reference either to a commonly used distance or to another geographic feature. The second helps readers understand where precisely a place is. This is particularly important given the wide range of spatial literacy within the general population. If you are producing a map of settlements on the shores of Loch Ness in the Scottish Highlands, you can be sure that *somebody* will know where Drumnadrochit is, but most won't. Similarly, if you're producing a map of Denmark you can assume that most people will know where in the world it is, but there will be *someone* who won't. Therefore, it is always a good idea to show people how big places are and where in the nation

Mapping Totals

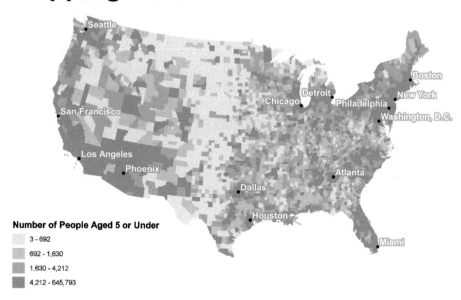

Number of People Aged 5 or Under

- 3 - 692
- 692 - 1,630
- 1,630 - 4,212
- 4,212 - 645,793

Mapping Percentages

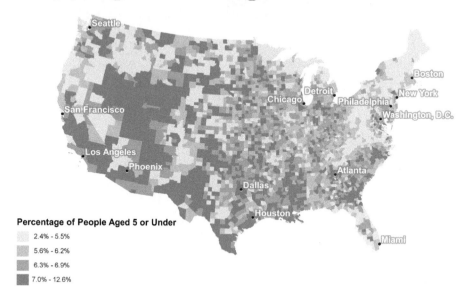

Percentage of People Aged 5 or Under

- 2.4% - 5.5%
- 5.6% - 6.2%
- 6.3% - 6.9%
- 7.0% - 12.6%

Figure 6.14   Non-normalised vs normalised choropleth map

or world they are. This is shown in the example in Figure 6.15 with a map of the local authority area of Oxford in the UK. In the bottom left of the map we have added a scale reference, in both metric and imperial measurement systems, to give readers a sense of the size of Oxford. Not everyone knows where within the UK it is, so in the top right we have added a simple inset map with a black dot showing where in the country Oxford is. If this were being produced for a global audience we might also have added a further inset to show where the UK was in the world. So, with the addition of a couple of small lines and a little inset map, we are able to better understand what we are looking at in the main body of the map.

2 km

1 mile

Figure 6.15   The importance of communicating map scale

6.5.10 Layout

If we bring all of the different elements above together in the right way, we still have to decide how they are laid out on a map canvas. This is another difficult topic, and it can make or break your map depending upon the choices you make. The different features and elements mentioned above all need to fit together in a coherent manner if your map is to be effective. In addition, you may also add other features, such as a north arrow (which we would argue is *not* always essential; it depends upon end use and context), data source notices, logos, charts, and authorship information. Ultimately, the map layout should be designed with a view to maximising visual communication and minimising cognitive overload. Again, this is a big topic and one that Gretchen Peterson clearly covers in *GIS Cartography*, so here we suggest five basic principles to stick to.

- **Title at the top:** most of your readers will follow the so-called F-pattern, whereby they first look at a page along two horizontal and one vertical lines, roughly resembling the letter F, from the top left. If you include a title in your map, therefore, it is best to situate it towards the top and often in the top left.
- **Details in the margins, map in the middle:** the most important thing about your map is the map. Make sure, therefore, that details (such as scale bar, legend, copyright notices, etc.) are kept in the margins of the map. Normally, these are best situated towards the bottom of the map but this is not always possible. Put the actual map front and centre.
- **Make the legend big enough:** a common mistake people make is to include the legend, but at a scale that makes it illegible. What may look okay on your screen may not work well on a large projector screen or on paper, so make sure that your legend is legible. If it isn't, there is a chance that your map will become a pretty, but useless, picture. Also, make sure the labels and headings make sense and are not simply the names your map layers or data had in your GIS software (e.g. *under_5_ct.shp*).
- **Attribution is essential:** so, you've produced a lovely map and you're proud of it, right? That's great, but you must also give due credit to whoever made the underlying data available, and you must also follow any licensing conditions set out by the data provider. This might mean adding a © copyright notice, or just a simple attribution. Having said this, some data providers, such as Natural Earth (who provide free geodata for the entire world), don't even ask for that, with authors Tom Patterson and Nathaniel Vaughn Kelso stating: 'No permission is needed to use Natural Earth. Crediting the authors is unnecessary.' But, as a rule, we would still say that attribution is essential.

- **Context defines content:** this is a general principle rather than a specific rule, but we believe it is helpful. So, if you are producing a map for navigation through the Amazon rainforest, things like an accurate scale bar and north arrow will be immensely important. On the other hand, if you're producing a map of the world for a Kindergarten wall using a whimsical font like Comic Sans and some rather bright colours, this will do very little harm, even if it doesn't produce a conventionally beautiful map. Likewise, if you're producing a map for an audience of urban planners in Madrid, there is little need to add an inset map showing the location of Madrid in the world. The only slight complication here is that with the advent of the Internet and particularly social media, maps can be and are frequently taken out of their original context and can end up looking rather odd, which can lead to a social media backlash.

6.6 CONCLUSIONS

In this chapter we have attempted to highlight some of the most important issues in the world of mapping, and particularly those that apply to maps in the media. Some of it does of course apply more widely. What we haven't explicitly said, yet hope you have realised, is that maps are inherently political representations of the world. Maps are not value neutral because they reflect an idea of the world and are a simplification of it. This means that when making maps we have to be very careful, particularly in areas of the world that are contested or where ownership is disputed. The very act of mapping something is, therefore, political. Of course, this applies to maps that may have nothing to do with politics, but we must always remember this. A recent example of this could be seen in Chinese passports in 2012 when a faint background map on one of the pages showed a map of China that included disputed areas of the South China Sea, which are also claimed by Brunei, Malaysia, Taiwan, the Philippines and Vietnam. Such examples are thankfully not too common, but they serve to emphasise the importance of the message that mapping is political, even if what we're mapping is not. When making maps in the media, where we have a potentially international audience, these issues cannot be overlooked.

The key principles of this chapter, if you are to take them on board and learn them off by heart, will help you both make effective maps and identify bad ones – both of which are important and highly valued skills. However, if we are to distil this chapter down into a series of key learning points, we would offer the following four. We trust that readers will take them on board as they look again at maps with a newly critical eye.

1   **Don't map unless you have to.** Despite the fact that maps can be fun, powerful, beautiful and highly influential, a bad map can also do harm. It may not cause a diplomatic incident, but it could cause a lot of confusion. Therefore we encourage readers to ask themselves whether a map is the best way to visualise data. If it is, great!

2   **All maps tell lies.** Some of these 'lies' are of the necessary kind, such as projecting a 3D earth on to a flat plane, or generalising line features so they are legible. But, as we have seen, some lies are rather more sinister. The example of gerrymandering highlights the fact that map making can be a quite devious practice and that the lies maps tell can have a big impact.

3   **Data decisions matter.** How we classify data and present it on a map matters hugely. As we saw with the example of mapping house prices, using different data breaks can lead to different geographic patterns and, therefore, different conclusions about the nature of the underlying data. This is also true in choropleth maps and the issue of normalisation. A non-normalised map can be quite misleading.

4   **Little things can have a big impact.** As we have tried to emphasise in the previous section, little things in map design and layout can make all the difference. If we forget to include a legend, a beautiful map can be rendered useless. Poor colour choices can make people look away and bad labelling can cause headaches. Okay, that might not be true, but it certainly won't make people want to look at your map or spend any time looking at it.

6.7 CONCEPTS LEARNED IN THIS CHAPTER

Map projections: the earth is close to spherical, so when we represent it on a flat screen or piece of paper we need to distort it somehow. Map projections provide a systematic way of doing this, but in doing so some compromises have to be made with respect to size and shape. As we have seen in this chapter, map projections can cause massive distortion and make areas look like they have the 'wrong' shape. This is why we need to understand what they are and what they do.

Gerrymandering: redrawing electoral boundaries so that the political party has a numerical advantage; this is a political problem, but it is also a statistical problem of data aggregation more generally. The way we draw boundaries on maps can have profound implications on the lives of individuals. Gerrymandering provides one of the most extreme examples of the power of maps and it is a persistent problem in some countries, particularly the United States.

Data classification: one of the most common types of data-driven map you'll see is the choropleth map. This kind of map assigns colours to areas according to a value (e.g. % voting for a particular candidate). The data being mapped is usually put into categories beforehand (e.g. 0–24.9; 25.0–49.9; 50.0–74.9; 75.0–100) and the number of categories can vary but is usually 10 or fewer. Sometimes people show raw totals in choropleth maps, but this is best avoided because if you do this your map will normally just end up showing which areas are most populated in the first place.

Generalisation: this is a key concept in mapping and it basically relates to simplifying the shapes we use to represent real-world things, such as coastlines, national borders or even the outline of a house. There are some complex mathematics behind the process but all you need to know here is that most maps you look at contain a degree of generalisation, normally to make them easier to read.

6.8 QUESTIONS FOR CLASS DISCUSSION

1   Is Greenland bigger than Africa? If not, why does it appear that way on some maps? Try to answer this question with reference to map projections.
2   How can a political party with far fewer votes than another party end up winning an election? There are in fact a variety of ways, but can you explain how this might happen from a geographical perspective, using a basic diagram?
3   How long *is* the coastline of Great Britain? This is not a trick question, and there is only really one correct answer!
4   It is said that all maps lie in some way or another: do you agree?

FURTHER READING

Field, K. (2018) *Cartography*. Redlands, CA: ESRI Press.
Tufte, E. (2001) *The Visual Display of Quantitative Information*. Cheshire, CT: Graphics Press.
Yau, N. (2013) *Data Points: Visualization That Means Something*. Indianapolis: Wiley.

REFERENCES

Daley, D. (2016) *Ratf**ked: Why Your Vote Doesn't Count*. New York: Liverlight.
Hawkins, E., McNeall, D., Williams, J., Stephenson, D. and Carlson, D. (2015) Scrap rainbow colour scales. Correspondence published in *Nature*, 519, 291.
Mandelbrot, B. (1967). How long is the coastline of Britain? Statistical self-similarity and fractal dimension. *Science*, 155, 636–8.

McGann, A., Smith, C. A. and Latner, M.. (2016) *Gerrymandering in America, The House of Representatives, the Supreme Court, and the Future of Popular Sovereignty*. Cambridge: Cambridge University Press.

Monmonier, M. (1991) *How to Lie with Maps*. Chicago: University of Chicago Press.

Openshaw, S. (1984) *The Modifiable Areal Unit Problem*. Norwich: Geobooks.

Peterson, G. (2009) *GIS Cartography: A Guide to Effective Map Design*, Second Edition. Boca Raton, FL: CRC Press.

Smith, A., Campbell, C., Bott, I., Faunce, L., Parrish, G., Ehrenberg-Shannon, B., McCallum, P. and Stabe, M. (2019) Visual Vocabulary (Version 5). Available at https://github.com/ft-interactive/chart-doctor/tree/master/visual-vocabulary

7 Mapping patterns and people: 'Why does geography matter?'

Key concepts

spatial aggregation, political maps, classifying people and places (geodemographics), the ecological fallacy, the 'modifiable areal unit problem'

7.1 INTRODUCTION

This chapter tries to convey the idea that geography matters. That is, the way we apply geographic units in statistical analysis can have a big influence on how we understand the world. For example, if someone asks you 'what's the population of New York?', you might be tempted to answer 'about 8.5 million people', because that is roughly the population of the five boroughs of New York City. Yet someone else might answer 'about 20 million' and they wouldn't necessarily be wrong, because this is the population of the wider Metropolitan Statistical Area (MSA) of which New York is a significant part.

This may seem like an obvious point, yet too often these kinds of geographical questions are overlooked, and it can lead to confusion and erroneous assumptions as we will see later in the chapter. When we deal with social statistics more broadly, we often make assumptions about individuals based on data relating to larger geographic units, such as a neighbourhood or city. For example, we might assume that in an area defined as 'poor' using an income measure (such as wages) all individuals in that area are poor. This *may* be the case, but it's more likely that there will be many people who are *not* poor, and a majority who are. However, it is also possible that the majority may not even fit our definition of 'poor' if there's a few *very* poor households skewing the average. If we narrow things down to the building level, we may again find that we have a mix of people who are 'poor' and those who are not. The problem in statistical analysis, however, is that we often have to make assumptions about individuals based on data for larger geographical areas, and doing so can be fraught with difficulty. Just be aware here that with larger geographical areas, we normally have to assume a higher level of variation within those areas in relation to the characteristics of people who live there, compared with smaller areas.

Therefore, in this chapter we look more closely at how, why and when geography matters in spatial statistical analysis (i.e. mapping people and places). We begin by looking at the seemingly simple question of mapping points and how we can make sense of them through aggregation into geographic units. Following on from this, quite appropriately, we look at political mapping and the case of the 2016 EU Referendum in the UK. Then we look at the variety of ways in which people and places are classified and how this information is used. Because this deals with people *and* places simultaneously, this is known as geodemographics.

Before ending the chapter, we look at two sources of error and bias. The first is something called the '**ecological fallacy**', which is where we make false assumptions about individuals based on the characteristics of a group they belong to (like when we assume *everyone* in a wealthy area is actually wealthy). The second is called the '**modifiable areal unit problem**'. This is the phenomenon whereby using different geographic units to aggregate data can lead to completely different results. If this sounds slightly 'cloak-and-dagger', that's because it is, so it's best to be aware of these issues before you try to understand maps that deal with people and places.

7.2 'THAT'S JUST A BUNCH OF DOTS, ISN'T IT?'

Geographers are keen to tell you that 'everything happens somewhere', and although this is both mostly true and blindingly obvious, it is not very helpful. But it is a good starting point for talking about how we can make sense of geographic point data. In Figure 7.1, you will see an example of this, where a large number of points (2,000 in total) are shown in the Greater London area; you can also see London Borough boundaries on the map. These kinds of maps feature in the media quite a lot, for example in relation to where crimes have occurred (e.g. the *Chicago Sun Times*' 'Homicides in Chicago' interactive map). We are using fictional data here (i.e. randomly generated points), but let's imagine each dot represents a single event, such as a crime: how might we begin to make sense of this from a geographic point of view? That's the question we try to answer here.

From the map, we can very quickly do a visual check and see that there appear to be more crimes in the north west (top left) corner of Greater London, in the south east corner (bottom left) and in a few other areas. Well, perhaps you may see something different. Some parts of Greater London seem quite empty by comparison. In order to test if this assumption is correct, we can perform a 'point in polygon' count: a simple GIS operation that tells us how many points there are within a given set of areas. It literally counts how many points there are

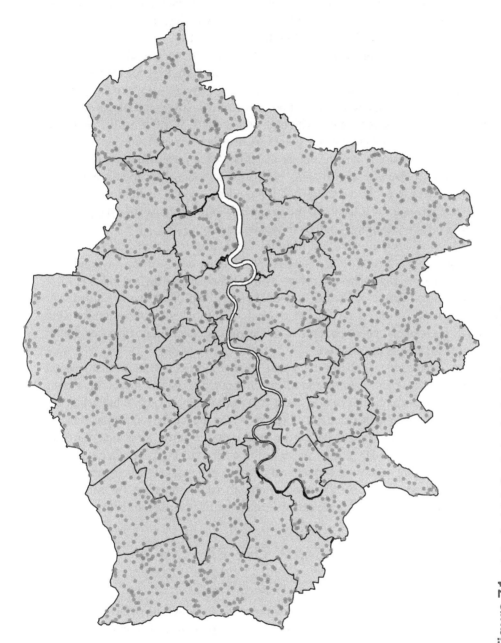

Figure 7.1 Lots of points in Greater London (one dot = one crime)

within each 'polygon' (GIS jargon for an area). We've shown the result of this in Figure 7.2, using London Boroughs as the geographic unit, and we've added a number to show how many points there are within each polygon. From this, we can see that there are 209 points in one area (Bromley, in the south east) and only three in another (the City of London, in the centre).

This process of **aggregation** can help us understand spatial patterns more clearly, but it comes with its own problems. The most obvious one here is the varying size of the geographic units we've used above. Bromley was probably always likely to have the highest number of points because it covers the largest area. The same goes for most other areas with high point counts. What we really need to do if we want to understand how the points are distributed is use some kind of standardised spatial unit to count the points, and this is what we have done in Figure 7.3, using equally sized hexagonal areas, each 2 km in width. This approach is sometimes referred to as 'hex-binning' and it provides us with a spatially standardised way to aggregate point data. We use hexagons simply because they happen to be quite good at tessellating (i.e. they fit together neatly).

We can now say for sure that there are clear clusters of high values in central London but also several other clusters on the outer edges of the city, and elsewhere. Many hexagons have no points within them, and the highest value is 14, in the north west corner of Greater London. In a few steps, then, we've moved from looking at what was effectively just a bunch of dots, where we could make some rough guesses on spatial patterns, to a clearer understanding of the geographic nature of the point distribution.

If we wanted to take things further, we could also think about how many people lived in each area, for example, and whether this ought to be taken into account in our analysis. For example, if one hexagonal area has 48 crimes within it but is home to 1,000 people and another area has 48 crimes within it but only 100 people, it makes much less sense to compare these areas, even if they do cover the same geographic extent. For now, though, just be aware that in order to make sense of a big mess of geographic point data, some further analysis and aggregation is usually a necessary and useful first step and the aim should normally be to 'normalise' (or standardise) the data in some way so that we can make meaningful comparisons between areas.

7.3 THE POLITICAL MAP: THE EU 2016 REFERENDUM

A good example in the real world of the ways in which boundaries really do matter is in the field of politics, and political mapping in particular. US President Donald Trump has in recent years demonstrated his fondness for political maps, and public announcements that 'the president likes maps' (MSNBC, 2017)

Figure 7.2 Count of points by London Borough

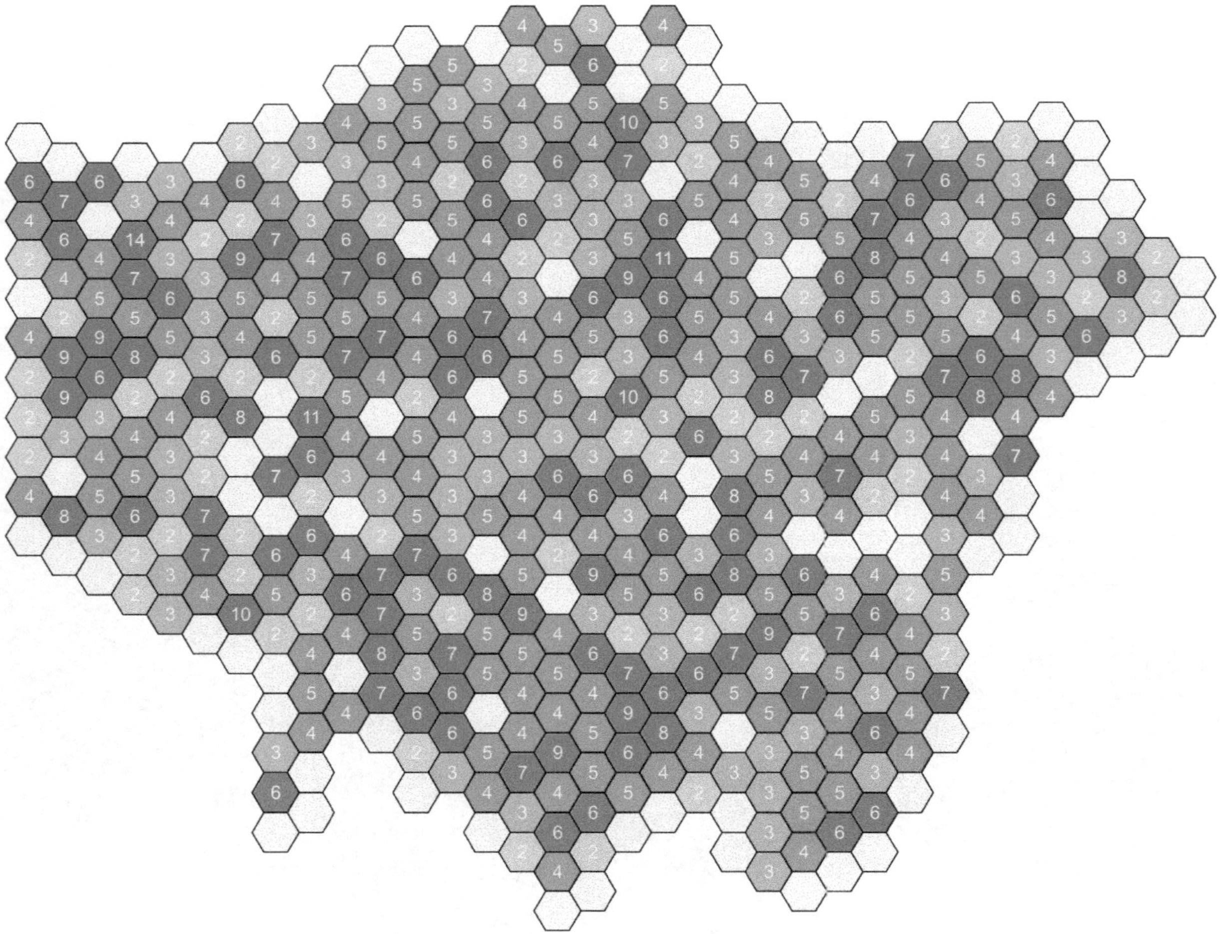

Figure 7.3   Count of points using hex-binning

have reinforced this view and helped popularise the subject. We also like maps, though we want to emphasise the need for a little caution when interpreting them. When we're dealing with political maps, a *lot* of caution is generally required. Of course, it is certainly easier to unquestioningly accept political maps if you are on the winning side of an election campaign, yet we must also be aware of the fact that political maps in particular often hide more than they reveal. There are two crucially important points here in this regard.

The first is that the geographic units we used to count votes can have a massive impact on what a map actually looks like. The second is that when we are mapping **binary** categories like 'Republican/Democrat', a lot of data is simply ignored because each area ends up being coloured for one or the other. This also applies in cases when there are more than two possible outcomes, of course, like when there are multiple parties contesting an election, as is the case in most countries. When we combine these two principles in a map, strange things can happen. For example, a political map from a US presidential election that was mostly red in colour (for the Republican Party) may actually represent a Democratic victory, owing to the fact that the blue areas on the map where most Democratic voters live (e.g. most major cities) are geographically smaller but more densely populated relative to some of the larger, emptier areas with Republican majorities which tend to dominate US presidential election maps. This may seem like an obvious point to those who understand the underlying principles of maps and data, but very often it is not well understood.

A great recent example of this kind of binary political mapping, and the confusion it can cause, can be seen in the results of the UK's 2016 EU Referendum, which was based on a simple 'Leave'/'Remain' choice about whether or not people wanted to stay in the European Union. A total of 33.6 million votes were cast, and these were counted in 399 referendum counting areas across the UK, plus Gibraltar. In total, 17.4 million people voted to leave the EU and 16.1 million voted to remain. The results were presented by almost every media outlet in map form, which often looked like Figure 7.4 below, where each area is coloured for 'Leave' or 'Remain'. This helped solidify in the minds of voters that the UK was made up of 'Leave' areas or 'Remain' areas. The truth was more complex, as it often is. For example, it would be easy to assume from the map that there were very few people in Scotland who voted 'Leave', because all 32 areas indicate that this was the case. It looks like an open and shut case. Yet of the 2.7 million people in Scotland who voted in the referendum, 38% (1 million people) voted to leave the EU. This is impossible to discern from the map. In one area in the north of Scotland (Moray) the vote was very close indeed, with 50.1% voting to remain in the EU and 49.9% voting to leave. In absolute numbers, in Moray there were only 122 more votes to remain in the EU than to leave. Yet the fact that 'Remain' voters were the majority in every local authority means the map in Scotland looks solidly 'Remain' and all areas, including Moray, have the same shading. Yes, Moray was a 'Remain' area, but only just.

Figure 7.4   Leave/remain map

A slightly different phenomenon is evident in England, where it looks like voters overwhelmingly backed leaving the EU, with 85% of the total map area coloured for 'Leave'. The result in England (53.4% Leave, 46.6% Remain) was a lot closer than in Scotland (62% Remain, 38% Leave), but the impression given by the map is a resounding victory for 'Leave' in England. Coincidentally, across the UK map as a whole, 53% of the surface area is coloured for 'Leave' whereas 47% represents 'Remain'. In one sense this is of course tied to the way elections are reported on, where a majority in one area leads to the colour of the winning party or organisation representing the whole area. This is not necessarily misleading, but it does mean we need to be careful about how we interpret political maps and what we infer from them.

An important question arising from all this, then, is what we can do to help deal with the problem of mapping binary categories – or multiple categories where there is a single 'winner' in one area, as in most electoral maps. We also need to think about how to deal with the issue of larger, less populous areas dominating such maps and leading people to make erroneous assumptions in relation to vote share as a direct result. On this latter issue, we refer readers to the discussion in Chapter 6, where our discussion of electoral mapping raised this very point and showed how representing political constituencies as equally-sized hexagons is one way to over-come the problem of unequal populations and variation in the size of geographic units. In relation to the question of how we might show a more nuanced view of the 2016 EU Referendum in the UK, we take a different approach. In Figure 7.5, we have presented the referendum results in a more nuanced way, where the result is shown not simply in relation to which side won the vote in each area, but is instead illustrated using a graduated colour classification based on banded percentages, making sure to have a break point at 50% because in this instance that is the critical value. We've also shown the number of areas which fall into each map category, in order to give the reader some further information to help process the map from a cognitive point of view and to help offset the perennial problem of larger areas dominating the map from a visual perspective. We can't help but wonder whether a more nuanced approach to mapping the results of this vote, by the media, might have an important role to play in helping to break down some of the divisions in society that currently characterise some nations, such as the UK and the United States. The point here is that we are perhaps not always as different or divided as maps suggest.

When we look at things from the perspective of Figure 7.4, the referendum result seems pretty clear cut: it's a resounding victory for 'Leave', at least in England. This is the dominant image we saw in media representations of the result, with few exceptions. Yet if we presented it in a more nuanced manner, as we have done in Figure 7.5, a different picture emerges. Certainly the map is less visually striking, more messy and probably less attractive, yet it also contains more information, and this is a crucial point. From the first map we are only able to discern which side won or lost in each area, which is important in itself. Yet we cannot say anything about how close the result might have been or how this compares with other areas, as we can in the second map.

With Figure 7.5, the story in Scotland changes slightly and we can see that in many areas (16) between 50 and 60% of voters opted for Remain, and in the other 16 the Remain vote was over 60%. Likewise, the pattern appears to change somewhat in England, with a concentration of areas with 40% or fewer voting for Remain in the east of the country and only London and a small number of other places with a vote share of 60% or above for Leave. By adding the number of areas in each category to the map's legend, we are also able to say that in a quarter of areas the Remain vote was between 24 and 40%, but it was only in 12% of areas where the Remain vote exceeded

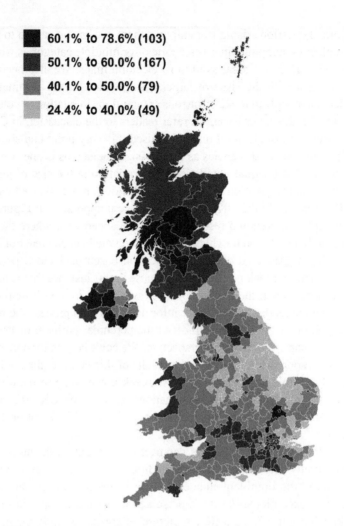

60.1% to 78.6% (103)
50.1% to 60.0% (167)
40.1% to 50.0% (79)
24.4% to 40.0% (49)

Figure 7.5   A more nuanced view of the Brexit vote

60%, and as we can see from the map these areas are concentrated in London, Northern Ireland and Scotland. There are many more patterns we could explore here.

Ultimately, the way we present such results is not necessarily a simple choice, because it depends upon multiple factors, not least of which is who the results are aimed at. We also want to emphasise that neither option here is right or wrong, and our preference would be to use both maps. In a media context, the BBC and *Financial Times* in particular have been very successful in presenting election results in a more nuanced way by taking a variety of approaches in order to highlight the underlying complexity of electoral outcomes. That's why if you look at the results of the referendum on the BBC News website (2016) you will see the kind of map shown in Figure 7.4 but also variations on what we have presented in Figure 7.5.

The point here, before we move on, is that there is no single optimal way to map election results. However, through a combination of approaches using the variety of methods at our disposal (including the hex cartograms mentioned in Chapter 6), we can present our data in richer, more meaningful ways that help illustrate the underlying complexity and nuance with data that is too often presented only as a simple either/or.

7.4 GEODEMOGRAPHICS: CLASSIFYING PEOPLE *AND* PLACES

So far in this chapter we've focused on issues of representation, and how we can do a better job of presenting spatial data in order to obtain meaning from it. To do this, we have used aggregation and classification, both fundamental principles of geographic data analysis. An important and widely used approach to understanding people and places, based on both aggregating *and* classifying data, is therefore the subject of this section. **Geodemographic segmentation**, or geodemographics for short, has a long lineage and is very widely used across areas as diverse as retail planning, electoral strategy, government welfare policy and urban planning. In the media, such approaches are often used as a shorthand way of understanding and describing people and places. For example, when Richard Webber, one of the world's leading geodemographic pioneers, moved house, the *Daily Mail* in the UK published a story with the following headline: 'Postcode Professor sells up in Alpha Territory (and at £6 million Bedsit Beneficiaries won't get a look in)' – where 'Alpha Territory' and 'Bedsit Beneficiaries' are two of the groups in Webber's own Mosaic classification.

Here we explain what geodemographic classifications are, where they came from, and how they are used today.

Geodemographic segmentation is (at its simplest) a way of putting small areas into different categories based on the aggregate characteristics of the people who live there. It's normally done at the small-area level (e.g. UK postcodes or US zip codes) using a variety of different variables such as age, ethnicity, employment status, health, income, and so on. These variables are then combined using more complex statistical approaches, such as cluster analysis, in order to identify groups of areas that have similar profiles. For example, if we performed such an analysis, we might identify one group of areas characterised as being predominantly white, low income, of average health, with low levels of employment. Another group of areas might be more ethnically diverse, have higher than average incomes and employment levels, but poorer health. These groups of areas then become the basis for further segmentation and are often given descriptive names which help people understand the characteristics of the people in them. To put this into some kind of context, let's take the example of the Office for National Statistics' UK geodemographic classification from 2011. There are many other geodemographic classifications.

The Output Area Classification (OAC) was built in partnership with the UK's Office for National Statistics and was created entirely from 2011 census data. It uses methods very similar to other geodemographic classifications, though others often include data from a wider range of sources. The OAC is based on a total of 60 variables, relating to *demographic structure* (e.g. % persons aged 0 to 4), *household composition* (e.g. % households with no children), *housing* (e.g. % who live in a flat), *socio-economic characteristics* (e.g. % households with two or more cars) and *employment* (e.g. % aged 16 to 74 in employment). A clustering method is then applied to these indicators and, in the case of the OAC, a '*k*-means' method was used. Put simply, this approach looks for groups of areas with similar characteristics and clusters them together so that we end up with a fixed number of groups that have similar characteristics. For more detail on this particular approach, readers should see Gale et al. (2016), which explains the method in detail.

Once the clustering is complete and we have a number of different area groups, the usual approach is to give each cluster a name which helps illustrate the characteristics of the people and areas with a good degree of similarity. With the 2011 OAC, these were as follows:

1   'Rural residents'
2   'Cosmopolitans'
3   'Ethnicity central'
4   'Multicultural metropolitans'
5   'Urbanites'
6   'Suburbanites'
7   'Constrained city dwellers'
8   'Hard-pressed living'

7.1 Examples of Output Area Classification 'pen portraits' from the OAC

3 Ethnicity central

The population of this group is predominantly located in the denser central areas of London, with other inner urban areas across the UK having smaller concentrations. All non-white ethnic groups have a higher representation than the UK average, especially people of mixed ethnicity or who are Black, with an above average number of residents born in other EU countries. Residents are more likely to be young adults with slightly higher rates of divorce or separation than the national average, with a lower proportion of households having no children or non-dependent children. Residents are more likely to live in flats and more likely to rent. A higher proportion of people use public transport to get to work, with lower car ownership, and higher unemployment. Those in employment are more likely to work in the accommodation, information and communication, financial, and administrative related industries.

8 Hard-pressed living

The population of this group is most likely to be found in urban surroundings, predominantly in northern England and southern Wales. There is less non-White ethnic group representation than elsewhere in the UK, and a higher than average proportion of residents born in the UK and Ireland. Rates of divorce and separation are above the national average. Households are more likely to have non-dependent children and are more likely to live in semi-detached or terraced properties, and to socially rent. There is a smaller proportion of people with higher level qualifications, with rates of unemployment above the national average. Those in employment are more likely to be employed in the mining, manufacturing, energy, wholesale and retail, and transport related industries.

Most of the OAC groups above are quite easy to interpret, though we need to emphasise here that the nature of the groupings will of course vary by country. For example, in Spielman and Singleton's 10-cluster geodemographic classification of the United States in 2015, categories included 'Low income, minority mix', 'Native American' and 'Low Income African American'. These categories are then given further meaning with descriptive 'pen portraits', as shown in Box 7.1 for the 'Ethnicity central' and 'Hard-pressed living' categories from the OAC (ONS, 2014).

As you can see from the descriptions of these clusters, geography really does play an important part in geodemographic classifications. This can be seen in the fact that 'Ethnicity central' is predominantly located in London and 'Hard-pressed living' has significant concentrations in the north of England, as in Figure 7.6.

The fact that we can take 60 indicators, subject them to a complex algorithm and then observe how clustered they are spatially is a clear sign that the so-called 'First Law of Geography' is valid. Invoked by the late Waldo Tobler in a short paper in 1970, this law states that 'everything is related to everything else, but near things are more related than distant things' (1970: 236). It is a nice, simple way of explaining why things tend to cluster geographically, whether it be high house prices or people with similar political views. Tobler himself was quite surprised at the way his 'law' has taken on a life of its own, and actually said, 'I was just having fun doing an animation in order to bring time into geography more

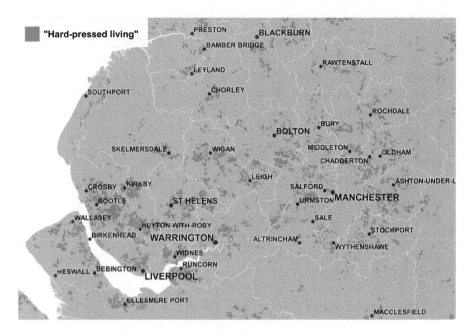

Figure 7.6   'Hard-pressed living' from the OAC 2011

explicitly' (2004: 308). Nonetheless, it remains a very useful reference point in geographical analysis.

Tobler recognised that his statement of a first law of geography 'was not terribly novel', and the same might be said of today's geodemographic classifications, at least in relation to the underlying principle they are based on. The principle, put simply, is the idea of classifying people *and* places simultaneously, in order to put areas into a limited number of categories, which we can then use as a shorthand way to understand the world. This is not without its own problems, of course, and we discuss some of these below, but the simplicity of the underlying idea and the fact that it has many real-world applications mean that there are many different geodemographic classifications in existence today.

If we go back to the late 1880s, however, this truly was a new idea and was pioneered by English social researcher and reformer Charles Booth in London. As part of his meticulous and richly detailed *Inquiry into Life and Labour in London* (1886–1903), Booth and his team of researchers produced a set of maps which classified streets into one of seven types. However, these were not based on in-depth analysis of census variables using a clustering algorithm, but a long period of in-depth, street-by-street fieldwork that also produced 450 notebooks on London from the late 1880s to the early 1900s. This archive, available online via the Charles Booth Archive at the London School of Economics and Political Science, also includes a fascinating set of maps and is a wonderfully rich source

of information on life in London at the turn of the nineteenth century (LSE, 2018).
Twelve maps were published in 1888–9 as 'Maps Descriptive of London Poverty,
1898–99' and they cover a large area of inner London. You can see in Figure 7.7
how streets have been given different shades and in the map legend below you can
see the descriptors used for each type, which do of course seem rather sweeping
and even derogatory from a contemporary perspective, particularly the 'Lowest
class, Vicious semi-criminal' category. We should always be careful, when classifying people, not to assign stereotypical attributes to some groups unfairly – by
today's standard, Booth didn't do this very well!

A good question arising from all of this is 'what are geodemographics actually
used for?'. Well, the answer might surprise you. Whereas Charles Booth and his
team were really attempting to understand the 'life and labour' of the people of
London in an early piece of qualitative urban sociology, modern geodemographic
classifications are used to influence, predict and even prevent different kinds of
behaviours. One example of this is in election campaigns, where geodemographic
classifications have been used by political parties to better target their advertising
to particular groups. Another example is in retail, where supermarkets tailor their

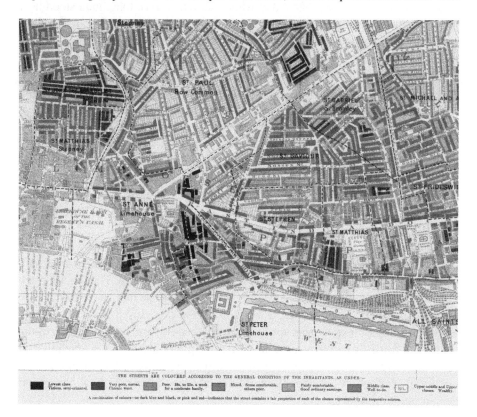

Figure 7.7   Extract of Charles Booth map of East London (Sheet 1 – Eastern District)

marketing mailshots and locate new stores based on geodemographic analysis. In healthcare, it might be used to help mitigate the growth of health conditions that disproportionately affect poorer, inner-city residents. So, although geodemographic classifications are very interesting in their own right, their real-world usefulness is the reason for their proliferation and longevity, and in some ways it is best to think of the approach as commercial social science.

In their study of geodemographics in the United States and UK, Singleton and Spielman (2014) chart the development of such analyses over time, and how by the mid-1970s there was significant commercial interest in the approach on both sides of the Atlantic as two early classifications emerged: A Classification of Residential Neighbourhoods (ACORN) in the UK; and Potential Rating Index for ZIP Markets (PRIZM) in the United States. Today, there are dozens of these classifications in existence across the world, including freely available geodemographic classifications like OAC, described above. The principal reason for this is that they are useful across a wide range of subject areas in relation to understanding society, not least of which is consumer behaviour, as described in *The Predictive Postcode* (2017), by geodemographics pioneer Richard Webber and renowned urban sociologist Roger Burrows. They state that while marketers have long understood how such classifications are extremely useful for understanding variations in purchasing behaviours (and thereby capitalising upon these behaviours), policy-makers and academic social scientists have been much slower to recognise their utility.

Today, the number one use for geodemographics remains retail planning and marketing, where retailers may have a limited marketing budget and need some way of targeting certain customer segments for particular products. It can also be very useful when it comes to planning new store locations. You may not realise it, but even some of what you may consider 'junk mail' that arrives at your mailbox or letterbox has reached you as a direct result of geodemographic segmentation. In this way, as Webber and Burrows note, your postcode (or zip code) has *predictive* power and that is why the approach is now even more widely adopted, across areas such as healthcare (e.g. to predict need), politics (e.g. to target likely voters), or e-commerce (e.g. to target advertising).

The fundamental truth of Tobler's First Law of Geography is the reason for the persistent utility of the geodemographic approach. Yet it is also true that, sometimes, birds of a feather do not flock together, as it were. That is, although Tobler has been proved right, it is not always the case that 'near things' are more related than distant things, a fact not always recognised in the media and elsewhere. Sometimes we are *not* like our neighbours, and as we discuss in the next section, this can have quite important implications. From a media point of view, however, such nuance is often not mentioned (perhaps for reasons of brevity or bias) yet it is critically important that we understand how places and demographics interact.

7.5 BEWARE THE ECOLOGICAL FALLACY: OR, 'WHY VICTOR ISN'T AN URBANITE'

In order to demonstrate one of the potential downsides to understanding the world in an aggregate, broad-brush way, let's take an example from the 2011 Output Area Classification we described above. There are eight different types of areas in this classification and I (Alasdair Rae), like everyone else in the UK, live in one of them. According to the 2011 OAC, I am classified as an 'Urbanite', so let's see how closely this matches reality. According to the descriptor for 'Urbanites', they are most likely to be located in urban areas in southern England and in less dense concentrations in cities elsewhere in the UK. Since I live in the city of Sheffield in the north of England, this seems fair enough. 'Urbanites' are more likely to live in flats or terraced housing and, since I live in a terraced house, this is also accurate. Urbanites are more likely to speak English as their main language, which is also correct for me. It also tells me that if I am in employment there is a good chance I'll be working in one of a few employment sectors, including education. Again, this is correct. So far, so good, even if I am originally from the Highlands of Scotland and don't feel like an 'Urbanite', but that's another issue altogether.

In most geodemographic classifications, you can actually drill down to sub-categories, as is the case with the OAC. The first subgroup for 'Urbanites' is 'Urban professionals and families', who have a higher proportion of children aged 0 to 14. Well, how about that? I am married and I have two boys aged 5 and 12, so that's just spot on. But surely everyone in my area doesn't have these characteristics. Well, in order to demonstrate this, let's take the example of Victor, my next-door neighbour (not his real name, but he *is* real). Victor is single, is non-white, works in healthcare and does not speak English as his first language. He therefore does *not* fit nicely into the 'Urbanite' category, or the 'Urban professionals and families' or 'Ageing urban living' subgroups (because he has no children, and he is not 65 or over). So, if we were to assume from the classification of the area he lives in that Victor was an 'Urbanite', as described above, we would be incorrect. In social science, we describe this kind of error as the 'ecological fallacy'.

The reason it is referred to as the 'ecological' fallacy is that it relates to the relationships between individuals and their physical surroundings (i.e. their wider group). Variables used to describe groups of individuals, instead of the individuals themselves, are in biology termed 'ecological' and are used where the analysis of individual-level data is either not possible or not feasible. This is most often the case in socio-economic studies of the kind we are describing here. Thus, we use the characteristics of the group as a kind of shorthand to describe and understand individuals, but it is of course not always safe to do so.

So, the ecological fallacy is a kind of error where you make incorrect assumptions about individuals based on group-level data. In the geodemographics example, if we assume that Victor fits the description of 'Urbanite' because he lives in an 'Urbanite' area, this would be a mistake. Victor does not fit the profile of an 'Urbanite', even though, on average, most people in the area probably do. Therefore, this example also directly contradicts Tobler's First Law of Geography. The point here is that even though spatial aggregation and analysis are very powerful and often very useful, they are not foolproof methods, so we must always retain a degree of caution in the interpretation of results. We should not assume that everyone (or even most people) who lives in a 'poor' neighbourhood is actually poor or that everyone in a 'rich' neighbourhood is rich. This applies in academic social science as much as it does in the media, though in the case of the latter it can often be more difficult to communicate nuance because of editorial and time constraints.

7.6 THE MODIFIABLE AREAL UNIT PROBLEM (MAUP)

Another kind of geographical aggregation problem deserves mention before we end this chapter. Although it may not sound terribly exciting, the modifiable areal unit problem (MAUP) *is* sometimes worth getting excited about. Well, perhaps. At the very least, it is important that anyone reading, producing or trying to understand geographic data knows about this potential source of statistical bias and how it works. In order to demonstrate this, we'll shortly return to the idea of mapping points that we used at the beginning of the chapter.

The modifiable areal unit problem arises from the fact that the lines we draw on maps to divide up countries, regions, cities, towns, neighbourhoods are mostly arbitrary, in contrast to features like coastlines, over which we normally have no control. So, while the borders between US counties, the dividing lines between census tracts, or the precise placement of city limits are important in many ways, they are largely artificial and can in theory be redrawn. This potential for modification – even if it never actually occurs – is the source of the MAUP and is the reason why we need to be particularly careful when interpreting results based on aggregate spatial data. There are parallels here between the MAUP and the ecological fallacy in that both are concerned with the relationship between individuals and groups, and in both cases the end result may be misleading. If we aggregate our data using different geographies we will often get different results, and this may lead to different conclusions about what the underlying data is telling us. Put simply, then, the MAUP is the situation whereby using different boundaries to group together features leads to different results. To illustrate this, we're going to use a simplified version of the point-to-polygon example we began the chapter with.

In Figure 7.8a, we can see a simplified example of the MAUP in action. There are four areas within a city (labelled 'Area 1', 'Area 2', and so on) and each is home to a different number of people, some of whom are rich (smiley face), and some poor (sad face) (we'll explain the relevance of this later on). Area 1 has the highest population, at 16, followed by Areas 2 and 3 with 10 and Area 4 with 8 people. If we modify the size and shape of the areal units, as we have done in Figure 7.8b, we can see that our areas now contain different numbers of people. The overall population remains the same, at 44, but our areas are now home to 13, 13, 7 and 11 people respectively. This alone is significant since it shows how summary statistics can change when we modify the boundaries we use to aggregate data. However, if we take things a step further, we can see how the MAUP could affect the way we might end up understanding the world, and our response to it.

If we were doing some statistical analysis on the relative wealth of a city comprising four neighbourhoods, we would see that in Figure 7.8a, Area 1 has 15 rich people and only 1 poor person. Therefore, this area could very simplistically be classified as 94% rich, 6% poor. In Area 2, on the other hand, we have six poor people and four rich people, so it would be 60% poor, 40% rich. Area 3 is 60% rich and Area 4 is 100% rich, a nice result if you happen to live there.

In our modified boundary example in Figure 7.8b we perform the same analysis but we arrive at different results. This time, the area we call 'Area 1' is 92% rich and 8% poor. Area 2 has changed from being 60% poor in the first example to 46% poor in the second example and is now a majority-rich area. Area 3 is now 29% poor, compared with 40% in the first example, and Area 4 has moved from 100% rich to only 82% rich. The total population has remained the same and the number of rich and poor people has remained the same, but the story of the data appears to have changed when in fact all that has changed is where we drew the boundaries between the four areas.

A comparison showing the result of these different zoning arrangements is given in Table 7.1, where we can see the effects of the modified boundaries on the summary statistics. Area 1 doesn't change much in terms of its wealth profile, just like Area 4. Their populations *have* changed but they still remain very wealthy places overall. Areas 2 and 3, on the other hand, now look different. Area 2 has moved from having a poor majority (60% vs 40%) to a wealthy majority (54% vs 46%) and Area 3 has increased from 60% rich to over 70% rich.

This is a highly simplified, trivialised example of the MAUP in action, yet it can have very important implications in reality. In both cases, there were

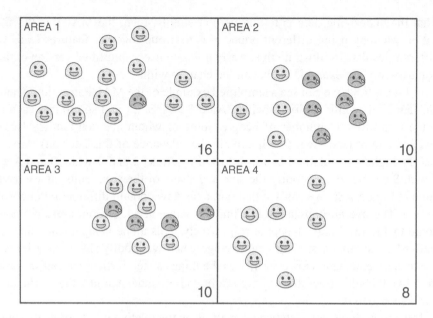

Figure 7.8a   The modifiable areal unit problem, version 1

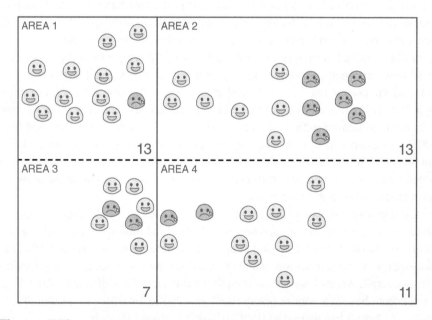

Figure 7.8b   The modifiable areal unit problem, version 2

Table 7.1   Comparison of results based on different zonal arrangements

Zone	Figure 7.8a		Figure 7.8b	
	% Rich	% Poor	% Rich	% Poor
Area 1	94	6	92	8
Area 2	40	60	54	46
Area 3	60	40	71	29
Area 4	100	0	82	18

11 poor people out of a population of 44, a full quarter of the population. However, in the first example only one area was majority poor and when we modified the boundaries the issue simply disappeared, so our fictional city of 44 people now has no areas where poor people are in the majority. If a government decided to offer additional welfare funding to areas of cities where the percentage of poor people exceeded 50%, then in the first example Area 2 would have been eligible and the poorest residents could have received much needed support. Yet in the second example, by virtue of shifting boundaries, the residents of Area 2 are no longer eligible and would not receive much needed assistance owing to the fact that 'Area 2' was now 54% 'rich'. It might seem surprising, but this kind of thing does actually happen in the real world.

Geographers have been aware of this problem for decades, yet it is still not yet widely known, and very rarely finds its way into media reports which use aggregate geographic data. First identified by Gehlke and Biehl in 1934 (in part), the 'modifiable areal unit problem' as we refer to it today was formally described by Openshaw and Taylor in 1979 and it can have an impact on many different kinds of analysis. It can also lead to the kind of boundary shifting we discussed in Chapter 6 in relation to gerrymandering. In the EU, for example, regional economic development funds have historically been available in regions whose GDP per capita is below 75% of the EU average. These funds are aimed at accelerating the economic development of so-called 'lagging' regions and are based on a division of the EU into what is known as 'NUTS 2' regions, of which there are 273 across the EU, with populations between 800,000 and 3 million. It could therefore be argued that there is an incentive for individual nations to modify regional boundaries in order to obtain more funds, though of course there is no suggestion here of any impropriety on the part of individual nations. We are just highlighting the fact that should an EU member state wish to increase its share of regional funding, it would benefit from fully understanding the MAUP. It is perhaps for this reason that the EU, through its ESPON programme (2006), has published a 254-page report on this very topic!

Before we move to the end of this chapter, two final points are worth noting. The first is the fact that in the MAUP example used here we can also see how the ecological fallacy might apply. In a population of 44, a quarter of residents within our fictional city were classified as poor, yet only in one scenario were they in the majority in any one area. In the case of Figure 7.8b, where all four areas were majority rich, people may infer from the aggregate data that there were no poor people, or that on the whole poverty is not a problem, even though a full quarter of the population at the individual level is classified as poor. To make this assumption about individuals would of course be an error. It is only in the first example, in Figure 7.8a, where a majority in any one area are classified as poor and this might therefore be picked up as significant. The second point is that were we to map this data by classifying areas as *either* rich or poor, Figure 7.8b would contain only rich areas, whereas Figure 7.8a would have three rich areas and one poor area. Different boundaries lead to different results.

7.7 CONCLUSIONS

We began this chapter by posing the question of the population of New York and explained that, based upon the boundaries you use, it's possible to arrive at different answers to such simple questions. This helps explain why, in the media, we often see different numbers used to refer to the same thing. This is the fundamental principle underlying what we have written here and it demonstrates that in statistical analysis geography really *does* matter. The way we group together people and places has a direct influence on the results of our analyses and, as we just saw with the modifiable areal unit problem in the previous section, such spatial organisation questions can even lead to differing conclusions on the same data, as in the case of Area 2, which changed from majority poor to majority rich, owing to modified boundaries. If we understand this better, we can understand data in the media better.

All this might lead you to conclude that any kind of geographic data analysis is so fraught with complexity and laden with caveat that it is not worth pursuing. This is not the case. The message we *really* want to drive home is the need to be aware of the potential impacts of how data is grouped, and the underlying spatial units we use for analysis. This is an important principle whether we are aggregating points to polygons (e.g. murders), mapping the results of the EU Referendum (e.g. using a binary in/out classification vs a more nuanced gradation), producing geodemographic classifications ('poor' vs 'rich'), or avoiding error and bias, as in the ecological fallacy and the modifiable areal unit problem. Taken together, what does all this mean? It means that geography matters and that we need to be cautious in our interpretation of aggregate geographic data, as indeed we should be with any other kind of data. Next time you pick up a newspaper and you see a map, keep all this in mind!

7.8 CONCEPTS LEARNED IN THIS CHAPTER

Aggregation: this word just means bringing things together, or grouping or clustering them. So when in this chapter we talked of dealing with datasets comprising hundreds, thousands or even millions of points, we use aggregation to make sense of underlying patterns. This is commonly done with crime data, for example, where points may be aggregated to hexagons or perhaps some other kind of spatial unit in order to get a sense of how crime is distributed spatially in a given area. It could also be done with polygons, but in this chapter we looked at aggregation of point data only.

Problems with binary map classification: the idea here is not that mapping the results of a 'yes'/'no' referendum or a 'Trump'/'Clinton' election are inherently wrong, but that they inevitably conceal significant, and quite important, variation. Every area falls into only one category or the other, giving the impression of total dominance in one area for a certain category, when in fact things may be much more complex. This is a perennial problem, yet we think it is worth (i) raising awareness of it and (ii) suggesting potential alternatives that provide the opportunity for more nuance, even if they are used alongside a binary map. 'Life is messy, and so is data.'

Geodemographic segmentation: this is a well-established approach to classifying people *and* places. It is based on the idea that people who live near each other have similar characteristics and behaviours (as in Tobler's First Law of Geography) and that it is possible, and useful, to group similar neighbourhoods into classes based on these characteristics and behaviours (such as income, political affiliation, age, employment, and so on). Geodemographic classifications have many applications today and are widely used by consumer organisations, political parties and local and national governments.

The ecological fallacy: this may sound like it has something to do with plants, but it's really about when we assume the features of a group apply to all individuals in that group. So, if we assume that someone is rich just because they live in a 'rich' area but in fact they are very poor, this would be an example of the ecological fallacy. The reason it happens is because almost without exception when we work with data we do not have individual-level information, so we have to make certain assumptions about individuals based on the characteristics of larger groups. When those assumptions are wrong, it's known as an ecological fallacy.

The modifiable areal unit problem: this might not sound like the most exciting concept, but it really is so important. The basic idea is that if we modify the areas we use to understand things (like the population of a city), we can get very different results. As we explained above, there are many different ways to divide up geographic space into areal units, so we must be aware of this when conducting any kind of geographical analysis or interpreting the results.

7.9 QUESTIONS FOR CLASS DISCUSSION

1   If you had a dataset with a million geographic points in it, each one representing a crime in a particular city, how might you begin to understand the underlying spatial pattern of the points?
2   What are some of the problems associated with mapping election outcomes where a map is depicted using two colours as an either/or result (such as 'yes'/'no' or 'Republican'/'Democratic')?
3   Name some uses of geodemographics, and write down a list of possible problems with this approach to understanding people and places (e.g. privacy, erroneous assumptions).
4   Can you think an example where the ecological fallacy might benefit an individual? (Hint: let's imagine you are only eligible for a scholarship if you live in a poor area.)
5   Without looking at the example earlier in this chapter (or doing so only briefly) sketch out an example of the modifiable areal unit problem on a piece of paper and compare your results with others.

FURTHER READING

Dorling. D. (1996) *Area Cartograms: Their Use and Creation, CATMOG 59*, Geo Abstracts, Norwich. Available online: https://alexsingleton.files.wordpress.com/2014/09/59-area-cartograms.pdf

Monmonier, M. (2018). *How to Lie with Maps*, Third Edition. Chicago: University of Chicago Press.

Openshaw, S. (1981) *The Modifiable Areal Unit Problem, CATMOG 38*, Geo Abstracts, Norwich. Available online: https://alexsingleton.files.wordpress.com/2014/09/38-maup-openshaw.pdf

Robinson, W. S. (1950) Ecological correlations and the behavior of individuals'. *American Sociological Review*, 15(3), 351–7.

REFERENCES

BBC (2016) 'EU referendum: The result in maps and charts', 24 June. Available at https://www.bbc.co.uk/news/uk-politics-36616028 (accessed 12 June 2018).

Booth, C. (1889) *Life and Labour of the People*, Vol. I. London: Macmillan.

ESPON (2006) *The Modifiable Areas Unit Problem: Final Report*. Luxembourg: ESPON.

Gale, C., Singleton, A., Bates, A. and Longley, P. (2016) 'Creating the 2011 area classification for output areas (2011 OAC)'. *Journal of Spatial Information Science*, 12, 1–27.

Gehlke, C. and Biehl, K. (1934) Certain effects of grouping upon the size of the correlation coefficient in census tract material. *Journal of the American Statistical Association*, 29, 169–70.

LSE (2018) Charles Booth's London: Poverty maps and police notebooks. Available at https://booth.lse.ac.uk/ (accessed 12 June 2018).

MSNBC (2017) When it comes to intelligence briefings, 'the president likes maps', 2 February. Available at www.msnbc.com/rachel-maddow-show/when-it-comes-intelligence-briefings-the-president-likes-maps (accessed 12 June 2018).

ONS (Office for National Statistics) (2014) 2011 Area Classification for Output Areas, 18 July. Available at http://webarchive.nationalarchives.gov.uk/20160128184749/http://www.ons.gov.uk/ons/rel/regional-trends/area-classifications/2011-area-classification-for-output-areas/index.html (accessed 12 June 2018).

Openshaw, S. and Taylor, P. (1979) A million or so correlation coefficients: three experiments on the modifiable areal unit problem. In N. Wrigley (ed.), *Statistical Applications in the Spatial Sciences*. London: Pion. pp. 127–44.

Singleton, A. and Spielman, S. (2014) The past, present and future of geodemographic research in the United States and United Kingdom. *Progress in Human Geography*, 66(4), 558–67.

Spielman, S. and Singleton, A. (2015) Studying neighbourhoods using uncertain data from the American Community Survey: a contextual approach. *Annals of the Association of American Geographers*, 105(5), 1003–1025.

Tobler, W. (1970) A computer movie simulating urban growth in the Detroit region. *Economic Geography*, 46, 234–40.

Tobler, W. (2004) On the First Law of Geography: A reply. *Annals of the Association of American Geographers*, 94(2), 304–10.

Webber, R. and Burrows, R. (2017) *The Predictive Postcode: The Geodemographic Classification of British Society*. London: Sage.

8 Understanding uncertainty in estimation: 'Are you sure?'

Key concepts

uncertainty, probability, margin of sampling error, confidence intervals, statistical significance, replication

8.1 INTRODUCTION

On 20 February 2016, British Prime Minister David Cameron announced a referendum on whether the UK would remain in the European Union. The vote was seen by many as the most important political decision facing the country in decades. In hindsight, it's easy to wonder why the Prime Minister would have agreed to hold the vote in the first place, risking his leadership and political legacy (he resigned the day after the results were announced on 23 June 2016: 51.9% voted to leave the EU, 48.1% to remain). *The Guardian*'s data journalist Pamela Duncan noted that 'of 168 polls carried out since the EU referendum wording was decided ... fewer than a third (55 in all) predicted a leave vote' (2016). So, what happened? Were the polls really that off the mark?

While there are many potential explanations (e.g. a shift in support for Brexit due to the well-organised Leave and troubled Remain campaigns: Behr, 2016), we're going to focus our attention here on the concept of uncertainty surrounding numbers reported in the media. Because many of our techniques for analysing data are based on samples taken from a larger population, they introduce a degree of imprecision to the things we are trying to find out. This imprecision is commonly referred to as **uncertainty**.

How does uncertainty apply to polling data? As we learned in Chapter 4, taking a random sample of data from the population comes at a cost – each individual poll result will fall within a range of possible values. For most polls, which have a sample size of 1,000 respondents, the uncertainty is three percentage points in either direction (later in this chapter we'll see how this uncertainty is calculated, which helps explain why most polling companies settle on this sample size).

If we look at the polls reported in the news the week before the Brexit vote took place, only one of seven online polls showed Remain in the lead (BBC News, 2016), and that was by a single percentage point; four polls showed Leave ahead by no more than two points; the final two even showed a tie. These results tell us that the vote was going to be quite close and possibly in favour of Leave. And this is what happened. Yet, the consequences of failing to account for uncertainty can be devastating: as voting closed on 24 June, *The Daily Telegraph* reported that the 'Brexit vote wipes $2 trillion off global stocks and knocks pound to 31-year low'! If you think back to Chapter 2, you'll realise just how big £2 trillion is!

In this chapter, we're going to learn more about the concept of uncertainty in understanding the results of data analysis, which is often under-appreciated and misunderstood when making sense of data in the media.

8.2 PROBABILITY AND STATISTICAL INFERENCE

Before we can see how to incorporate uncertainty into our data analysis, we need to consider the scary 'p-word': probability. **Probability** is the likelihood that an event will occur, given the set of all possible events that could occur. For example, the probability of rolling a 1 on a single die is $\frac{1}{6}$, or about 0.17, because there is one way to roll a 1 out of six possible and equally likely outcomes (a standard die has six faces resulting in six possible outcomes: a 1, 2, 3, 4, 5 and 6). Probabilities always fall between 0 and 1 because events must be mutually exclusive (i.e. it's not possible to roll a 1 *and* a 6 on a single die at any time). A probability of 0 means that an event will never occur, and a probability of 1 means that it will always occur. In reality, most probabilities fall somewhere in between these two endpoints.

At this point, you might be asking yourself why we need to introduce probability to interpret data in the media. Well, the answer is that probability is crucial because it allows us to use an observed sample of data to make inferences about an unobserved population. Pretty amazing, right? This process of extrapolation from a sample to the population is known as statistical inference. **Statistical**

inference is guessing what we don't observe from what we do observe. That is, when we collect data – say, for example, a survey about views towards guns and gun ownership in the United States as reported by the Pew Research Center (Igielnik and Brown, 2017) – we don't want to know only about the sample. While it's interesting that three in 10 survey respondents in that study revealed that they owned at least one firearm, what we really want to know is what this data tells us about gun ownership among *all adult Americans*. In other words, we want to use the sample of 3,930 people to be able to generalise to the population. How do we do that?

We can use the laws of probability to make the leap from a sample that we observe to the true value in the population. Let's see how this works in practice. First, the **Law of Large Numbers** tells us that if we perform the same experiment many times, we'll approximate the long-run average of these repetitions. The Law of Large Numbers is perhaps easiest to understand with repeated coin flips. For each coin flip, we can observe only one of two options, heads or tails. As we can see in Figure 8.1, the first coin flip results in heads, so the proportion of heads from this single event is 1.0. If we were to stop the coin flipping experiment after only flipping one coin, we might falsely conclude that flipping a coin always results in heads. Yet, the Law of Large Numbers states that with a large enough sample of coin flips – in this case, about 100 or so – we should arrive at

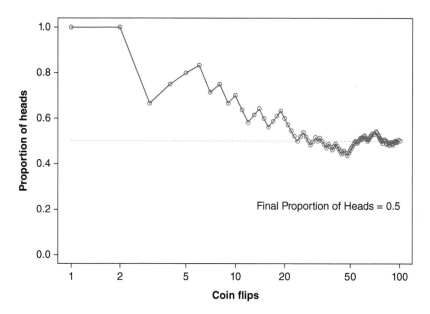

Figure 8.1   Demonstration of the law of large numbers using 100 simulated coin flips

the expected proportion of heads, which is 50% of the time. That's all there is to the Law of Large Numbers.

Second, the **Central Limit Theorem** (CLT) tells us that if we take repeated samples, then the distribution of sample means will approximate to a **normal distribution**, or bell curve (see Box 8.1 for a fuller discussion of distributions). In other words, any given result can be thought of as a single draw from a wider range of potential results, and we know that they follow the normal distribution. This is incredibly useful because, if we can work out how wide the spread is of that distribution, then we can determine how sure we are about our single result.

8.1 Distributions and Their Shapes

Recall that a **distribution** refers to the way in which data is dispersed, and this dispersion has a surprising impact on the approach to our data analysis. Though we can summarise a distribution of data by using summary statistics like its mean and variance, the best way to really understand how data is dispersed is by visual inspection. One method is by creating a histogram, which summarises the distribution of data over a continuous interval (or time period). A histogram looks similar to a bar chart, but it uses bins to capture the number of observations that fall within each discrete range of values. With bar charts we're interested in the height of the bars, while with histograms it's the area of the bins that matters. Figure 8.2 shows an example of a histogram of the Brexit vote share (votes for Leave divided by the total number of ballots cast) by UK voting areas (local authorities) in the 2016 EU Referendum. In this graph you can see that the distribution is skewed with most of the data falling above 50% vote share for Leave. But we should also be mindful that different graphs show us different things (think back to Chapter 5). For instance, you might be wondering why a majority of the bins in Figure 8.2 are above 50% if only 51.2% of citizens voted Leave. Why is that? Well, the reason is that bins represent voting areas and these vary massively in population – Remain voters were concentrated in the big places!

Another method for visualising the distribution of data is with a kernel density plot, which modifies the histogram with an algorithm that smooths out the clunky bits of the histogram (Figure 8.3). Like a histogram, the peaks of a density plot show us where values are concentrated, yet the advantage of the density plot is that it isn't affected by the number of bins displayed.

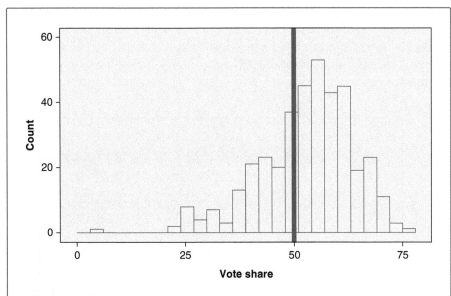

Figure 8.2   Histogram of Brexit vote share

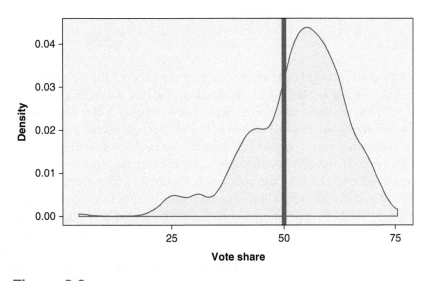

Figure 8.3   Density plot of Brexit vote share

(Continued)

The normal distribution, or bell curve, is one of the most important distributions in statistics because so many of our analytical tools are based upon the assumption of normality. Figure 8.4 shows an example of the normal distribution.

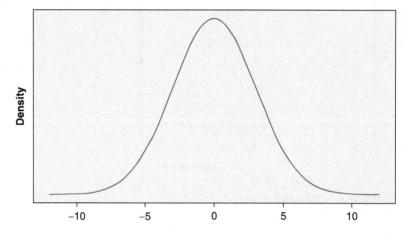

Figure 8.4   The normal distribution

Now let's put this together to determine the proportion of people in the United States that own a gun. Recall that the sample of the Pew Research Center survey was 3,930, and we know that the US population is roughly 330 million people (at the time of writing this book). In the sample 3 in 10 people owned a gun; however, we know that the true proportion in the population might be a bit higher, or might be a bit lower. If we were to take many different samples, they would produce a nice bell-shaped plot (like the one shown in Box 8.1). The distribution of the sample estimates of the proportion of gun owners would form a normal curve, and the mean 0 – the highest point on the normal curve – would be the true proportion of gun owners in the United States. The Pew **estimate** will be somewhere on the curve. If we're lucky, it will be bang on the true average (i.e. the middle of the normal curve). But more likely it will be a bit higher or a bit lower than that value. But how much higher or lower? One way to determine the true value would be to take many samples from the population to see how much higher or lower they turn out to be. But it turns out we don't need to do that – we can work it out on the basis of just our single sample. We find out how in the next section.

8.3 UNCERTAINTY IN ESTIMATION

Now that we've seen how probability helps us make the jump from observed values in the sample to the (unobserved) true value in the population, let's look more closely at how we calculate the uncertainty that affects every estimate that comes from samples. Remember that no matter how carefully data is collected, any time we take a sample from a larger population we introduce some amount of random error into the process. **Random error** is the difference between the value we observe in the sample and the true value in the population. It is the cost of relying on a sample rather than the entire population to make our inferences.

8.3.1 Margin of Sampling Error and Confidence Intervals

Uncertainty can be expressed in various ways depending upon the type of data analysis. For polls in the media, for example, the degree of error that occurs can be expressed by a statistic called the **margin of sampling error (MoSE)**. The MoSE tells us just how far the estimate from a sample would be, on average, from the true value from the population. How does it do that?

The results from any media poll can be understood within the context of repeated samples: while a single sample from the population of interest reflects one set of possible outcomes, another sample of survey respondents would likely produce slightly different results. If we were to repeat this process many times with unique samples, we could construct an interval that reveals where the true value in the population is likely to be located. As long as we can assume that the sample has been randomly selected – that is, there's no systematic bias in the way that the observations were chosen or how people choose to participate in the poll – then the MoSE can be calculated as the average distance from the mean estimate, across all our samples. But it turns out we don't need to take repeated samples to work this out. If we have one sample, we can estimate the MoSE using a simple formula. In this case, the MoSE is largely determined by the sample size and our desired level of confidence in the estimate.

Perhaps the easiest way to see exactly how the MoSE works in practice is with a specific example. Near the end of former President Barack Obama's second term in office in 2015, the news media reported polling data from a CNN/ORC poll and claimed that Obama was less popular than his predecessor, former President George W. Bush. Consider these headlines:

> *National Review*: 'New Poll Finds George W. Bush More Popular Than Obama' (Porterfield, 2015)

Daily Mail: 'Obama less popular than every living president – including George W. Bush!' (Chambers, 2015)

But was that really true? The polling data was collected by telephone from a nationally representative sample of 1,025 American adults, including a sample of mobile phone users to ensure coverage of different subpopulations (think back to Chapter 4). In the poll, 49% of respondents said they had a favourable opinion of Obama, while 52% said the same of Bush, which is a difference of 3 percentage points. The question for us is whether these percentages fall within the MoSE, thus making it impossible to determine whether Bush was more popular than Obama, or vice versa.

First, we need to calculate the **standard error** of Obama's favourability. The standard error tells us how much the values of Obama's favourability would vary from the mean if we were to collect data from many polls. We can do this using the following formula:

$$\text{Standard error} = \sqrt{\frac{\text{proportion}(1-\text{proportion})}{\text{sample size}}}$$

In our example, the standard error can be calculated using the proportion of favourability in the sample, or 0.49, and the sample size of 1,025:

$$\text{Standard error} = \sqrt{\frac{0.49(1-0.49)}{1,025}} = 0.0156$$

Working through the formula, we find that the standard error is 0.0156, or 1.56%. This tells us that we would expect the values in the population to deviate from the true proportion by about 1.6 percentage points on average. Thus, we're able to use data observed from a single sample to make inferences about the degree of variation in the percentage of favourability in the population.

But we're not quite finished. We need to translate this estimate of error into a range of values knows as a confidence interval. A **confidence interval** (CI) uses probability and the Central Limit Theorem to provide us with a range of values that are likely to include the true value in the population a certain proportion of the time. This proportion is determined by the **confidence level**, which refers to the degree of uncertainty that we are willing to accept when moving from the sample to the population. Stated differently, what proportion of the time (i.e. in repeated samples) will the true value fall within the range of values specified by the CI?

We can choose any confidence level that we want, but it does directly affect the range of values included in the confidence interval: the greater the confidence level, the wider the resulting confidence interval (and vice versa). The most common confidence level is 0.95, which implies that the true value in the population will fall within the confidence interval we calculate from our observed sample of data 95 out of 100 times. Most researchers believe that this is a reasonable tradeoff between being fairly sure about our result, while also ending up with a range that isn't so big that we can't tell anything about our estimate. But this depends somewhat on the scientific discipline – in physics, for instance, when astrophysicists found evidence for the Higgs boson, they used a confidence level associated with just 1 in 3.5 million (Lamb, 2012)!

The confidence level we choose is associated with a **critical value** from a standard normal distribution. For instance, the confidence level of 0.95 has a critical value of approximately 1.96, which corresponds to the number of standard deviations from the mean at each tail of the distribution (5% in total; 2.5% in each tail of the symmetric bell curve). If we multiply the critical value by the standard error, we obtain the margin of sampling error:

$$MoSE = \text{critical value} \times \text{standard error}$$

Using values from our favourability example,

$$MoSE = 1.96 \times 0.0156 = 0.031$$

This means that the MoSE was 3.1% in either direction. Now we have all of the information necessary to calculate the range of values in the 95% CI:

$$95\% \text{ CI} = [\text{proportion} - MoSE, \text{proportion} + MoSE]$$

In this equation, the 'proportion' refers to the 49% of the sample, or 0.49, that held a favourable opinion of Obama. By subtracting the MoSE from the proportion, we obtain the lower bound of the CI; by adding the MoSE to the proportion, we find the upper bound:

$$95\% \text{ CI} = [0.49 - 0.031, 0.49 + 0.031] = [0.459, 0.521]$$

Based on this single sample of data we collected, we know that Obama's true favourability in the population could have been as high as 52.1% (49 + 3.1 = 52.1) or as low as 45.9% (49 − 3.1 = 45.9). It is still possible that our sample is extreme – the 95% CI implies that 5 samples out of 100 will fall into this category (the problem is that we'll never know for certain whether this is the case, and the only way to reduce this possibility further is to calculate a wider CI such as the 99% CI). So, while this specific poll showed that less than half of Americans had a favourable view of Obama, the headline is misleading because Obama's true favourability among American adults could have been higher or lower. In fact, the MoSE also applies to Bush's favourability, too, which at 52% of the sample implies that his true favourability could have been as low as 48.9% or as high 55.1% of the public. You may see what we're getting at with this example: Obama's and Bush's true favourability in the population could be reversed due to sampling error! Thus, it's unwise to jump to the conclusion that Obama was less (or more) popular than Bush – we simply don't know whether this is the case given the observed data.

Now there's one caveat to this interpretation: This 3.1% MoSE described above is valid for a 95% CI. If we wanted to increase our level of confidence that the estimate would fall within a certain range of values – let's say for 99 out of 100 samples – then we would need to adjust our CI, which would include a wider range of values, unless we collect more data. The MoSE using a 99% confidence level (the critical value is now 2.576) is 4.0, which means that Obama's support could have ranged from 45 to 54%. In general, the higher the desired level of confidence, the wider the range of values must be to accommodate this increased confidence (unless we increase the sample size). Usually, if a CI is not specified, it's safe to assume that a 95% confidence level has been specified.

8.3.2 Sample Size and Sampling Error

In Chapter 4, we learned that many polls reported in the news rely on samples of roughly 1,000 individuals. Why is this sample size so popular among survey researchers? The short answer is that a sample of 1,000 respondents provides a nice balance between having a relatively low margin of sampling error and the added cost of collecting a larger sample. Survey research is expensive work, so if we're going to sample more people, we want to be sure that we're getting our money's worth. But it turns out that there are diminishing returns beginning around a sample size of 1,000 respondents, which corresponds to an MoSE of approximately ±3.1 percentage points (for a 95% CI). It's easy to see this in Figure 8.5.

In contrast, a sample size of only 100 respondents has too large an MoSE—nearly 10 percentage points in either direction! And if we collect more data, a sample size of 2,500 only reduces the MoSE from the original sample of 1,000 by about 1 percentage point. That's a lot of extra work for a small reduction in the MoSE.

Ultimately, the MoSE is important because it allows us to make the jump from estimated results to the true value in the population. Thus, we can actually learn a great deal about the population from a single sample. Yet, we also need to be

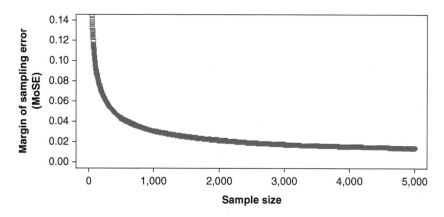

Figure 8.5   The tradeoff between sample size and sampling error

careful to avoid discussing specific point estimates as if they were the true value; instead, we'd be better served to include some degree of uncertainty in our statements to account for sampling error. We shouldn't confidently say that 49.1% of Americans held positive views towards Barack Obama, but we can say that around half of Americans did.

8.3.3 Subsamples and Uncertainty

Another concern with respect to sample size and uncertainty in polls is that we often want to compare the results from different groups in society. For instance, how might the opinions of women differ from men? Or how about younger from older people? The wealthy from the poor? Republicans from Democrats? The possible comparisons are numerous, and they help us better understand interesting relationships in the data. In other words, this information suggests *why* we observe certain patterns in the aggregate numbers.

Dividing the data into smaller groups is called **subsampling**. One important consequence of subsampling is that it can drastically reduce the size of the sample used for calculating the MoSE. Recall that the MoSE is inversely related to the sample size, which means that as we divide the original sample into smaller portions, we increase the error associated with our estimates. In practice, the greater the uncertainty associated with our estimates, the more difficult it is for us to make inferences from the data.

To illustrate this concept, let's consider the Scottish independence referendum that took place on 18 September 2014. In this referendum, nearly 85% of eligible Scottish voters turned out to decide a single issue: 'Should Scotland be an independent country?' While the 'No' side against Scottish independence ultimately won with 2 million votes, or 55.3% of the total ballots cast, opinion polls leading up to the election suggested a close decision. In fact, most surveys showed that the gap between the sides had narrowed to just a few percentage points with enough undecided voters to swing the decision either way.

One interesting narrative that emerged in the media was how young people voted – particularly 16 and 17 year olds – given that they had just been granted the franchise by the Scottish Parliament back in June 2013. Based on a single poll, the media claimed that young people overwhelmingly favoured Scottish independence, making the referendum much closer than it would have been had young people not been allowed to vote. For instance, *The Guardian* (Anon., 2014) reported the results of an Ashcroft Poll indicating that 71% of 16 and 17 year olds voted 'Yes' in the referendum. That certainly seems like strong support for independence among young voters.

Let's investigate this number in more detail. The Ashcroft poll surveyed 2,047 respondents from an electorate of about 4.3 million voters. In the aggregate, the results of this poll are almost spot on: 54.6% of respondents said that they voted 'No', which is very close to the actual vote total of 55.3%. For the entire sample, the MoSE is plus or minus 2.2 percentage points for a 95% confidence level. Thus, we would have expected the true value from the population to fall between 52.4 and 56.8%, which it does. This much is reassuring.

But if you look carefully at the subsamples in the Ashcroft poll, there are only 14 respondents out of 2,046 people in this 'young voter' age category. That's just 0.6% of the entire sample! Now let's calculate what the MoSE is for a sample size of just 14. According to the UK census, the population of young voters is estimated at 100,000. So just how much error does this introduce? The MoSE for this subsample of young voters is plus or minus 26.2%. Now that's a pretty large confidence interval!

Thus, the Ashcroft poll revealed that 71% of sampled young voters (16–17 year olds) indicated that they voted 'Yes' in the referendum, but now we know that comes with an MoSE of ±26.2%. This means that the true value of support for this group of young voters could be as high as 97.2% (71 + 26.2 = 97.2) or as low as 44.8% (71 − 26.2 = 44.8). This high level of uncertainty in our estimates suggests that we probably shouldn't be drawing any conclusions from this relatively small number of observations. There's simply too much uncertainty in our estimates to say anything meaningful about how young Scots aged 16 and 17 voted.

So the next time you see different groups being compared in a poll, just make sure that you know how much uncertainty is associated with these smaller sample sizes. If that information isn't available, you should probably be sceptical. The margins of error we are calculating here assume that our sample is representative (see

Chapter 4). If we have an unrepresentative sample, this can add bias to our results, meaning the true value in the population could actually be well outside of our calculated confidence intervals. Chapter 4 deals with this problem in a bit more depth.

8.3.4 Uncertainty in Measurement

There's also uncertainty introduced in our quantitative measures, which are often coarse tools of assessing social and political phenomena. Measurement is an important (yet often overlooked) part of whether we should trust the underlying data analysis. **Measurement** is how we quantify objects and events, so that we can make comparisons among them. In the natural sciences, our ability to accurately measure the world around us comes down to the precision of the instruments. The better our tools, the more accurate our results. For example, in chemistry we might want to measure the heat given off by a thermal reaction, or in physics we may want to study fluid dynamics to learn how liquids and gases move. In these cases, our tools have become quite sophisticated and allow for very accurate measurements.

However, when we study people or organisations in the social sciences, our measures are usually far less accurate. For example, if we want to know how someone feels about a social or political issue, we usually must ask them directly or observe their behaviour. The difficulty is that we can only indirectly measure what goes on inside someone else's head, which is why it is sometimes referred to as the 'black box' – we simply don't know what's actually going on there.

For some issues, directly asking survey respondents what they think is relatively straightforward. Most people have no problem providing their opinion about things going on in their everyday lives. For instance, they probably won't have a problem revealing how they feel about the weather, commuting to and from work, or whether they generally listen to music on their journey. But for other issues, it can be quite difficult to get people to reveal their opinions to accurately measure public opinion. For instance, some people may find it hard to answer questions about foreign policy. They may not have a strong sense, for instance, of the best strategy for US–Russian relations. In these cases, measuring public opinion can be challenging because people generally spend less time thinking about these types of issues and don't have enough information to provide an accurate answer. Other people may not want to respond or might even lie, perhaps because they are embarrassed to admit to a particular view that could be socially unacceptable.

In sum, all measures introduce some degree of error. For some areas, this error may be relatively small, while in others it may be quite large and consequential. Being aware of the measures used in the dataset will help us determine the quality of the evidence. Ultimately, even if we have a representative sample of data and have carefully reviewed the methods, we should consider the measures themselves. As the saying goes: 'garbage in, garbage out'.

8.4 STATISTICAL SIGNIFICANCE

When researchers report the results of their data analysis, they sometimes include the phrase 'statistically significant'. **Statistical significance** can be a complicated concept to fully grasp, but it essentially refers to whether or not the result we observe in our sample generalises to the whole population. In other words, is our result likely a real thing, or might it have simply occurred because of random chance? In most of the social sciences, we determine that a result is unlikely to be due to chance by calculating a statistic called the probability value, or 'p-value' for short. The **p-value** (usually) tells us the probability of finding something (a relationship, or value) as extreme as (or greater than) what we observed in the data, if there was actually no relationship, or a zero value, in the population. The lower the p-value, the less likely the result is due to chance alone.

Statistical significance is determined by the variability of the estimate (its standard deviation) and the square root of the sample size. If the estimate has relatively little variability – that is, values are clustered tightly around its mean – then the standard error and, by extension, the corresponding p-value will be smaller. Likewise, if the sample size is large, then the p-value will be smaller. In fact, one reasonable criticism of p-values is that in large samples, many estimates from the analysis will be statistically significant simply because the denominator, or bottom number, is increasingly large.

Researchers often use p-values as a shortcut for determining whether there is sufficient evidence to support a particular conclusion. The norm in most of the social sciences is to use a p-value of less than 0.05 as this threshold. That is, a p-value smaller than 0.05 tells us that there's less than a 0.05 probability (or 5% chance) of that result popping up randomly. There's nothing inherently special about $p < 0.05$ – it's just an arbitrary rule of thumb to help us determine whether the result will generalise to the population. We could just as easily specify that $p < 0.01$ or $p < 0.001$, and so on, but there's a tradeoff between the error of finding something that is a result of chance and failing to find something that is actually there. If our p-value threshold is too high, we're likely to do the former; too low and we're likely to do the latter. Confused? So are many people who learn about p-values. But the important thing to remember is that a p-value isn't the final answer but helps us decide whether a finding is likely to exist in the real world (Ziliak and McCloskey, 2008).

Of course, whether a result is statistically significant tells us nothing about its effect size. In contrast, **practical significance** refers to whether a result has a meaningful impact on the outcome of interest. For instance, a study may include a statistically significant finding at the $p < 0.05$ level, yet the effect size associated with the finding may be quite small, sometimes even approaching zero.

Over the years a problem has arisen regarding the way in which p-values are used as decision-making tools. For instance, a p-value of less than 0.05 is often a key determinant of whether a study will be published in an academic journal. One real concern with this arbitrary threshold is that it contributes to **publication bias,** which is also known as the 'file-drawer problem'. The file-drawer problem was first coined by Robert Rosenthal and used to describe the practice of reporting only studies that have statistically significant results (at the $p < 0.05$ level), while leaving those with non-significant findings ($p > 0.05$) 'in the file drawer'. The problem with this practice is that it means there are far more published studies with significant results than should be possible, which implies that some of these findings could be due to random chance alone.

Focusing on statistical significance and p-values also encourages binary decision making about the importance of results. If the results from a data analysis show $p < 0.05$, then the tendency is to conclude that we have support for our preferred argument (and it should be published). If not, then there are often incentives to conduct additional tests or ways of slicing the data to 'nudge' the results so that they have $p < 0.05$. Or we might use weasel words to try to sell our result as significant (see Figure 8.6 which captures this idea quite nicely).

Alternatively, we might just keep testing lots of different things until we find significant results. The problem with this is that random chance will sometimes give us significant results: 5% of the time, in fact! That is, if we run 20 different tests (e.g. of relationships between variables), chances are we'll find at least one test that appears statistically significant, even if there isn't any truth to it. This practice has been referred to as **'p-hacking'**, but although this sounds malicious, it's quite easy to do accidentally, by changing our research question based on what we see in the data.

Ultimately, we should be testing specific theories with data and considering statistical significance, rather than testing lots of things and only writing up the ones that are statistically significant. If we do the latter, then many studies will end up with findings that are actually untrue, and different results will be found when people try to replicate the results (see Box 8.2).

'Chocolate accelerates weight loss' was a headline in the UK's *Daily Express* and repeated in many news organisations around the world (Barns, 2015). This was the result of a published scientific study – an experiment where people who were given chocolate appeared to have more weight loss than a group of people who did not. However, it turns out that this was a hoax study, where the author deliberately used p-hacking to find a result (Bohannon, 2015). He did this by testing lots of different outcomes – as well as weight loss, he also looked for changes

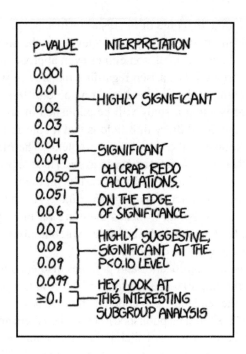

Figure 8.6   Statistical significance and p-hacking

Source: xkcd.com by Randall Monroe

in sleep patterns, cholesterol, general well-being, and so on. Because it tested so many possible outcomes, the chances of finding a significant effect just by chance was really high: 5% of those outcomes were always going to give a p-value of less than 0.05.

Ultimately, the important lesson is that we shouldn't focus solely on p-values for determining whether a result from a single study is worthy of our attention. Instead, many researchers have moved away from this practice and will consider the estimate in terms of its substantive effect. Remember that a p-value should only provide one piece of information that we use to decide whether an observed effect is meaningful.

8.5 REPLICATION AND ROBUST RESULTS

How can we be sure that the results we have found are real and not the result of chance? Or perhaps more relevant for this book: how can we know if a finding in a news story has occurred by chance? To test whether results are robust, we really want to know two things: would the same results happen if we ran the test again; and would a different method produce the same result?

Replication means using the same procedures to gather and analyse new data. The idea is that although a single study could potentially produce biased results due to random chance, multiple studies will eventually converge on the average effect. If we've carefully designed our data collection and measures, then the average of the effects from multiple replications should give us the true estimate in the population according to the Law of Large Numbers. But how can we be sure that this will occur?

Let's take a closer look at replicating one of the most (in)famous psychology experiments of all time. The experiment into obedience to authority was first conducted in the early 1960s by Yale psychologist Stanley Milgram. It was designed to investigate how seemingly 'normal' people could commit atrocities like those witnessed during the Second World War. Milgram (1963) showed that an authority figure allows people to shift the responsibility of harming others to someone else. Subjects in his experiment were told that it was a scientific study of memory and learning, and that the goal was to determine how punishment might improve an individual's ability to remember word pairs. Unbeknownst to participants, they were always allocated to the role of the teacher (who would be asked to administer punishments), while actors working with the research team were assigned to the role of the learner. The task was simple: teachers read word pairs to test the learners' ability to recall the correct pair. Incorrect answers were supposedly punished with a brief shock, which was administered by the teacher in 15-volt increments up to 450 volts (a potentially lethal dose of electricity!) for each wrong answer. Although the participants didn't know this at the time, no actual electric shocks were administered; the experiment worked because participants believed that they were giving shocks.

In 2008, news outlets published the results of a modern-day replication into the effects of obedience to authority. The *Daily Mail* and BBC News ran headlines like '"Disturbing" study reveals most of us would torture others if ordered to' (Foreign Service, 2008) and 'People "still willing to torture"' (Anon., 2008), respectively. The BBC even aired an hour-long programme about the replication, called 'How Violent Are You?', to examine just what makes humans capable of committing extreme acts of violence against one another (Horizon, 2009).

So, how did subjects fare in the modern-day replications? Just as they did in the original study, the majority of British respondents in the BBC replication continued administering what they believed could be lethal electric shocks to another human being. What's even more disturbing about this finding is that it occurred with what appeared to be harmless individuals. Moreover, replication efforts in the United States (Burger, 2009) and Poland (Doliński et al., 2017) also showed similar results, adding to the evidence of the effect. In short, replication ensures that we haven't been led astray by a single errant result.

8.2 The Replication Crisis in the Social Sciences

There is an ongoing replication crisis facing a number of social science disciplines. For example, attempts to reproduce experiments in psychology (Open Science Collaboration, 2015) made national headlines when it was reported that only 39% of replication attempts found statistically significant results, and less than half of the 100 studies reported similar effect sizes to the original experiments (Yong, 2016). Similarly, a group of economists reported that only 61% of results in a selection of economics papers replicated, which means that two out of every five studies didn't replicate, a far greater share than what we should have observed (Camerer et al., 2016).

Notwithstanding these replication efforts, attempts to reproduce existing research findings are relatively rare in the social sciences – only a tiny fraction of empirical papers in social science have been subject to formal replication tests. As a result, the credibility of the discipline rests on our ability to make replication easier and less expensive, which in turn will help increase the accountability of researchers and raise the bar of future research quality.

As one of the lead researchers on the psychology replication effort stated:

> Humans desire certainty, and science infrequently provides it. As much as we might wish it to be otherwise, a single study almost never provides definitive resolution for or against an effect and its explanation … Scientific progress is a cumulative process of uncertainty reduction that can only succeed if science itself remains the greatest skeptic of its explanatory claims. (Open Science Collaboration, 2015, aac4716–7)

8.6 CONCLUSIONS

In this chapter, we have seen how probability can take us from learning about a single sample to the entire population. Yet, we shouldn't forget other sources of error that can skew the results. The news media like to report 'horse race' polls of candidates during an election year. These types of polls – so named for their focus on the political candidates rather than the party platforms and political issues – are easy for people to follow and generally (though not always) provide an insight into who might win the upcoming race. For instance, in 2015, a general election was held in the UK, and pollsters had predicted a very close election outcome, so close in fact that it wouldn't produce a majority government. Here are a few headlines from leading national news agencies:

> *The Guardian*: 'Election 2015: it's too close to call – so what will happen next?' (Helm, 2015)

> *The Independent*: 'General Election 2015: 2 charts that show why this election is too close to call' (Dathan, 2015)

> *Daily Mail*: 'Fears mount over knife-edge election producing no "credible" government …' (McTague, 2015)

Yet in fact, the 2015 General Election resulted in a sizeable lead for the Conservative Party over their nearest rival: they finished with 331 seats to Labour's 232, a difference of nearly 100 seats (out of 632 in England, Scotland and Wales). We now know that these horse race polls likely suffered from unrepresentative samples (see Chapter 4), which biased the results (Sturgis et al., 2016). In other words, the plus or minus three percentage point margin of sampling error in polls is just one source of error (and not necessarily the most important one at that!).

Ultimately, uncertainty is something that is often misunderstood, and rarely explained. People think that statistics 'prove' something, when in fact the opposite is true – they tell us how sure (or rather, how unsure) we are about a particular result. So when we see findings in the news, we should think about how much certainty we really have about the reported findings. We should think about how wide the confidence intervals are – if they are very wide, it might not tell us very much of interest at all.

8.7 CONCEPTS LEARNED IN THIS CHAPTER

Estimate is a quantity that is approximated using statistics from the observed data.

Uncertainty is the imprecision of our estimates due to error introduced by samples and the process of quantification.

Probability is the likelihood that an event will occur given the set of all possible events (there are other definitions of probability, see e.g. Box 8.1).

Statistical inference is the process of extrapolating from what we observe (i.e. the sample of data) to the population.

Census is an official count of all units in the population.

Law of Large Numbers tells us that if the same experiment is repeated many times, we will obtain the long-run average of these repetitions.

Central Limit Theorem tells us that if the same experiment is repeated many times, the long-run average approximates the normal distribution.

Distribution shows the frequency of all possible values for a variable; it describes the dispersion of the data.

Normal distribution tells us that the dispersion of a variable is bell shaped.

Random error is the difference between the value we observe in the sample and the true value in the population.

Margin of sampling error is how close on average the estimate from a sample would be from the true value in the population.

Standard error is the dispersion of means taken from repeated samples around the population mean.

Confidence interval uses probability and the Central Limit Theorem to provide a range of values that are likely to include the true value in the population a certain proportion of the time.

Confidence level is the proportion of time (in repeated samples) that the true value in the population will fall within the range of values specified by the confidence interval.

Critical value is the value of the test statistic that must be exceeded to reach statistical significance.

Subsampling is dividing a sample into smaller groups.

Measurement is how we quantify objects and events, so that we can make comparisons among them.

Statistical significance means that the observed result generalises to the population because it is unlikely to occur due to random chance (e.g. $p < 0.05$).

P-value is the probability of getting a result as extreme (or greater) than what we observed in the data: the lower the p-value, the less likely the result is due to chance alone.

Hypothesis testing is a process of falsification by specifying a directional statement and testing whether it can be rejected by the test statistic derived from the observed data.

Null hypothesis is a specific statement that we expect to refute with the observed data.

Regression is a statistical technique for fitting a line to a set of observed data points. The slope of the line indicates the effect of the predictor variable on the outcome of interest.

Practical significance is when the observed result is meaningful because the effect size is sufficiently large.

Publication bias refers to the practice of only publishing results that are statistically significant; it implies that some reported research could be due to random chance rather than a real effect.

P-hacking is performing multiple tests on a dataset until you find a 'statistically significant' result. These results will be meaningless, because, given enough tests, some results will appear statistically significant just by chance.

Replication means using the same procedures to gather and analyse new data.

8.8 QUESTIONS FOR CLASS DISCUSSION

1   Investigate how the margin of sampling error (MoSE) from an opinion poll is affected by changes to the size of the sample and desired confidence level. Find an opinion poll reported in the news media by visiting a specific news site or searching for the word 'survey' or 'poll'. Calculate the MoSE for the entire sample using the formula introduced in this chapter. Now calculate the MoSE for at least one subsample reported in the poll or discussion of the results (note: this may not be possible if the methodology section is not sufficiently detailed). Did the news agency convey the degree of uncertainty associated with these estimates in its reporting? Overall, what did you learn from this exercise?

2   The data journalism website FiveThirtyEight (or 538, for the number of votes in the US Electoral College) has an interactive tool to help you understand p-hacking. Visit the website to see if you can 'Hack Your Way To Scientific Glory' (https://projects.fivethirtyeight.com/p-hacking/) by getting a p-value of less than 0.05, which as we learned in this chapter is a commonly accepted threshold for publishing social science research. Explain what choices you made and whether that resulted in a statistically significant p-value. What does this tell us about findings in social science? Now read this associated article from 538 and provide your thoughts about its overarching conclusions: https://fivethirtyeight.com/features/science-isnt-broken/.

3   Twenty-nine independent research teams were given an identical dataset and tasked with investigating a research question about racial bias in sports: 'Are football players with darker skin tone more likely than those with lighter skin tone to receive red cards from referees?' The results of this crowdsourced research (i.e. data analysis conducted by multiple research teams) were surprising. The analytical approaches varied drastically among research teams, as did their conclusions: 20 teams (69%) found a statistically significant

positive effect (nine teams retained the null hypothesis of no differences by skin tone). Read the article (and commentary) and discuss what this means for publication bias and academic research.

Original article: Silberzahn, R., Uhlmann, E. L., Martin, D. P., Anselmi, P., Aust, F., Awtrey, E., Bahník, Š., Bai, F., Bannard, C., Bonnier, E. and Carlsson, R. (2018) Many analysts, one data set: making transparent how variations in analytic choices affect results. *Advances in Methods and Practices in Psychological Science*, 1(3), 337–56.

Commentary: Silberzahn, R. and Uhlmann, E. (2015) Crowdsourced research: many hands make tight work. *Nature*, 526(7572), 189–91. www.nature.com/news/crowdsourced-research-many-hands-make-tight-work-1.18508

FURTHER READING

Silver, N. (2013) *The Signal and the Noise: The Art and Science of Prediction*. London: Penguin.

REFERENCES

Barns, S. (2015) Chocolate accelerates weight loss: research claims it lowers cholesterol and aids sleep. *Express*, 30 March. Available at https://www.express.co.uk/life-style/health/567211/Chocolate-weight-loss-lowers-blood-cholesterol-aids-better-sleep (accessed 13 November 2018).

BBC News (2016) EU Referendum poll tracker. 22 June. Available at https://www.bbc.co.uk/news/uk-politics-eu-referendum-36271589 (accessed 16 May 2019).

BBC News (2008) People 'still willing to torture'. December 19. Available at http://news.bbc.co.uk/1/hi/health/7791278.stm (accessed 13 November 2018).

Behr, R. (2016) How remain failed: the inside story of a doomed campaign. *The Guardian*, 5 July. Available at https://www.theguardian.com/politics/2016/jul/05/how-remain-failed-inside-story-doomed-campaign (accessed 13 November 2018).

Bohannon, J. (2015) I fooled millions into thinking chocolate helps weight loss. Here's how. *Gizmodo*, 27 May. Available at https://io9.gizmodo.com/i-fooled-millions-into-thinking-chocolate-helps-weight-1707251800 (accessed 13 November 2018).

Burger, J. M. (2009) Replicating Milgram: would people still obey today? *American Psychologist*, 64(1), 1–11.

Camerer, C. F., Dreber, A., Forsell, E., Ho, T.-H., Huber, J., Johannesson, M., Kirchler, M., Almenberg, J., Altmejd, A., Chan, T. and Heikensten, E. (2016) Evaluating replicability of laboratory experiments in economics. *Science*, 351(6280), 1433–6.

Chambers, F. (2015) Obama less popular than every living president – including George W. Bush! *Daily Mail*, 3 June. Available at: https://www.dailymail.co.uk/news/article-3109475/Obama-popular-living-president-including-George-W-Bush.html (accessed 13 November 2018).

CNN/ORC Poll. (2015) Obama economy poll, June 3. Available at: https://www.daily mail.co.uk/news/article-3109475/Obama-popular-living-president-including-George-W-Bush.html (accessed 13 November 2018).

Dathan, M. (2015) General Election 2015: 2 charts that show why this election is too close to call. *The Independent*, 30 March. Available at: https://www.independent.co.uk/news/uk/politics/generalelection/general-election-2015-2-charts-that-show-why-this-election-is-too-close-to-call-10142955.html (accessed 13 November 2018).

Doliński, D., Grzyb, T., Folwarczny, M., Grzybała, P., Krzyszycha, K., Martynowska, K. and Trojanowski, J. (2017) Would you deliver an electric shock in 2015? Obedience in the experimental paradigm developed by Stanley Milgram in the 50 years following the original studies. *Social Psychological and Personality Science*, 8(8), 927–33.

Duncan, P. (2016) How the pollsters got it wrong on the EU referendum. *The Guardian*, 24 June. Available at: https://www.theguardian.com/politics/2016/jun/24/how-eu-referendum-pollsters-wrong-opinion-predict-close (accessed 13 November 2018).

Foreign Service (2008) 'Disturbing' study reveals most of us would torture others if ordered to. *Daily Mail*, 19 December. Available at: www.dailymail.co.uk/news/article-1097941/Most-torture-ordered-study-reveals.html (accessed 13 November 2018).

Helm, T. (2015) Election 2015: it's too close to call – so what will happen next? *The Guardian*, 15 March. Available at: https://www.theguardian.com/politics/2015/mar/15/election-2015-too-close-call-whats-next (accessed 13 November 2018).

Horizon (2009) How violent are you? BBC Two, 12 May. Available at: https://www.bbc.co.uk/programmes/b00kk4bz (accessed 13 November 2018).

Igielnik, R. and Brown, A. (2017) Key takeaways on Americans' views of guns and gun ownership. *Pew Research Center*, 22 June. Available at: www.pewresearch.org/fact-tank/2017/06/22/key-takeaways-on-americans-views-of-guns-and-gun-ownership/ (accessed 13 November 2018).

Lamb, E. (2012) 5 Sigma What's That? *Scientific American*, 17 July. Available at: https://blogs.scientificamerican.com/observations/five-sigmawhats-that/ (accessed 13 November 2018).

McTague, T. (2015) Fears mount over knife-edge election producing no 'credible' government as new poll reveals 70% of voters don't want the SNP having ANY say over English laws. *Daily Mail*, 6 May 6. Available at: www.dailymail.co.uk/news/article-3070063/Fears-mount-knife-edge-election-producing-no-legitimate-government-new-poll-reveals-70-voters-don-t-want-SNP-having-say-English-laws.html (accessed 13 November 2018).

Milgram, S. (1963) Behavioral study of obedience. *Journal of Abnormal and Social Psychology*, 67(4), 371–8.

Munroe. R. (n.d.) P-Values. Available at: https://www.xkcd.com/1478/ (accessed 13 November 2018).

Open Science Collaboration (2015) Estimating the reproducibility of psychological science. *Science*, 349(6251), 943.

Porterfield, J. (2015) New poll finds George W. Bush more popular than Obama. *National Review*, 3 June. Available at: https://www.nationalreview.com/2015/06/cnn-presidential-poll-george-w-bush-more-popular-than-obama/ (accessed 13 November 2018).

Sturgis, P., Baker, N., Callegaro, M., Fisher, S., Green, J., Jennings, W., Kuha, J., Lauderdale, B. and Smith, P. (2016) *Report of the Inquiry into the 2015 British General Election Opinion Polls*. London: Market Research Society and British Polling Council.

The Guardian (2014) Scottish independence: poll reveals who voted, how and why. 20 September. Available at https://www.theguardian.com/politics/2014/sep/20/scottish-independence-lord-ashcroft-poll (accessed 13 November 2018).

Yong, E. (2016) Psychology's replication crisis can't be wished away. *The Atlantic*, 4 March. Available at: https://www.theatlantic.com/science/archive/2016/03/psychologys-replication-crisis-cant-be-wished-away/472272/ (accessed 13 November 2018).

Ziliak, S. T. and McCloskey, D. (2008) *The Cult of Statistical Significance: How the Standard Error Cost Us Jobs, Justice, and Lives*. Ann Arbor: University of Michigan Press.

9 Ranking with league tables: 'What's the best?'

Key concepts

construct validity, multilevel models, shrinkage, random variation, regression to the mean

9.1 INTRODUCTION

Rankings and league tables, where individuals or organisations are compared against each other in some way, are everywhere. If you're a student, you might have found yourself on a league table based on your exam results. If you play sports competitively, you or your team may be ranked in a league. Of course, sports league tables often cover a good proportion of newspaper back pages. But increasingly, other organisations are also ranked in newspapers and online. Countries are ranked on their economic growth, their level of democracy and their attitudes to minority rights. In some countries, school league tables are an important part of some parents' decisions about which schools to send their children. Universities are ranked too, for example on their students' satisfaction or research quality, as are police forces on crime statistics, and many other public bodies on a whole raft of performance indicators.

What is perhaps less clear is that there are often lots of different ways that league tables can be calculated, meaning that no one league table is likely to give the definitive answer when comparing the performance of organisations. This can have substantial implications for those being ranked and those with an interest in them. How a sports league is designed affects the way that participating teams act, as we will see in the next section. Similarly, if school league tables are designed in such a way as to encourage schools to behave in a particular manner, that has implications for how teachers teach, the things that students learn, and what parents look for in a good school.

Public sector league tables in particular have, as a result, often been a source of controversy, with some calling for them to be banned, while others see them as essential so people can exercise an informed choice over the school/university/hospital that they use. But despite this, league tables have the potential to be very useful: in helping decide what the best option is in a range of circumstances, to seeing how well your favourite football team is doing.

This chapter will delve into that controversy, while looking at some key statistical concepts that are part of the controversy. We'll start with sport as a way into the ideas behind league tables and the way they can make teams behave in certain ways. We'll then go on to look at two examples of league tables in the UK public sector – school league tables and university league tables – so if you are uninterested in sport, please bear with it – it will help you understand the stuff that comes later! Through these examples, we'll be able to explore the causes of the controversy that league tables inspire, and see the good and the bad things that they can offer. We will see that league tables/rankings are trying to measure certain specific things, and what those things are, and how they are measured, affect the way that we should use them.

9.2 LEAGUE TABLES IN SPORT

In general, we think of sports league tables as fairly objective indicators of performance. If a team wins the league, it is reasonable to think that this is a result of its being the best team over the course of the season. For the most part this is a reasonable thing to assume, but even in the world of sport where winning and losing are clearly defined, there are situations where things are not as objective as we might think.

In professional football (or soccer depending on where you live), there was a shift in the way points were awarded between 1981 and 1995. Previously, teams were given two points for a win and one point for a draw. From 1981 in England, and later for other countries, this was changed to give three points for a win. This was done to encourage teams not to settle for a draw and to play more attacking football, because, in comparison with a draw, teams have more to gain (two points) from winning a game than they would miss out on (one point) from losing. In other sports, extra points are awarded for high scoring – for example, an extra point in some rugby union games for scoring four tries.

Thus, how we choose to set up our sports league will depend on the things that we value in sport. The point is that these league tables are not absolute measures of quality – they can be adapted to help incentivise certain behaviours in such a league, or disincentivise other behaviour. In the example above, the league itself incentivises attacking football. The same can apply to other league tables as well – their presence can change the behaviour of the groups being ranked. Often these effects can be positive – creating more attacking football, for example. But in other cases, they can lead participants in the league to 'game' the system. Participants in a league can do things that boost their ranking that were unintended by the league organiser and that might not fit with the purpose of the league.

A classic example of this happened in a qualification game between Barbados and Grenada in the 1994 Football/Soccer Caribbean Cup. Before the match, Barbados were bottom of the league table, and needed to win the game by a two-goal margin to reach the final (see the left-hand side of Table 9.1). The tournament had an unusual 'golden goal' rule (football's governing body, FIFA, was experimenting a lot with such rules at the time), where, if the match is still drawn after 90 minutes, extra time is played and a goal in that period counted as two goals.

With Barbados leading the match 2–1, and struggling to find a third goal to get them through, they went for an unusual strategy – to score an own goal that would level the match, allowing them the period of extra time to score a third goal that would count double and see them through. Now, however, Grenada realised that scoring at either end would help their qualification. Barbados therefore had to defend the goals at both ends of the pitch for the final three minutes of the game (which they did). They then scored in extra time, winning the game 4–2 and qualifying for the next round (see right-hand side of Table 9.1).

This is not the only such occasion where teams have deliberately scored own goals to meet their own ends. While creating a fascinating example for sports nerds to ponder over, the Barbados vs Grenada match didn't go as the organisers

Table 9.1   The 1994 Caribbean Cup qualifying group 1 league, before and after the match

| | Before the match | | | | After the match | | |
Team	Played	Points	Goal difference	Team	Played	Points	Goal difference
Grenada	1	3	+2	Barbados	2	3	+1
Puerto Rico	2	3	−1	Grenada	2	3	0
Barbados	1	0	−1	Puerto Rico	2	3	−1

intended, and Grenada fans might well have felt cheated by how it happened. After the 1994 qualifying tournament, that particular 'golden goal rule' wasn't used in a football match again. But it shows that league tables are not passive instruments of measurement. They can change the way in which those participating in the league behave.

Not only that, but even in the best cases, league tables are not always particularly good measures of the quality of the teams they are trying to measure. As humans, we have a tendency to vastly underestimate the importance of random chance in deciding how well we do on a given occasion. When we do well, we assume that we did something particularly clever, while we scold ourselves when we perform particularly badly. However, the reality is that even the best players have bad days, and the worst teams sometimes perform well, for no reason other than that performance varies. While over a whole season we might expect this sort of bad luck to even out, in the shorter term, this variation can have a big effect on results. We're often caught out by this. We're surprised when sportspeople come into and go out of form, expecting their real-life performance to match our image of their ability. Sportspeople are often taken on by teams on the basis of their current (good) form, and fans get annoyed when that run of form doesn't last. This is known as '**regression to the mean**', and is also responsible for the '*Sports Illustrated* cover Jinx', whereby highly ranked sports stars appear on the front page of *Sports Illustrated* magazine, only to see a decline in form. It's as likely that the high performance that led to the appearance on the front cover is an outlier, and the decline in form is simply a return to normality. The same thing seems to occur with the award of 'manager of the month' in the English football league.

By considering sports, we've seen that league tables are never neutral rankings of objective ability. We've seen that sometimes they can be 'gamed' in unexpected ways. And we've seen that even when they are accurate measures of performance, they're susceptible to the **random variation** that can lead to higher performance that is simply the result of chance rather than a sports team/person possessing particularly high quality.

9.2.1 All-Time Rankings of Formula One Drivers

How might we go about solving these problems to create rankings that are, in some way, meaningful? Some of these problems are inherent – we might want to rank something, and the choice of exactly what that something is will always be subjective. However, there are also some statistical procedures we can implement to account for random variation caused by luck, or we can remove other factors that could be causing a difference in performance that is nothing to do with a sportsperson's ability.

In 2016, the *Daily Mail* 'revealed the best Formula One driver of all time according to SCIENCE' (O'Hare, 2016, emphasis in original). This was based on research by us (Bell et al., 2016). The aim of this paper was to produce a ranking of drivers, through the history of the sport, that (i) accounts for the fact that some Formula One teams are better than others, and (ii) avoids a short, lucky run by drivers inflating their ranking more than is appropriate.

Formula One is an interesting sport in that it contains two leagues: a driver league and a team league. Teams vary greatly in their quality, and drivers race for their team as well as for themselves. A high-quality driver in a poor team is likely to do badly, while a low-quality driver in a good team could do relatively well. That is, a driver's high performance is rarely caused solely by that driver's ability – other factors affect their performance as well (see the next chapter), in particular the team that the driver races for. In ranking drivers, we want to take out all that other stuff so that the ranking is based only on the drivers' ability. Fortunately, drivers often change teams, meaning that attempts to separate the effect of drivers from the effect of their team are possible given enough data over time.

Another way of saying this is that we want to be able to divide up the 'variation' – that is, to divide all the differences in race results that exist into those which are caused by the driver, those caused by the team, and those caused by random fluctuation. We can do this using a thing called a **multilevel model** (see Box 9.1) that divides the variation in Formula One performance (i.e. all the different results, from first to last, in each race) into levels: a driver level, a team level, and a final level that incorporates all the other causes of random variation (see Figure 9.1). By doing so, the model is able to isolate the 'driver' variation from all the rest of the variation caused by teams, and also by random chance and other factors that we are not so interested in.

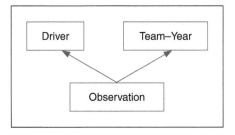

Figure 9.1   The multilevel structure of Formula One race results. Observations (the position a driver obtains in a given race) can be 'nested' within drivers, and within teams.

9.1 Multilevel Models

Often statisticians will create regression models that look at the relationship between variables. One problem with these models is that they assume that the people in the model are all independent of each other – that is, they aren't related to each other or influencing each other in some way. This is often problematic – thinking about schools, two students in the same school will in general be more similar than two students from two different schools. Such models also assume that the relationship between two variables is the same for everyone. In reality, such correlations are different for different types of people.

Multilevel models aim to solve this problem. They treat individuals as belonging in contexts – students belonging in schools, for example – and then are able to model relationships that happen at both levels.

This allows many questions to be answered that couldn't be answered otherwise. It allows us to say how much school characteristics matter (in comparison with student characteristics), and it allows us to produce league tables based on school-level effects that are adjusted based on their reliability (see Box 9.2).

The models can be used in a range of different data structures and in a range of different subject areas.

For more on multilevel models, see Snijders and Bosker (2012).

9.2 Shrinkage

Can we trust the estimates that a statistical model gives us? Often those estimates will be varied and based on a very small number of data observations, so the answer to that question is often 'no'. We generally want to adjust the results based on their reliability – that is, based on how accurately we think they measure what they are trying to. This is what a multilevel model does when estimating higher level effects, such as school effects that are used in 'Value Added' scores that are sometimes used in school league tables (see Section 9.2).

If a school is inaccurately measured – based on only a small fraction of students' results – we want to bring that school closer to the average, to shrink it back towards the average school. If a school is very accurately measured – based on almost all its students – we don't want to shrink it back very much at all because we are very confident about the originally measured school effect. Thus, we end up being much more sure about the more extreme results that we find, meaning we can be justified in making policy decisions on the basis of them.

   This shrinking is done automatically in multilevel models, and allows us to be more confident that the results we find are real and based on genuine differences between schools, and not just based on a random aberration.

The result is a ranking of drivers, based on their average performance net of their team's performance. But what about drivers who have participated in only a few races? An example of this is Prince Bira, who competed in only one Formula One race, in which he came second. We don't want to rank him highly, even though his average performance is exceptionally high (based, as it is, on only one observation). Fortunately, multilevel models account for this in the level effects. Drivers who have raced in only a few races are 'shrunk' back to the overall mean, (see Box 9.2). As such, high-performing drivers not only need to perform well on average, but also to perform consistently well over a relatively lengthy career.

Figure 9.2 shows the top 20 drivers. Those in the know about Formula One will recognise many of the names as top drivers, both current and past. Other names might surprise you. Christian Fittipaldi, for example, was never placed in a race, and is perhaps best known for accidentally flipping his car on the finish line of the Italian GP in 1993. However, he never raced in a high-performing car, but consistently beat his teammates (often simply by keeping a low-quality car on the track). Thus, the model ranks him highly. Other results may surprise the reader too, but our perception of drivers as particularly good or bad is not necessarily based on their performance, but also their team's performance, or how exciting they were/are to watch. Michael Schumacher has won more championships than anyone else, but his many championship wins were as much the result of his team's (Ferrari) as his own (undoubtedly high) ability, which is why he doesn't appear as high as many might expect.

You may be wondering, especially if you're not particularly interested in sport, why we have spent so much of this chapter talking about sport rather than about data in the media. It turns out that many of the issues we've been discussing are central to league tables that appear in the media on the front, as well as the back, pages. In fact, the issues which we have discussed so far are even more severe in the non-sporting world of league tables.

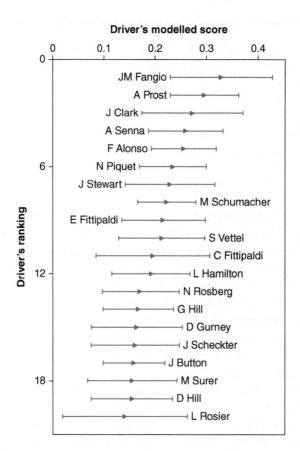

Figure 9.2   The top 20 Formula One drivers of all time, according to the model described here. These are measures of the 'Shrunken Residuals' assigned to each driver by the model, after team effects have been controlled out statistically. A higher score indicates a better driver, so Fangio is estimated to be the greatest driver of all time. The uncertainty (how sure we are about the position of each driver) is indicated by 95% confidence intervals (see Chapter 8) around each point. Adapted from Bell et al. (2016), figure 1.

9.3 SCHOOL LEAGUE TABLES

Those uninterested in sport can switch back on now! This section considers school league tables – that is, rankings of schools that are produced in a number of countries, including the UK, the United States and Australia. While in some countries (such as France), there's no choice for students and their parents in what schools they attend, in the UK parents do have a level of choice, and school league tables are published in local newspapers and online, especially in England, giving an indication to readers which schools in their local area are the highest performing and which are doing less well. This, in theory, allows parents to make informed choices while simultaneously allowing the government and public to hold schools accountable. However, as with sport, what 'highest performing' means is somewhat contested, and often multiple school league tables are published, each focusing on a different performance indicator with a different meaning. As with sport, these league tables are sometimes manipulated by schools, through means that don't necessarily lead to the best outcomes for students. These league tables can also be beset by random variation in school performance, with small schools being particularly variable and vulnerable to 'regression to the mean'.

Of course, such league tables have a number of potential uses. Students, and their parents, may not want the performance of their schools to be hidden from them. If a school is failing to educate its students, then parents, the government and the students themselves are likely to want to be warned, and to expect that something should be done to rectify it. Moreover, a public league table puts in place incentives for schools to keep doing as well as they can. It makes it much more difficult for schools to just continue being mediocre, since parents, students, government funders and taxpayers will complain to them if they do.

But what do school league tables actually measure? Ideally we want them to measure school performance – how well a school improves the ability, intelligence and all-round 'good-ness' of their students. But defining such a wishy-washy term is rather difficult, and somewhat politically charged. Can we really measure intelligence, or 'goodness'? If a student becomes cleverer but less socially capable, should that count as a good thing? Are some subjects more important than others in defining ability? Should we prioritise ability in (for instance) science and maths, over ability in art, or history? The answers that you give to these questions will depend on your values and what you think is important in society, and what you think the role of schools is in improving those things.

In England – there are different systems in Wales, Scotland and Northern Ireland – there are a number of different measures that are or have been used to try to measure how well schools perform. A crude measure used for many years was simply to list the proportion of students in a school that achieved a grade C or higher in at least five GCSEs (the exams sat by most students in the country at age 16, where A* is the highest grade and G the lowest). While this measure of student attainment is particularly easy to understand, it has a number of problems:

- Schools with lower performing students in their intake will perform less well through no fault of their own. Thus, schools in economically poorer areas will often appear 'low-performing' even when they're helping the students to improve greatly, because that improvement happens from a low base.

- The measure encourages schools to enter students in subjects they perceive as easier, meaning students miss out on arguably important subjects like maths and science.
- The measure encourages schools to focus effort and resources on students that are borderline, between grades D and C, and perhaps ignore students that will definitely achieve at least a grade C and students that definitely won't achieve a grade C.
- Schools that are small end up with highly variable, and therefore misleading, results, reflecting only random variation rather than the quality of the school.

The astute reader will recognise the parallels between these problems and those mentioned with regard to sport. In both, we have regression to the mean. Like the sport stars coming into and going out of form, for small schools there's a lot of variability in the results. Like the unusual 'golden-goal rule' described above, there are perverse incentives that lead schools to act in ways that are detrimental to some students. And there are other factors (like high levels of deprivation in the school intake) that mean the measure isn't a pure measure of school quality (i.e. confounding – see the next chapter).

As with the sporting examples, some of these can be solved by changing the way school league tables are measured. One attempt to do this was the so-called 'Contextual Value Added' (CVA) measure, which operated in England between 2006 and 2010. This was explicitly a measure of academic *progress* during secondary schooling rather than attainment at the end of secondary schooling, meaning it attempted to solve the problem of school differences in the composition of student intakes. It also attempted to avoid the problem of random variation in school attainment that will occur naturally in smaller schools. It did this using a similar technique to that in the Formula One example: it used a multilevel model to disentangle the school and student-level variation (see Box 9.1). It also took into account ('controls for') the attainment of the student when entering the school (see Chapter 10), meaning that the measure is not of attainment, but progress, a fairer measure with which to judge the school. It also controlled for some important factors that might affect attainment, such as levels of deprivation in the school's area. The multilevel model also uses shrinkage (Box 9.2) so that smaller schools are 'shrunk' to the mean across all schools, and thus are less susceptible to random fluctuations across schools, with confidence intervals being published to further express the level of uncertainty. To measure student progress, the CVA score used the eight best exam results that students attained when they were 16, but this didn't solve the problem of students being encouraged to do easier subjects; however, there was no arbitrary threshold of approval (grade C in the crude attainment measure), so there were fewer incentives to prioritise some students (like grade C/D borderline students) over others.

The latest (2018) headline school performance measure in England is called 'Progress 8'. This considers eight of a student's set of GCSE grades, but there are rules about which eight subjects are allowed to be included. Maths and English must be included and are double weighted, and three of the eight must be specific academic subjects: science, computer science, geography, history and languages. Thus, the incentive to enter students for subjects they find easier is somewhat removed, since students have to perform well in the key subject categories for their schools to do well in the latest league tables. Thus, the introduction of Progress 8 can be seen as an attempt by the government to alter the way schools behave, encouraging them to focus on more academic subjects. The measure is compared with the average for students with the same prior attainment, making it, like the old CVA score, a measure of progress rather than attainment.

Progress 8 is used not only for parental school choice, but also for government purposes. Schools that on average score less than half a grade lower than the national mean for students with the same prior grades are judged to be 'underperforming', and therefore face increased government scrutiny and potential takeover by other bodies (Leckie and Goldstein, 2017; for a readable introduction to this paper, see also Goldstein and Leckie, 2008). As such, these school league tables really matter to schools – the jobs of the school leaders could depend on them!

So, the measures of progress attempt to assess school quality, or, at least, how much a school's students improve academically during secondary schooling. However, these measures are still politically informed, being based for instance on the subjects that the UK government considers to be important. They're also open to gaming, in some ways that are predictable and in others that might not be. If a school decides to stop teaching maths and only teaches students how to dance, this will be reflected badly in the league tables, and most people would probably say it's right for that to be the case. However, if a particular student is particularly good at dance, the measures may well lead schools to actively discourage that student from pursuing such a vocation, and instead encourage the student to pursue subjects like maths and science that, while highly valued in society generally, might not be best for this student. Thus, students will increasingly be treated as uniform (forgive the pun), with specific subject areas being deemed 'important' and others less so.

Is this appropriate? That is for the reader to judge. You may think that expecting a certain level in key priority subjects is entirely appropriate. Or you may think that encouraging an exceptional dance student, and ensuring that this student doesn't become disillusioned with education more generally, is more important. The key point is that the choice is not a valueless one, and the people in charge of forming the measures of performance (and, perhaps, the people that elect them) will be the ones deciding which values are most important.

However, it's still unclear whether the league table acts as a useful source of information for parents who want to use it to choose what school they should send their child to. We've already discussed that there's some random fluctuation in schools that makes league tables less certain than we might think. But we haven't yet considered another source of uncertainty: time. School league tables reflect the exam results of students for the current year. But parents are interested in the potential exam results of their own children, and they won't be sitting their exams for, in most cases, another five years. A lot can change in a school in five years – teachers can come and go, funding levels can change, as can school policies – and all of these could have a positive or negative effect on school performance. As such, while we might be relatively sure that a school is doing a good job at the moment, we can be much less sure what that means for the school's performance when it matters for our child. Current and future performance are certainly correlated to each other, but they aren't perfectly correlated, so there's additional uncertainty from trying to predict one from the other.

Research by Leckie and Goldstein (2009) attempts to quantify this uncertainty. They find that there's so much uncertainty that it is impossible to reliably tell the difference between any schools. That is, there is a decent chance that the worst school will become much better, or the best school much worse, meaning that such league tables really have very little benefit in terms of school choice for parents and their children.

So, school league tables might play an important role in holding schools to account. We might be pleased to know our public services are working, or that our tax money isn't being wasted. But it's unclear whether they do much in terms of giving parents information to help them choose schools for their children. And they can also produce a number of problems that arguably aren't worth the benefits.

School choice is something that's usually only taken up by people that are relatively rich, or live in wealthy areas. For instance, there's evidence that well-off parents sometimes move house in order to be closer to a 'good school', while poorer families can't afford to do so. As such, the publication of league tables can replicate and reinforce social inequalities, with richer parents sorting themselves off from their less well-off peers to live near a 'good' school. Those schools might then attract the best teachers and even funding. This may be desirable for some parents, but it's probably not such a good thing for society in general, and may be harmful to bright but poor students.

Hopefully, it should be clear to the reader that, while statistical issues are important in the creation of league tables, these are often inextricably tied up with political and social issues. Statistics are sometimes presented as a boring and technical exercise that produces objective results. In reality, they are rarely objective, and are often politically charged and controversial. The choices made in measuring schools can have big effects, so we need to be careful in understanding what league tables are really measuring, and how they might make some schools behave.

9.4 UNIVERSITY LEAGUE TABLES

Schools aren't alone in being ranked in league tables. In fact, many public service providers are ranked in some way, either publicly or not. When registering for a GP (general practitioner, as in doctor) in the UK, you can see how different practices rank against each other in a number of categories. Police forces are also ranked in some parts of the UK. And it's not just public services: if you wish to choose a restaurant, there are plenty of websites telling you which are the best, based on public reviews. The same goes for buying pretty much any other product. All of these have their own quirks, and their own criteria that produce the rankings.

One of the quirks that the authors of this book know a fair bit about is the ranking of the institutions in which they work, in university league tables. There are loads of league tables ranking universities: some are global, others national; some rank research quality, others student experience or teaching quality. In each case, the methodology is different, and in each case there are decisions that are made as to what aspects of university life to prioritise.

If you are currently studying for a university degree (which, let's face it, is probably why you're reading this book) then the chances are that you've encountered university league tables prior to choosing your course of study. You'll probably know, better than we do, the extent to which they helped you decide what course to study. You'll also know that the league tables do not all agree with each other. At the time of writing, our own university (The University of Sheffield) is ranked 32nd nationally in the Complete University Guide table, 40th in the Guardian league table, 104th globally in the Times Higher Education Rankings and 82nd globally (13th in the UK) in the Quacquarelli–Symonds Rankings. Meanwhile, Sheffield was ranked 'Silver' in the Teaching Excellence Framework of 2017, and where it ranked in the 2014 Research Excellence Framework (a ranking of universities' research quality) depends on which subject you are interested in. Meanwhile, Sheffield is the third best university in the country according to the 'Student Experience Survey'.

Confused? You aren't the only one. With universities increasingly keen to attract students, you can be forgiven for thinking they're all saying they are 'one of the best' based on some kind of statistical measure – indeed universities will often advertise the league tables that position them well, but not those league tables that rank them poorly. Of course this doesn't mean that the measures are meaningless. It makes perfect sense that some universities are better than others academically, and those universities don't necessarily provide students with the best student experience more broadly. But it's worth thinking about how differences in these league tables can come about, and when they are (and are not) measuring the thing they're supposed to assess. The latter is called '**construct validity**' – the extent to which the measurement actually measures the thing it is meant to.

The academic standard of degrees can be measured in a number of different ways. First, you can measure grades: how many students achieve the top grade in their degrees. But this can create perverse incentives – there's nothing to stop universities simply awarding students more firsts! Second, you can judge how much the university spends on students' education. Again, this isn't a measure of quality – a very wasteful (or rich) institution will potentially do very well on this measure. Alternatively you can ask students what they think about their courses, as is done in the National Student Survey in the UK. While this might seem like a good idea in theory, there are problems with it. Lots of things can influence how students perceive their lectures. For example, different students have different expectations – some might expect to be spoon-fed answers, whereas others might not. League tables could (much like school league tables that use raw measures of attainment) become more a measure of the expectations, or even social class, of students than the quality of the teaching they receive. It has also been shown that students are influenced by the characteristics of lecturers, for example ranking female teachers less highly than male teachers (Jaschik, 2015). There are clear incentives created here as well. Would it really be in the students' interests if universities hired only male lecturers, or if lecturers ensured their subject content was easy? That might be one way to improve student feedback, but it would not be good for students in the long run. Another fundamental problem when measuring student satisfaction via surveys is that response rates vary across universities, and those who respond can differ in their opinions from those who do not, leading to biased measures of what's really happening in each institution (see Chapters 3 and 4 for more on making samples representative of the population they're measuring).

Part of the problem is that university league tables often attempt to combine many things: student satisfaction, quality of teaching, quality of research, reputation, employability of students and so on. All of these are imperfectly measured, because they're very difficult to measure. It is also difficult to know how to weight them. What is more important – quality of teaching, or social life, or job prospects in the future? The answer will be different depending on who you ask, and, indeed, different rankings put different emphases on different characteristics of a 'good' university. The result is something that might or might not be useful, but is at best imperfect. That's not to say such league tables don't have value. But we should be appropriately sceptical of university league tables, and consider what exactly they are measuring before using them to make decisions. If we are choosing a university to study at, we want to decide what we really want from it (lots of contact hours, good research, good reputation, and/or student satisfaction?) and use university rankings that take those things into account.

But, again, this is not to say that university rankings are useless and should be completely ignored. League tables give an imperfect but useful measure of university quality. Which league table you trust might depend on what factors you consider to be important for your university experience. Some might want a league table that ranks reputation highly; others might want one that ranks student experience above all else. The important thing is to understand the limits of these rankings and the ways that they might measure things they aren't intending to measure. As ever, information and data are almost always imperfect, and understanding their limits is important in making them useful to us.

9.5 CONCLUSIONS

This chapter has considered a number of different types of rankings such as sports, school and university league tables. You may want to consider others that you've encountered, and think about the ways in which they might be useful or problematic, or which might lead you to judge things in a very particular way.

Overall, we've shown that league tables can often help users to make choices, or help government bodies decide if public services are performing as well as they can be. However, all rankings are imperfect. The creators of league tables have to make a number of difficult choices: what measure(s) to use, how to balance different measures, and what things to leave out entirely. Their choices will reflect, in some ways, the values that they see as important. However, perverse incentives can be created when institutions attempt to perform as well as possible in those league tables, which might not be appreciated by the reader.

Whatever the league table (whether in sport, public services or private companies), how we understand it will depend on a number of things: (i) what the league table is designed for; (ii) what the league table is aiming to rank; and (iii) how the league table operates in practice. First, a league table designed for consumer choice might not be best used for accountability, and vice versa. Second, even seemingly subtle differences in what is being ranked and the aims of the league table creator (like the difference between attainment and progress in league tables) can make a big difference to the rankings. And finally, even if the creator of the league table intends it to rank institutions based on a specific dimension, this doesn't necessarily mean that's what will ultimately be ranked if the way the measure that has been constructed has some kind of flaw, or the institutions being ranked attempt to game the system in some way. Readers of league tables: beware!

9.6 CONCEPTS LEARNED IN THIS CHAPTER

Construct validity: put simply, this is the extent to which a measure accurately measures what it is supposed to measure. So, for example, raw measures of attainment will have poor construct validity as measures of school quality, because they are as much measuring the intake of the school.

   Multilevel models: a model that accounts for variation at a number of different 'levels'.

   Shrinkage: in multilevel models, the estimated effects of level units (such as schools) are 'shrunk' back to the mean based on their reliability. Thus, estimates that are based on very few observations (e.g. very few pupils in a school) will be shrunk to be closer to the mean than would otherwise be the case.

   Random variation: in the social world we usually cannot predict exactly how something will be measured. There are lots of factors, and chance occurrences, that lead people to score differently from what we might expect. This is called 'random variation', and its size and importance are often underestimated by the public.

   Regression to the mean: when an individual scores unusually highly on a particular occasion (because of random variation), it is likely that when measured again on another occasion the score will no longer be as high – it will regress to the average or mean.

9.7 QUESTIONS FOR CLASS DISCUSSION

1   Should league tables be banned? Discuss in relation to schools, universities or another type of league table in the public sector.
2   Take a league table used in the public sector and look at how it is constructed. How might you improve it so it tells you what you really want to know?

FURTHER READING

Ball, S. J., Bowe, R. and Gewirtz, S. (1996) School choice, social class and distinction: the realization of social advantage in education. *Journal of Education Policy*, 11(1), 89–112.

Bird, S. M., Cox, D., Farewell, V. T., Holt, T. and Smith, P. C. (2005) Performance indicators: good, bad, and ugly. *Journal of the Royal Statistical Society, Series A*, 168, 1–27.

Foley, B. and Goldstein, H. (2012) Measuring success: league tables and the public sector. Policy Centre report, The British Academy.

REFERENCES

Bell, A., Smith, J., Sabel, C. E. and Jones, K. (2016) Formula for success: multilevel modelling of Formula One driver and constructor performance, 1950–2014. *Journal of Quantitative Analysis in Sports*, 12(2), 99–112.

Goldstein, H. and Leckie, G. (2008) School league tables: what can they really tell us? *Significance*, 5(2), 67–69.

Jaschik, S. (2015) Rate my word choice. *Inside Higher Ed*. Available at https://www.insidehighered.com/news/2015/02/09/new-analysis-rate-my-professors-finds-patterns-words-used-describe-men-and-women (accessed 6 November 2017).

Leckie, G. and Goldstein, H. (2009) The limitations of using school league tables to inform school choice. *Journal of the Royal Statistical Society: Series A*, 172(4), 835–51.

Leckie, G. and Goldstein, H. (2017) The evolution of school league tables in England 1992–2016: 'Contextual value-added', 'expected progress' and 'progress 8'. *British Educational Research Journal*, 43(2), 193–212.

O'Hare, R. (2016) Revealed: the best Formula One driver of all time according to SCIENCE. *Daily Mail*, 14th April. Available at https://www.dailymail.co.uk/sciencetech/article-3539605 (accessed 24 September 2019).

Snijders, T. A. B. and Bosker, R. J. (2012) *Multilevel Analysis: An Introduction to Basic and Advanced Multilevel Modelling*, Second Edition. London: Sage.

10 When a relationship (doesn't) mean causality: 'How did that happen?'

Key concepts

observational data, correlation, causality, spurious correlation, experiments

10.1 INTRODUCTION

One important way that we learn about the latest scientific discoveries is through the news. It seems almost daily that new research comes out to tell us what to eat, how much to exercise, and which behaviours are most risky. But have you ever noticed how many of these news stories seem to contradict one another? Nowhere are these contradictions more evident than in news reporting about health.

Take coffee, for instance. Although people have been drinking coffee for centuries, we still don't know for certain whether the net effect to our health is positive or negative. And it's unclear how much coffee we would need to consume daily to affect our health. A quick scan of some news stories reveals a confusing mix of reporting on this topic:

Daily Mail: 'Could coffee be making you fat? (De Graaf, 2018)

The Telegraph: 'Too much coffee damages fertility for men' (Knapton, 2014)

USA Today: 'Coffee can help you live past 90, study says' (Manzullo, 2018)

The Independent: 'Drinking three cups of coffee could be "good for the heart", study finds' (Young, 2018)

The Telegraph: 'Six coffees a day could save your life' (Donnelly, 2018)

So which is it? Does drinking coffee make us fat? Does it lead to infertility in men? Or does it increase life expectancy and improve cardiovascular health?

The answer to this question isn't so easy because these headlines aren't just made up; they're based on the results from many real scientific studies. In fact, some published research suggests that drinking coffee may protect against certain types of cancer, stroke, diabetes and cognitive disease. Yet, other research studies link coffee to an increased risk of heart attack, cholesterol and arthritis. And we know that coffee can also be addictive (which is bad), but a large study reported that those who drink at least six cups per day had lower mortality rates (which is good; Loftfield et al., 2018). So perhaps it's not quite fair to blame the media when there are so many different studies responsible for producing these contradictory results.

(Spoiler alert: the Mayo Clinic has considered all of the available evidence to date from many different studies and concluded that coffee consumed in moderation likely provides more health benefits than risks, but there is certainly a need to collect more evidence to answer these questions definitively (Hensrud, 2017).)

These headlines are just a sample of the conflicting news reports about a single beverage. Imagine how difficult it would be to sort through all of the health news, which must inspire more confusion than confidence in what's really best for us. And we thought data was supposed to help us make sense of the world!

One reason for this confusion is related to the distinction between observational and experimental data. In this chapter, we're going to learn about these differences, and why they're crucial to making sense of data in the media. We're also going to discover how much trust we should put into a single research study, and how we can use different approaches to gain more confidence in the results.

The ultimate aim of this chapter is to determine whether we can say that one thing *causes* something else. Science can definitely help us find causal links in the real world; for instance, we're now very confident that smoking tobacco causes cancer (Cancer Research UK, n.d.). But even that conclusion required very specific evidence to ensure the relationship was causal. Therefore, being sure about this **causality** is very difficult, and it depends on the sort of data we collect and the ways in which we've analysed it.

This chapter goes through the different types of data that we can use to consider the relationships between variables, and whether those relationships are causal. In doing so, we will come across some of the different methods that are used and the problems that can arise from them.

10.2 OBSERVATIONAL DATA

One of the main reasons for the conflicting news reports about health and many other stories in the media is that they are often based upon analysis from observational data. **Observational data** is collected whenever we record quantitative measures without control over the things that are happening in the dataset. This includes most datasets collected in the 'real world'. In these situations, we choose what we record, but we don't change what is happening in that world.

Survey data, which we learned about in detail in Chapter 3, is a good example of observational data because, although we may have responses to many different questions, we aren't aiming to change things in the study; thus, we can't be certain that one variable leads to another variable (we'll learn more about why this is the case in the next section). Data that is collected at a single point in time is called **cross-sectional data**. The term 'cross-section' comes from mid-eighteenth-century engineering sketches that were used to reveal the inner workings of an object that could not be seen from the outside (Online Etymological Dictionary, n.d.). Applied to the social sciences, the term now refers to taking a snapshot of data at a specific time point.

With observational data, we can investigate how variables are related, but it's much more difficult to be sure about causality. Instead, we can use this type of data to describe patterns and relationships between variables. It can also be used to make predictions about future outcomes (recall the maxim: 'the best predictor of future behaviour is past behaviour'). The vast majority of data used in the social sciences falls within the category of observational data. However, in the social sciences we often want to move beyond description. Instead, we want to know *how* or *why* something occurs – that is, we care about explaining causal relationships among variables.

People often make the mistake of drawing causal inferences that simply aren't possible with observational data. To understand why this is the case, let's turn back to our coffee example. Recall that we were presented with a mix of news stories, some reporting negative health outcomes, while others showed positive ones. Now let's take a closer look at that sensational headline from *The Telegraph* which reported that drinking 'six coffees a day could save your life'. How did the journalist – or more likely the researchers – come to that conclusion?

To find out, we need to know more about the data and design of the original study. This information should be available in the main body of the news story or a detailed footnote. In our case, details about the data are presented near the bottom of the article. Here, we learn that the data comes from the UK Biobank, which 'followed the 498,134 participants, aged 38 to 73, from 2006 until 2016, during which time 14,225 of them died'. The word 'followed' suggests that this isn't simply a cross-sectional design because there were measures of coffee consumption and mortality at more than one time period. Instead, this is an example of **panel data**, which tracks the same individuals or organisations over time.

How do we know that the data is observational and thus not ideal for making strong causal claims? In this case, the lead researcher reminded readers that 'the results were based on observation [so] they cannot prove cause [and] should be treated with caution'. In other cases, it may be less clear and may require more digging into the original research paper. One clue that an analysis is based upon observational data is that the term 'association' (or its variants) will be used instead of stronger causal language. For instance, the lead researcher is quoted as saying: 'Coffee drinking was inversely *associated* with mortality, including among those drinking eight or more cups per day.' And unless it's explicitly stated otherwise, it's generally safe to assume that the data is observational. In short, we're not saying that drinking six to eight cups of coffee a day cannot produce these amazing health benefits – a reduction in death rates of 14 to 16% – just that the available evidence does not support this strong causal link.

10.2.1 Correlation

A **correlation** means that there is a connection between two things – like, in the above example, coffee and mortality. Two variables may be related because one causes the other. However, they may also be linked by a third factor, which is known as a lurking variable (or 'omitted variable'). A **lurking variable** is related to both of the variables believed to be linked causally, and it gives the appearance that those two things are related, when in reality the association is actually due to this third variable. Lurking variables are quite common in observational data and probably to blame for many of the conflicting results reported in the news.

In statistics, a correlation can be quantified using something called Pearson's r. You may have noticed that certain quantities are named after the person who came up with the statistic. In this case, you guessed it: Pearson's r is named after Karl Pearson, a British mathematician and founder of modern statistics (Magnello, 2005). In 1911, he even founded the world's first university statistics department at UCL (University College London, n.d.)!

Pearson's r ranges from −1 to +1, with 0 indicating no linear correlation between two variables. A correlation of −1 indicates a perfect negative linear relationship: when one variable increases, the other variable decreases by a consistent amount (or vice versa). A correlation of +1 indicates a perfect positive linear relationship: when one variable increases, the other variable also increases by a consistent amount (or if one decreases, the other decreases too). The closer the correlation is to −1 or +1, the more the data pattern falls on a straight line. Thus, Pearson's *r* provides a measure of the strength of the linear relationship between two variables.

Correlations are probably easiest to understand with a visualisation called a scatterplot. Recall in Chapter 5 that we learned about the importance of visualising relationships, particularly that Anscombe's quartet shows that four very different data patterns can have the exact same correlation. This occurs because the data pattern in some instances was **non-linear**: that is, taking a pattern that is more complicated than a straight line. The patterns in Figure 10.1 demonstrate the correlation coefficient associated with different data patterns, including what happens when we have non-linear data (Boigelot, 2011).

Notice that the correlations indicate how aligned the data points are in the scatterplots. However, what correlations don't tell us is the rate of change between variables, which is measured by how steep the slope of the line is (look at all the different relationships in the second row of the figure). For this, we would need to use a technique called linear regression, which tells us how much an increase in one variable is associated with another variable (see Box 10.1 for more details). They also don't tell us about the shape of the relationship – two variables can be strongly related while still having a zero linear correlation (see the third row in the figure).

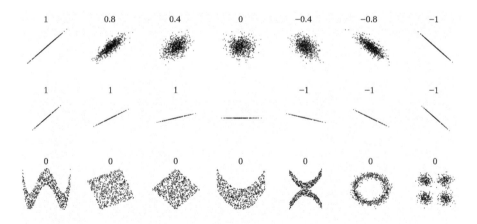

Figure 10.1   Data patterns and correlation coefficients

Source: Created by Denis Boigelot.

10.1 Regression Models in Social Science

When we think about a model, we think about a simplified representation of reality. A model aircraft, for instance, is a simplified representation of an actual aircraft. A statistical model is the same: it's an attempt to simplify things so that we can see, beneath all the uncertainty and white noise that exist in the world, what's really going on. The most helpful models are parsimonious, which means that they are as simple as can be allowed to capture the key theoretical concepts of the model.

One of the most important types of models that social scientists estimate is called linear regression. Linear regression is a technique for fitting a line to a set of observed data points – that is, the linear relationship between a set of predictors (sometimes called independent variables) and some outcome of interest (also know as a dependent variable). If you think back to our discussions about scatterplots, in which values of x (predictor) and y (outcome) are plotted against one another, the linear regression model is a process of adding a line of best fit to capture the linear trend in the data. The constant tells us where the regression line intersects the y-axis, the estimated value of y when all of the predictors are set at zero. The slope of this line tells us the effect of one or more predictor variables on the outcome – that is, how much a one-unit increase in the predictor changes the outcome, accounting for all of the other variables included in the model. These other variables are sometimes known as control variables because it means that we're showing how each predictor affects the dependent variable above and beyond the other predictors in the model.

If we are interested in health, for example, a linear regression model might be able to tell us the extent to which our health (the outcome) is related to our age, how much we drink, or the neighbourhood in which we live. That isn't to say that everyone will be influenced in the way suggested by the model. Rather that, in general, these factors are associated with our health. The stuff that the model doesn't explain – the random stuff that we don't understand – is separated away (the 'residual') so that we can see the general relationships that we are really interested in.

Many news stories that use numbers will be based on a statistical model like linear regression.

10.2.2 Correlation Does Not Always Imply Causation

A classic example of why correlation does not always reveal a causal link occurs with ice-cream sales and swimming deaths. The two variables are correlated:

when ice-cream sales increase, so too does the number of drownings. Yet, we wouldn't conclude that ice-cream sales *cause* swimming deaths. Here, the missing causal link is hot weather, which boosts both ice-cream sales and swimming deaths (because people are more likely to go swimming in hot weather and thus more likely to have fatal accidents in the water). An association between two variables that occurs because of a third lurking variable (or simply coincidence) is called a **spurious correlation**.

To illustrate this concept, it's sometimes helpful to find silly correlations that couldn't possibly be the result of a causal process. For example, let's consider the 'Redskins Rule', which states that whenever the National Football League's Washington Redskins win their last home game before a US presidential election, the incumbent party will win (conversely, when the Redskins lose their last home game, the incumbent party will lose the election). Since the Redskins relocated from Boston to Washington, DC in 1937, the rule has held in 17 of 20 presidential elections, or 85% of the time (Wikipedia, 2018). While most people don't take the Redskins Rule too seriously (nor should they!), news outlets still find time to write about it during election years. For instance, Fox News published this headline the day before the 2016 US presidential election: 'Why The "Redskins Rule" Is Bad News For Donald Trump' (Barrabi, 2016). The Redskins won their last home game 27–20 that year, predicting a win for the incumbent party – Democratic candidate Hillary Clinton. While she did get nearly 3 million more votes than her opponent, Republican Donald Trump, we now know that the Redskins Rule failed for only the third time in nearly 80 years. Of course, it's implausible that the outcome of a local sports match was responsible for the election outcome; hence, it's a spurious correlation.

Here's another fun example of a spurious correlation reported by the news agency Reuters: 'Eat chocolate, win the Nobel Prize?' (Joelving, 2012). For chocolate lovers, that's good news indeed! The relationship between a country's chocolate consumption and Nobel Prize winners was published in one of the world's leading medical journals, *The New England Journal of Medicine*, with the surprisingly strong correlation of $r = 0.79$ (Messerli, 2012). American physicist Eric Cornell, who won the Nobel Prize in 2001, joined in on the joke by saying: 'I attribute essentially all my success to the very large amount of chocolate that I consume.' Of course, this example once again highlights the dangers of making causal claims from observational data. Cornell later went on to clarify: 'Scientists look at hundreds and hundreds of different things, and every once in a while they will find two things that are surprisingly correlated with each other. Chocolate [may] be correlated with high-quality research, but there is no causal connection there.' In other words, the lurking variable is likely a country's wealth, which is also positively associated with its consumption of chocolate and support for academic research.

Tyler Vigen has a great book (2015) and accompanying website called *Spurious Correlations* that help us see just how ridiculous it would be to assume that some highly correlated factors really are meaningfully related with each other. For instance, did you know that the correlation between US spending on science, space and technology and suicides by hanging, strangulation and suffocation in the United States is 0.997? Figure 10.2 shows the surprising strength of the positive association between these two seemingly unrelated concepts. In fact, a correlation of 1 implies that these two variables are interchangeable because they could measure the exact same thing. (Notice that the y-axes on the left- and right-hand sides of the figure have been adjusted to make the line graph of the time series appear more related.)

Or, how about divorce rates in Maine and per capita consumption of margarine in the United States for a given year? The correlation between these variables is 0.992 (because the trends move in the same direction).

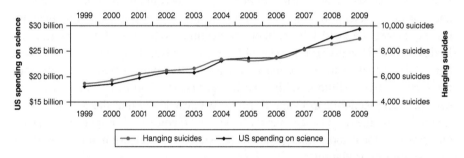

Figure 10.2   The correlation between US spending on science and suicides

Source: Spurious Correlations by Tyler Vigen (www.tylervigen.com/spurious-correlations).

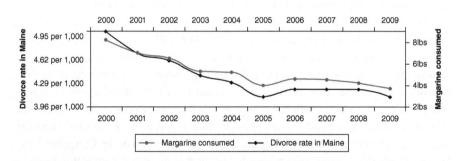

Figure 10.3   The correlation between US divorce rate and eating margarine

Source: Spurious Correlations by Tyler Vigen (www.tylervigen.com/spurious-correlations)

Ultimately, these extreme examples highlight the importance of not jumping from correlation to causation.

Hopefully by now it's clear that correlations are useful because they point to *potential* causal relationships, but that's not the same thing as identifying a *real* causal link between two things. So why is this distinction important? Often, we want to make sense of the world, so we use whatever data is readily available. This generally means that observational data intended for one purpose is used to test potential relationships between other things. This can provide important insights where we previously had little information, but it can also increase the chance of finding spurious relationships.

There's a funny story circulating round the statistics blogs to illustrate this concept (Cookson, 2012). A man is wandering the halls of a psychiatric ward with a spider in the palm of his hand. He sees the doctor and says, 'Look Doc, I can talk to spiders.' He says, 'Spider, go left!' and the spider duly moves to the left. He continues, 'Spider, go right.' The spider shuffles to the right of his palm. The doctor replies, 'Interesting, maybe we should talk about this in the next group session.' The man retorts, 'That's nothing Doc. Watch this.' He pulls off each of the spider's legs one by one and then shouts, 'Spider, go left!' The spider lies motionless on his palm. The man turns to the doctor and concludes, 'If you pull off a spider's legs, he'll go deaf!'

So, the next time you see an eye-catching headline, perhaps you should ask yourself whether the study was designed to identify a causal relationship or it's the result of a large observational dataset. Remember, correlation does not always imply causation.

Figure 10.4   Correlation doesn't always imply causation?

Source: xkcd.com by Randall Monroe

10.2.3 Can We Ever Make Causal Claims with Observational Data?

Sometimes we can come close to making causal claims with observational data – we just need to be very careful that there aren't other causes for the relationship that we find. Indeed, many of the most important findings in social science have come from observational data. Recall that we're now very confident that smoking tobacco is a major cause of cancer, and this conclusion came largely from the analysis of observational data.

So how might we determine causal links with observational data? First, we can think about the potential causes of a relationship between two variables. If the only plausible link is a causal one, then we might well be justified in making that claim. However, sometimes we cannot do this – often there are other things that could cause a particular relationship. For example, it might be that smokers are generally older than non-smokers, earn less money, have fewer years of formal education or eat poorly. All of these things might affect their health instead.

To counteract these potential confounds, we sometimes 'control' for these other factors, for example in a regression model (see Box 10.1). This means that we take account of those variables in our estimate of a given relationship. In the case of smoking and cancer, this was enough to give us a good deal of confidence that smoking does, indeed, cause cancer. However, sometimes there are things we haven't thought of, or things we have thought of but can't measure, that might be driving the relationship between these variables. In these situations, we shouldn't make causal claims, and might need to think about performing an experiment (we will explain it later in the chapter).

Another way to determine causality with observational data is through a process called triangulation. **Triangulation** means that more than one approach is used to collect and analyse new evidence. The term is a metaphor borrowed from navigational techniques, which used triangles to determine an unknown distance. The basic idea is that if we combine multiple data analysis techniques ideally on different datasets, we may be able to overcome the limitations that arise from analysing a single dataset. Just as we learned with replication (see Chapter 8), results that hold across many different study designs and independent samples are more 'robust' to errors in our estimates.

For example, we might want to investigate the effects of a candidate's gender on his or her ability to win elections. To explore this topic, there are several different methods that we could use to gather new evidence. First, we could look at existing election results to determine the effect that gender has on electoral success. Second, we might collect survey data with specific questions about how voters evaluate women running for office compared with men. Third, we could conduct detailed interviews with voters in group interviews asking them to discuss their thoughts and feelings about gender and politics, as well as how it might influence their vote choice. As we can see, these different methods of collecting evidence should help us to 'triangulate' on the true effect of gender in elections. The more data we collect on a given topic, the more likely we'll be able to discern the signal from the noise (Silver, 2012).

10.3 EXPERIMENTAL DATA

In the previous section, we learned that observational data can often lead us astray when trying to identify causal links between variables. So how do we determine when one factor is responsible for affecting the other? The answer is that we often need to use an experiment. **Experimental data** is collected when we expose participants to something that is manipulated by the researcher to test whether changes occur in the outcome variable. Because values of this 'treatment' are deliberately altered and everything else is kept the same (it's often called a treatment, even when it isn't a medical treatment per se), we can attribute any observed differences in the outcome to this treatment variable. With observational data, because any changes aren't controlled by the researcher, we can't be sure about the 'everything else is kept the same' part. For instance, if we were interested in the effect of gender on voting we could design an experiment pitting different candidates against one another in a mock election, making sure to hold constant all of their attributes except their genders. Doing this in an observational study is impossible because, while gender varies between real candidates, so too do other attributes – party, age, education, experience, competence, and so on – and many of these other attributes might affect vote choice, too!

Let's take a look at an example of using experimental data in more detail. In 2016, US news media outlets reported that guests using Airbnb, the global online marketplace for short-term lodging, were experiencing discrimination based on their public profiles (the platform gives hosts the discretion to decide whether to accept or reject guests after viewing their profiles) (Glusac, 2016). Some users of the platform claimed that they were routinely rejected by hosts because of their racial identity. In protest of this perceived mistreatment, some minorities vented their frustration on Twitter with the hashtag '#AirbnbWhileBlack' (W., 2016). One prominent case that made international headlines was that of Gregory Seldon, who filed a class action lawsuit against Airbnb after alleging that he was denied a booking request solely based upon his black racial identity. He claimed that when he requested the same accommodation with two new profiles switched with images of white males (rather than his real profile picture), his requests were immediately accepted (Whitten, 2016).

The observations of some users coupled with Seldon's mini experiment (manipulating the race of the user with different profile pictures) raises the real possibility of racial discrimination by Airbnb hosts. But Seldon's experiment could be done more systematically with a larger dataset, and indeed it was! Researchers at the Harvard Business School created a series of fake profiles on Airbnb and enquired about the availability of 6,400 listings across five different US cities (Edelman et al., 2017). The key manipulation involved whether the requestor had a black- or white-sounding name. Their experiment uncovered widespread racial discrimination: Airbnb guests with African-American names were 16% less likely to be accepted than those with stereotypically white names. While it only focused on the effect of having an African-American name, the Airbnb experiment raises the distinct possibility that other types of ethnic and gender-based discrimination occur on the platform. For example, the media reported that one Airbnb host was even hit with a $5,000 fine from California's Department of Fair Employment and Housing (DFEH) for cancelling an Asian woman's lodging explicitly because of her race (Perkins, 2017).

10.3.1 Causality and the Counterfactual

To understand how an experiment works, we need to introduce the concept of the counterfactual. The **counterfactual** tells us what would have happened if things in the treatment were different or had never occurred in the first place. While it sounds abstract, there are countless examples of this concept in popular media; for example, science fiction films that involve time travel are based around this idea. What would happen if George McFly never met his future wife in *Back to the Future*? What would happen if John Connor had never been born (in *The Terminator*)? In each case, time travel allows us to see two different worlds – one where something happens and another where it doesn't – to test how things would turn out in these alternate worlds.

Unfortunately (or perhaps fortunately?!), we can't travel back in time, which means that we can never perfectly rerun history. But we can approximate the logic of the counterfactual with a carefully designed experiment. For example, in the Airbnb experiment, the key manipulation is the racial identity invoked by the guests' public profiles. By comparing what happened when hosts received requests from black applicants with what would have happened in the counterfactual, we can create two different worlds, and by comparing the difference between those two worlds, we can estimate the causal effect. And because we are controlling the differences between the two worlds, we can be sure there isn't something else that has caused them (i.e. the differences).

10.3.2 Measuring Differences Between and Within Subjects

When considering experiments, it's useful to understand the two primary types of experimental designs, and how they help us disentangle causal relationships. In a **between-subjects design**, the treatment is assigned to one group of individuals (the 'treatment group'), while the other remains unexposed and serves as a comparison group. Participants assigned to this no-treatment group are known as the **control group** (Figure 10.5).

Usually individuals are assigned to the treatment and control groups at random, meaning ideally everyone has the same chance of being in either group. Random assignment to treatment and control conditions is crucial to between-subjects designs because it ensures that the only difference between groups is exposure to the hypothesised causal mechanism, while everything else is kept, on average, the same. In some academic fields (e.g. medicine), between-subjects designs are commonly referred to as **randomised controlled trials**. The Airbnb study is an example of a between-subjects design because stereotypically black- and white-sounding names were randomly allocated to hosts in the treatment and control groups, respectively. By comparing differences between the treatment and control group we were able to discern the causal effect of race on decisions to allow guests to stay with the host.

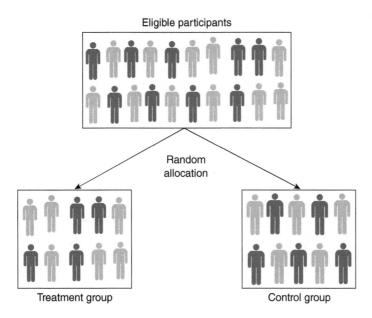

Figure 10.5   Between-subjects design

A drawback of the between-subjects design is that differences between groups can still occur even in the face of random assignment. This is because we often have small samples (meaning random differences between the groups can make a big difference) or there might be something wrong with the way we are assigning people to the groups. Also, while the groups may be relatively comparable between conditions, we don't actually get to observe the counterfactual for each individual. One solution to this problem is to examine differences that occur within individuals rather than between groups. This type of design is called a **within-subjects design**, and it means that measurements are taken before and after exposure to the treatment so that each person serves as their own comparison (Figure 10.6). The difference in these pre- and post-treatment measures provides the causal effect. The benefit of the within-subjects design is that individual differences no longer matter because any random variation between participants is not analysed. However, the downside to this approach is that there can be learning effects that result from using the same measures repeatedly.

Let's take a look at an example of a within-subjects design. In March 2018, the news media reported that a 22-year-old black man named Stephon Clark was shot and killed by police on his grandmother's property in Sacramento, California. Despite initial reports that he was armed, Clark was found without a weapon and carrying only a cell phone (Olmstead, 2018). An independent autopsy revealed that he had been shot 8 times (Robles and Del Real, 2018), and other reviews of the incident found that officers had fired a total of 20 times within 23 seconds of their encounter with Clark (Koetti, 2018). Like this one, other shootings of unarmed minorities by the police have been caught on camera and shared via social media. The shooting sparked widespread protests and has led some to wonder how the police could have mistaken Clark's cell phone for a gun (Bernstein, 2018).

To investigate this question, researchers have used a within-subjects design called the shooter bias experiment, which is also sometimes known as 'the police

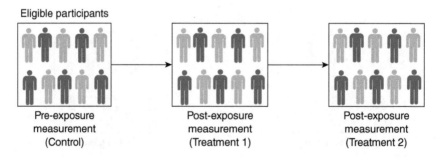

Eligible participants

| Pre-exposure measurement (Control) | Post-exposure measurement (Treatment 1) | Post-exposure measurement (Treatment 2) |

Figure 10.6   Within-subjects design

officer's dilemma' (Correll et al., 2002). In this experiment, participants are presented with a series of images of a black or white person holding either a weapon (e.g. gun) or a non-dangerous object (e.g. mobile phone) and must decide as quickly as possible whether to shoot the person. The task is intended to simulate the extremely quick decisions that police officers must make when encountering potential suspects who may be armed. A meta-analysis, which combines data collected from many different research studies, showed that participants were slower to avoid shooting unarmed blacks (relative to unarmed whites) and had a lower shooting threshold (i.e. were more trigger-happy when the target was black rather than white) (Mekawi and Bresin, 2015). Most importantly, these findings also include reaction time data from active police officers and show that despite their training, they demonstrate similar biases against minorities. The media have even reported research that people seem to carry their skin-tone biases over to robots, too: participants are quicker to shoot darker-coloured robots relative to lighter-coloured ones (Heggen and Attard, 2018). In sum, it seems that people's (un)conscious biases influence their ability to make rapid judgements that have life or death consequences.

Finally, it's worth noting that some studies combine between- and within-subjects experimental designs in what are called **mixed designs**. In mixed experimental designs, participants are randomly allocated to treatment and control groups, but multiple measures are taken at different points in time in both groups. This type of mixed design allows us to examine the causal mechanism in greater detail because we can test differences across groups, as well as see how this effect may change over time.

10.3.3 In the Laboratory or in the Real World?

Another important thing to consider is the location of the experiment, which may impact the types of generalisations we can make from the data. For instance, the shooter bias experiments we just learned about occurred in an artificial environment. These types of studies are often known as **laboratory experiments** because they typically occur in the confines of the lab. The advantage of using this type of setting is that it helps us ensure that the causal mechanism is the only thing that differs in the experiment because researchers have complete control over participants' environment. Yet, the main disadvantage is that this artificial environment may also be quite different from what participants would experience in their everyday lives. For example, the shooter bias experiment could never capture the real stress of being in a potentially life-threatening encounter. So while laboratory experiments may show how an effect *could* occur in the real world, they don't necessarily show how one *would* occur.

To remedy this issue, researchers can conduct an experiment that occurs outside of the controlled setting in the lab but still maintain control over the hypothesised causal mechanism. An experiment that occurs in the everyday environment of the participants is called a **field experiment**. The Airbnb experiment is an example of a field experiment because it was conducted in the real world.

Here's another example of a field experiment. In 2017 US National Public Radio published a news story about the effect of body-worn cameras on the behaviour of police officers (Greenfieldboyce, 2017). Police body-worn cameras (BWCs) have been suggested as a possible tool to reduce violent confrontations between the police and members of the public. The idea is based upon the 'Hawthorne effect', which stipulates that people behave differently under the watchful eye of the camera. In fact, a survey at the time suggested that nearly all US police departments are planning to implement them thanks in part to millions of dollars in funding to agencies from the US Department of Justice (Maciag, 2016).

Despite these claims, there is little causal evidence about whether police BWCs would actually reduce aggressive behaviour or complaints filed against departments. One group of researchers conducted a field experiment in Washington, DC involving 2,224 Metropolitan Police Department officers (Yokum et al., 2017). In the study, some officers were randomly assigned to wear cameras, while those assigned to the control group did not. Surprisingly, the researchers found a negligible treatment effect of BWCs on use of force and complaints filed, which suggests that there were no differences between officers in the treatment and control groups. Ultimately, this study provides some evidence that BWCs may not be the panacea many were hoping for to address rising instances of violent confrontations with the police.

10.3.4 A Word of Caution When Interpreting Experimental Data

It is worth noting that even when we have experimental data there are plenty of other concerns that may limit our ability to make causal inferences. For instance, experimental data may sometimes be affected by one or more **confounding variables**, which are related to the treatment but may also affect the outcome. Let's think about the field experiment designed to test the effect of BWCs on violent confrontations with the police. Imagine that during this field experiment, the police also instituted new training guidelines in response to increased media attention about police shootings. In this scenario, we would no longer be able to disentangle the effects of BWCs from those of the new training guidelines, which would make it impossible for us to identify each of their independent causal effects. The distinction between a lurking and confounding variable is that the former is not included in the study design and 'lurks' unobserved behind the scenes.

A confounding variable is observed and often measured, but we cannot determine its unique effect on the outcome.

Another way that confounding occurs is when individuals know that they are in the treatment group. If people know they are in the treatment group, it can lead them to respond more positively, even if the treatment itself doesn't make a difference (i.e. this is also called the placebo effect). In medical trials, it has been shown that this can have a surprisingly big effect. Even if the patient doesn't know which group he or she is in, if the doctor administering the treatment does know, this can have an effect, too! This is why medical trials are often '**double blind**', so neither the patient, nor the doctor, know who is in which group. This, of course, is much harder to do with some other experiments (such as those described above), where it would be impossible to hide which group people are in.

Of course, many other concerns that we learned about in previous chapters may also affect the strength of evidence from experimental data. For example, an experiment may suffer poor measurement of concepts, small or unrepresentative samples, and poorly designed stimulus materials, just to name a few. If not properly accounted for, each of these issues weakens the causal inferences we can make from an experiment.

10.4 CONCLUSIONS

In this chapter, we have learned about the distinctions between observational and experimental data, and why they're crucial to making sense of data in the media. We also discovered how much trust we should put in a single research study, and how we can use different approaches to gain more confidence in the results.

And, the next time you see headlines like these, just remember that correlation does not always imply causation!

> *Daily Mail*: 'Parasite caught from pet cats makes people more likely to start a business and take risks, finds study' (Allen, 2018)

> *The Guardian*: 'Can a cat-poo parasite turn you into a millionaire?' (Anon, 2018)

10.5 CONCEPTS LEARNED IN THIS CHAPTER

Observational data is collected when the researcher does not have control over potential causal mechanisms.

   Causality means that one variable is responsible for affecting the other.

   Cross-sectional data is observed at a single point in time.

Panel data tracks the same individuals or organisations over time. Also known as longitudinal data.

Correlation measures a linear association between two variables.

Lurking variable is not directly observed but is related to both the predictor and outcome variables, giving the appearance of an association.

Non-linear means that the data points do not follow a straight line.

Spurious correlation is a false association often due to a lurking variable.

Triangulation means that more than one method is used to collect and analyse new evidence.

Experimental data is collected when the researcher exposes participants to a treatment to test whether or not changes occur in an outcome.

Counterfactual reveals what would have happened if things in the treatment were different or had never occurred in the first place.

Between-subjects design (a.k.a. **Randomised-controlled trials**) occurs when the treatment is randomly assigned to one group of individuals, while the other remains unexposed and serves as a comparison group.

Control group is the comparison group of participants who are not exposed to the treatment.

Within-subjects design occurs when measurements are taken before and after exposure to the treatment so that each participant serves as his or her own comparison.

Mixed designs use a combination of between- and within-subjects designs.

Laboratory experiment tests causal relationships in an environment completely controlled by the researcher.

Field experiment occurs in the everyday environment of the participants.

Double blind means that neither the researcher nor the participant knows who has been assigned to what condition, which prevents them from behaving differently because of this knowledge.

Confounding variable makes it impossible to identify a clear causal link in experimental research because the variable is related to both the predictor and the outcome.

10.6 QUESTIONS FOR CLASS DISCUSSION

1   One way to improve your ability to spot correlations is to play a fun, interactive game called Guess the Correlation developed by Omar Wagih. Originally designed to collect data on people's ability to identify patterns from scatterplots, it's also a great way of learning. The game works by presenting randomly generated scatterplots and asking players to guess the numerical value of the correlation. The game has a 1980s retro feel to it,

quirky sounds, and can be quite addictive. Visit the Guess the Correlation website (http://guessthecorrelation.com/) and see how well you can do by playing this interactive game. What's your high score, and how many new games did it take to achieve it? Have they improved your ability to understand and spot correlations?

2   Google Correlate (https://www.google.com/trends/correlate) allows you to search patterns over time and location, many of which are spurious correlations. Use the interactive tool to see what you can discover. Just remember that correlations only show linear associations, and that the link could be due to other hidden (or sometimes obvious!) lurking variables.

3   Design an experiment to test a research question in the social sciences. First, identify the specific causal relationship that you are testing. What is the counterfactual? Next, explain the type of design you are using (e.g. between-subjects, within-subjects or mixed designs). Where would you collect the data, and how does this affect your ability to generalise your findings to the population (e.g. laboratory or field)? What are the treatment and control conditions? Make sure that you discuss how this design specifically tests the causal mechanism. What are its limitations?

4   Think of a research question in the social sciences. Now search for published research on this topic. Evaluate how strong the evidence exists testing your idea. Do the findings point in a similar direction? Have they been replicated? Do they use different methods (e.g. triangulation)? What new data would you collect to address any gaps in the evidentiary base?

FURTHER READING

Dunning, T. (2012) *Natural Experiments in the Social Sciences: A Design-Based Approach*. Cambridge: Cambridge University Press.

Gerber, A. S. and Green, D. P. (2012) *Field Experiments: Design, Analysis, and Interpretation*. New York: W Norton.

Mutz, D. C. (2011) *Population-Based Survey Experiments*. Princeton, NJ: Princeton University Press.

Pearl, J. and Mackenzie, D. (2018) *The Book of Why: The New Science of Cause and Effect*. New York: Basic Books.

REFERENCES

Allen, V. (2018) Parasite caught from pet cats makes people more likely to start a business and take risks, finds study. *Daily Mail*, 25 July. Available at www.dailymail.co.uk/health/article-5989699/Parasite-pet-cats-makes-people-likely-start-business-risks-finds-study.html (accessed 13 November 2018).

Anon (2018) Can a cat-poo parasite turn you into a millionaire? *The Guardian*, 25 July. Available at https://www.theguardian.com/lifeandstyle/shortcuts/2018/jul/25/cat-poo-parasite-turn-you-into-millionaire-toxoplasmosis (accessed 13 November 2018).

Barrabi, T. (2016). Why the 'Redskins Rule' is bad news for Donald Trump. Fox Business News, 7 November. Available at https://www.foxbusiness.com/features/why-the-redskins-rule-is-bad-news-for-donald-trump (accessed 13 November 2018).

Bernstein, S. (2018) Video of police shooting unarmed black man sparks protests in Sacramento. Reuters, 12 March. Available at https://www.reuters.com/article/us-california-police/video-of-police-shooting-unarmed-black-man-sparks-protests-in-sacramento-idUSKBN1GY39B (accessed 13 November 2018).

Boigelot, D. (2011) An example of the correlation of x and y for various distributions of (x,y) pairs. Available at https://commons.wikimedia.org/wiki/File:Correlation_examples2.svg (accessed 13 November 2018).

Cancer Research UK (n.d.) How smoking causes cancer. Available at https://www.cancerresearchuk.org/about-cancer/causes-of-cancer/smoking-and-cancer/how-smoking-causes-cancer (accessed 13 November 2018).

Cookson, G. (2012) Examples for teaching: correlation does not mean causation. Available at https://stats.stackexchange.com/q/443 (Accessed: 13 November 2018).

Correll, J., Park, B., Judd, C. M. and Wittenbrink, B. (2002) The police officer's dilemma: using ethnicity to disambiguate potentially threatening individuals. *Journal of Personality and Social Psychology*, 83(6), 1314–29.

De Graaf, M. (2018) Could coffee be making you FAT? The 'guilt-free' energy boost could affect hormones that fuel a belly bulge – but only if you drink too much. *Daily Mail*, 7 February. Available at www.dailymail.co.uk/health/article-5363831/Could-coffee-making-FAT.html (accessed 13 November 2018).

Donnelly, L. (2018) Six coffees a day could save your life. *The Telegraph*, 2 July. Available at https://www.telegraph.co.uk/news/2018/07/02/six-coffees-day-could-save-life/ (accessed 13 November 2018).

Edelman, B., Luca, M. and Svirsky, D. (2017) Racial discrimination in the sharing economy: evidence from a field experiment. *American Economic Journal: Applied Economics*, 9(2), 1–22.

Glusac, E. (2016) As Airbnb grows, so do claims of discrimination. *The New York Times*, 21 June. Available at https://www.nytimes.com/2016/06/26/travel/airbnb-discrimination-lawsuit.html (accessed 13 November 2018).

Greenfieldboyce, N. (2017) Scientists hunt hard evidence on how cop cameras affect behavior. National Public Radio. Available at https://www.npr.org/sections/alltechconsidered/2017/04/27/525081998/scientists-hunt-hard-evidence-on-how-cop-cameras-affect-behavior (accessed 13 November 2018).

Heggen, B. and Attard. M. (2018) We're racist towards robots, too, study finds. ABC News, 24 July. Available at www.abc.net.au/news/2018-07-24/we-are-racist-towards-robots-too-study-finds/10029548 (accessed 13 November 2018).

Hensrud, D. (2017) Does coffee offer health benefits? The Mayo Clinic, 4 March. Available at https://www.mayoclinic.org/healthy-lifestyle/nutrition-and-healthy-eating/expert-answers/coffee-and-health/faq-20058339 (accessed 13 November 2018).

Joelving, F. (2012) Eat chocolate, win the Nobel Prize? Reuters, 10 October. Available at https://www.reuters.com/article/us-eat-chocolate-win-the-nobel-prize/eat-chocolate-win-the-nobel-prize-idUSBRE8991MS20121010 (accessed 18 November 2018).

Knapton, S. (2014) Too much coffee damages fertility for men. *The Telegraph*, 20 October. Available at https://www.telegraph.co.uk/men/active/mens-health/11172506/Too-much-coffee-damages-fertility-for-men.html (accessed 13 November 2018).

Koetti, C. (2018) What we learned from the videos of Stephon Clark being killed by police. *The New York Times*, 7 June. Available at https://www.nytimes.com/2018/06/07/us/police-shooting-stephon-clark.html (accessed 13 November 2018).

Loftfield, E., Cornelis, M. C., Caporaso, N., Yu, K., Sinha, R. and Freedman, N. (2018) Association of coffee drinking with mortality by genetic variation in caffeine metabolism: findings from the UK Biobank. *JAMA Internal Medicine*, 178(8), 1086–97.

Maciag, M. (2016) Survey: Almost all police departments plan to use body cameras. *Governing*, 26 January. Available at http://www.governing.com/topics/public-justice-safety/gov-police-body-camera-survey.html (accessed 13 November 2018).

Magnello, M. E. (2005) Karl Pearson and the origins of modern statistics: an elastician becomes a statistician. *The Rutherford Journal*, 1. Available at www.rutherfordjournal.org/article010107.html (accessed 13 November 2018).

Manzullo, B. (2018) Alcohol and coffee can help you live past 90, study says. *USA Today*, 22 February. Available at https://eu.usatoday.com/story/news/nation-now/2018/02/22/alcohol-and-coffee-can-help-you-live-past-90-study-says/364878002/ (accessed 13 November 2018).

Mekawi, Y. and Bresin, K. (2015) Is the evidence from racial bias shooting task studies a smoking gun? Results from a meta-analysis. *Journal of Experimental Social Psychology*, 61, 120–30.

Messerli, F. H. (2012) Chocolate consumption, cognitive function, and Nobel Laureates. *New England Journal of Medicine*, 376(16), 1562–4.

Munroe, R. (n.d.) Correlation. Available at https://xkcd.com/552/ (accessed 13 November 2018).

Olmstead, M. (2018) Unarmed black man shot by police in Sacramento found to have been holding cellphone when killed. *Slate*, 21 March. Available at https://slate.com/news-and-politics/2018/03/unarmed-black-man-stephon-clark-killed-in-sacramento-by-police-over-fear-of-cellphone.html (accessed 13 November 2018).

Online Etymological Dictionary (n.d.) Cross-section. Available at https://www.etymonline.com/word/cross-section (accessed 13 November 2018).

Perkins, M. S. (2017) Airbnb host hit with $5,000 fine for cancelling on an Asian guest over her race. *Business Insider*, 14 July. Available at https://www.businessinsider.com.au/airbnb-racial-discrimination-asian-tami-barker-dyne-suh-2017-7 (accessed 13 November 2018).

Robles, F. and Del Real, J. A. (2018) Stephon Clark was shot 8 times primarily in his back, family-ordered autopsy finds. *The New York Times*, 30 March. Available at https://www.nytimes.com/2018/03/30/us/stephon-clark-independent-autopsy.html (accessed 13 November 2018).

Silver, N. (2012) *The Signal and the Noise: Why So Many Predictions Fail – But Some Don't*. New York: Penguin.

University College London (n.d.) Karl Pearson. Available at https://www.ucl.ac.uk/mathematical-physical-sciences/departments/statistical-science (accessed 13 November 2018).

Vigen, T. (2015) *Spurious Correlations*. New York: Hachette Books.

W., A. (2016) More Airbnb customers are complaining about racism. *The Economist*, 27 June. Available at https://www.economist.com/gulliver/2016/06/27/more-airbnb-customers-are-complaining-about-racism (accessed 13 November 2018).

Whitten, S. (2016) Airbnb sued for allegedly ignoring racial discrimination on its site. CNBC, 20 May. Available at https://www.cnbc.com/2016/05/20/airbnb-sued-for-allegedly-ignoring-racial-discrimination-on-its-site.html (accessed 13 November 2018).

Wikipedia (2018) Redskins Rule. Available at https://en.wikipedia.org/wiki/Redskins_Rule#cite_ref-9 (accessed 13 November 2018).

Yokum, D., Ravishankar, A. and Coppock, A. (2017) Evaluating the effects of police body-worn cameras: a randomized controlled trial. *The LAB @ DC*. Available at https://bwc.thelab.dc.gov/TheLabDC_MPD_BWC_Working_Paper_10.20.17.pdf (accessed 13 November 2018).

Young, S. (2018) Drinking three cups of coffee a day could be 'good for the heart', study finds. *The Independent*, 17 April. Available at https://www.independent.co.uk/life-style/coffee-drinking-three-cups-good-heart-health-conditions-caffeine-effects-a8308441.html (accessed 13 November 2018).

11 Surprising quirks in the media: 'Is that possible?'

Key concepts

Bayes' Theorem, Simpson's Paradox, the Birthday Problem, within- and between-group effects

Alice laughed: 'There's no use trying,' she said; 'one can't believe impossible things.'

'I daresay you haven't had much practice,' said the Queen. 'When I was younger, I always did it for half an hour a day. Why, sometimes I've believed as many as six impossible things before breakfast.'

Lewis Carroll, *Alice in Wonderland*

11.1 INTRODUCTION

So far in this book, we have seen many examples of statistics that have been misused, accidentally or deliberately, to make a point that is different from and often the opposite of what the data really shows. If you have read the preceding chapters, you will know that a threefold increase in the risk of cancer isn't actually as scary as it sounds; that an unrepresentative survey doesn't really tell you what you think it might; that a graph that looks like it shows something staggering might only look interesting because of a truncated axis; that there is lots more to school performance than school league tables; and so on, and so on, and so on.

In each case, there was a statistical idea underlying the reason why the use of statistics was misleading. It might be the idea of (un)representativeness, or the difference between relative and absolute risk, or even simple concepts like means, medians and modes. Each concept when used in certain ways implies something different from what the data really suggests. Hopefully, you will now feel comfortable spotting some of these when they are presented in the news media and elsewhere, and calling them out.

However, sometimes we are confronted with statistical ideas that are so surprising that even the most experienced data journalist might sit up and think 'huh?'. These are ideas that make facts appear fictitious, and vice versa. Statistics often work in such an unexpected way that we are surprised, and can't work out what happened. These 'statistical quirks' are the subject of this chapter.

In particular this chapter will consider some general examples where statistics surprise us, before focusing in particular on Simpson's Paradox and Bayes' Theorem. Some examples of the things we will show can be true are the following:

- If you are a student there are probably two people in your lectures who share a birthday. In a lecture theatre of 70, it's almost certain.
- If a test for a disease is 99% effective, and you test positive, you still probably don't have the disease.
- A treatment for a drug works for men, and works for women, but appears to make things worse when you look at both groups together.

Although these ideas sometimes rest on some complex-looking equations (and we'll point those of you so inclined to those equations), they can be explained perfectly well with words. We will see that the surprise comes down to the fact that two questions that sound very similar can actually be very different, and so produce very different answers. If we ask the wrong question, we get the wrong answer. For the rest of the chapter, nothing will be as it seems!

11.2 WHEN STATISTICS SURPRISE US

While in general we are happy to trust our brains, occasionally our brains deceive us. A classic example is shown in Figure 11.1. It shows two parallel lines, with additional lines forming arrows pointing in (for line A) or pointing out (for line B). It looks as if line B is longer than line A, but they are in fact the same length. Our brains are deceived by the arrow ends: they change the way that we perceive the image. This is known as the Müller–Lyer illusion, named after Franz Carl Müller-Lyer, who devised it in 1889.

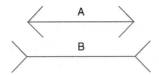

Figure 11.1   The Müller–Lyer illusion

Source: https://commons.wikimedia.org/wiki/File:Effetto_ottico_3_.png

What's particularly interesting (or perhaps particularly galling) about this is that even when we get out a ruler and check to make sure, our brains *still* tell us that line B is longer than line A when we look at it. The illusion works even when we know it's an illusion. It takes rational thought to understand how our brain was tricked, and what the truth is, and even then there is a part of us that remains unconvinced. Statistics can have a similar effect. We can be told that something is the case, but it remains difficult to believe because the illusion is so powerful. We need to really dig down into what's going on to understand how the impossible might in fact be true.

Next time you are in a lecture, or a newsroom, or even at a gathering of friends, look around the room. How likely is it that two people in the room share a birthday (as in the same day and month – not the same year)? It may be that you have already met someone that shares your birthday (you might even have a twin there!), but, more likely, you haven't. People sharing birthdays is something remarkable – it's exciting when you find someone sharing your birthday precisely because it's unusual.

The question really comes down to how many people are in the room. If there are only two of you in a lecture (if this is the case, unluckily, you probably can't get away with falling asleep!) the probability is much lower than if there are hundreds (you probably shouldn't sleep in this case either – the lecturer can see more than you think!).

What is surprising, though, is that the number of people you need in a room for this – to be more likely than not – is smaller than you might think. You might expect that, for there to be a 50% chance of a shared birthday, you would need, perhaps, around 183 people (to account for half the days in the year). But in fact, you only need 23 people to have more than a 50% chance of there being a shared birthday. There is a 99.9% probability of a shared birthday if there's 70 people.

How did our brains get this so wrong? The answer is that we tend to confuse things in our heads, and in this case we are confusing the chance of our sharing a birthday (this is, still, quite low) with the chance that *any two people in the room* will share a birthday. That combines lots of small probabilities (the probability that each person shares a birthday with each other person) to make a much bigger one. This, combined with a general sense that sharing birthdays is an unusual, interesting thing, primes our brains to think it is something rarer than it actually is.

So we can see, straight away, that we can't always trust our brains. This is part of the reason we use statistics, to check that what we think we know we actually do. The rest of the chapter will focus on a few examples of seemingly impossible things, and see how they are not only possible, but require careful reporting in the news media when newsworthy.

11.3 SIMPSON'S PARADOX

11.3.1 Are Wages in the United States Declining or Growing?

In 2013, *The New York Times* reported that 'Median Pay in US is Stagnant' (Norris, 2013a; Smith, 2013). In the article, it was reported that the median wage (for a reminder of what this is, see Chapter 2) had increased in real terms by about 1% since 2000. However, the same article stated that the median wage had declined in real terms for college graduates, those with some college education (but no bachelor's degree), those with only high school diplomas and those who dropped out of high school.

The astute among you will look at those categories and think: they account for all possible education levels. We could imagine most categories declining and the overall wage growing if there were another group whose wages grew dramatically. But that's not the case here. Given this, the statistics suggest that wages have risen (modestly) for everyone, but fallen for, well, everyone! How can this be?

The answer lies in a statistical quandary called **Simpson's Paradox**, which was first explicitly described by Edward Simpson in 1951 (hence the name). The effect explains how it is that a trend in several different groups of data (education groups in the above) can be completely different when combined.

Let's take a closer look at that pay growth data. A subsequent New York Times blog (Norris, 2013b) gives more detailed data, and we found similar data on the US government statistics website, which you can see in Table 11.1.

As you can see, the overall change is positive, but the changes of each of the individual groups are all negative. What on earth could be making this happen?

Table 11.1 Change in wages in the United States, in total and by education level

	2000 median weekly wage (2014$)	2000 working population (thousands)	2013 median weekly wage (2014$)	2013 working population (thousands)	Change (as % of 2000 wage)
High school dropouts	498	8,534	480	6,591	−3.61
High school graduates, no college	695	28,054	662	24,768	−4.75
Some college (but no bachelor's degree)	820	24,578	760	24,796	−7.32
Bachelor's degree or higher	1,226	27,564	1213	37,013	−1.06
Total	764	88,730	775	93,168	+1.44

Sources: Wage data from: https://www.bls.gov/opub/ted/2015/more-education-still-means-more-pay-in-2014.htm
Population data from: https://www.bls.gov/webapps/legacy/cpswktab5.htm

Note: We don't exactly replicate the figures from the blog, probably because of different inflation rates used to calculate the total wages. The basic point is clear, though!

The answer lies in the size of the population of each group. Between 2000 and 2013, the number of college graduates grew a great deal, while the other groups declined in size. Although the wages of college graduates have in real terms declined, they still get paid a great deal more than the other groups, and there were a lot more or them in 2013 than in 2000. In other words, while an individual in any of these groups saw a decline in wages between 2000 and 2013, because there are more people in the highest earning group than there used to be, overall, people in the country are earning more.

So which is correct? Did wages rise or fall? Well, both, actually – it depends on what you are interested in. If you are interested in an individual's wages, the **within-group effects** are the correct ones: wages are falling. If, however, you are interested in whether people in the population are generally being paid more in one group than another, the total figure is correct – people are, generally, being paid more, in part because there are more college graduates in the population than there used to be.

Part of the problem, in more statistical terms, is that we have a confounding variable (for more on this, see Chapter 10) that is affecting the relationship we are interested in. Specifically, we are interested in the relationship between time and people's wages, and there is a confounding variable, education, which is affecting what we find. When we separate out the data into the education groups, we are effectively controlling for education – keeping it constant within each of the groups – so we get the effect(s) as if the composition of the education groups hasn't changed in the period of interest. In contrast, when looking at the overall data, we are no longer controlling for those changes in educational composition. This figure is the amount that wages in the population have changed, but it is in part a result of education changes in that population. For more on controlling and confounding, see Chapter 10.

So both are correct – they are just answering slightly different questions, and, in this case, those different questions produce in opposite results. This is strange, because the two questions 'how have overall wages changed?' and 'how have individuals' wages changed?' don't really sound that different. But it turns out that this slight difference in wording makes all the difference.

11.3.2 Another Example: Gender Bias in Universities

One of the classic examples of Simpson's Paradox, which centres on accusations of discrimination in admissions to UC Berkeley (and which you can read about in Bickel et al., 1975), is mirrored by a more recent example of alleged discrimination in applications to the 'VENI programme', a research grants scheme that academics in the Netherlands can apply to, between 2010 and 2012. A paper in the journal *Proceedings of the National Academy of Science* (PNAS; Van der Lee and Ellemers, 2015) argued that there was gender discrimination in the awarding of grants from this programme, with nearly 18% of applications from men accepted, compared with less than 15% of applications from women. However, when this was broken down by academic discipline, the results were less clear: women were more successful than men in four out of nine subject areas, and men more successful in five. In no discipline were those differences significant in either direction.

How was this the case? The problem was that the more competitive subject areas were ones that happened to have more female applicants (Albers, 2015). So, for example, applications in the social sciences were the most competitive (with only 13.4% of applications accepted), and had a higher proportion of female applicants. In comparison, applications in the chemical sciences were much less competitive (with a 26.3% success) and had a much lower proportion of female applications.

As with the wage example above, the issue here is confounding. We are interested in the relationship between gender and the success rate of grant applications, but this effect is confounded with another variable: the competitiveness of the discipline of the applicant. We can also think of there being different effects within and between disciplines. Within disciplines, there appears to be no effect of gender; there are no statistically significant gender differences found within disciplines. In a given discipline, men and women have the same chance of being successful in a grant. However, there are differences between disciplines. That is, some disciplines give more grants to men than others, but this is because more men apply for grants in those disciplines than others. It so happens that those disciplines also tend to be the least competitive (for both men and women) to get into.

So, does this mean there is no discrimination? Not necessarily. While it seems within-discipline discrimination is not occurring, a decision has been made to fund female-dominated disciplines less than male-dominated disciplines (at least, relative to the number of applications in each). Because of this, the between-discipline effect is not neutral, so this gender bias cannot be dismissed as a statistical artefact as easily as we might think. Once again, how we interpret these results will come down to our own subjective leanings. Are disciplines with more women underfunded? Or are there just too many people in those disciplines to be able to fund as big a proportion of people? The point, though, is that the within- and between-group effects are different effects and neither is right or wrong: both are sometimes of interest. However, they are showing us potentially very different things about how the data has been produced. We should be careful not to confuse them.

Simpson's Paradox occurs when the question we think we are answering is more complex than we thought: there are different within-group and **between-group effects**, or there is a confounding variable, or the question we were asking isn't the one we intended to ask. In this case, we need to be more precise about the way in which the differences we found came about, and whether those differences are a problem or not. The latter applies to the examples that follow as well.

11.4 BAYES' THEOREM

11.4.1 How Likely Are You to Have a Disease?

Many of you will have been to a doctor to have tests to see whether you have a particular disease. Imagine you go in to take a test that will tell you whether or not you have a disease, and that 1 in 1,000 people in the population has this disease. You are told that the test is 99% effective – that is, there is a 1% risk of a positive result (a result that says you have the disease) when you are in fact disease-free. There is also a 1% risk of a negative result (a result that says you don't have the disease) if you do in fact have the disease.

This sounds like a pretty good test, meaning that, if you get a positive result, you might think you can be fairly sure (or about 99% sure) that the test was accurate. And yet, this is very wrong. In fact, in this situation, if you get a positive test, there is a 90% chance that you *don't* have the disease.

How can this be true? The test is 99% effective, yet we're telling you that if you get a positive test, there is a 90% chance that the result is wrong! The explanation lies in the question you are answering. The 99% figure represents the chance that, if you have the disease, you will get a positive result. In other words, that figure is for people who know they have the disease and are assessing the quality of the test. But as a patient, this isn't what you want to know at all. You don't know if you have the disease, but you do know the test result, so are interested in the chance of having the disease given the test. It's the other way round – the probability of a positive test result given you have the disease versus the probability of having the disease given you have a positive test result.

Does that really make that much difference? Well, sometimes, yes it does. Figure 11.2 shows how this can happen, in a population of 100,000 people. There are four possible situations in this example:

- you can get a positive test result and have the disease;
- you can get a negative test result and have the disease;

- you can get a positive test result and not have the disease; and finally
- you can get a negative test result and not have the disease.

We know from the description above that 1 in 1,000 will have the disease, so that's 100 people in the sample of 100,000 in the first two groups (the two 'have the disease' groups). The other 99,900 people will be in the latter two groups. Of those 100 people with the disease, we know that 1 in 100 will incorrectly receive a negative result, with the other 99 people having the disease.

This leaves the 99,900 people in the population that do not have the disease. Of those, we would expect 1 in 100 to be incorrectly diagnosed with a positive test (i.e. 999 people), while the rest (98,901 people) would have a correct, negative result.

The key thing is that, among those who received a positive test result, the group that doesn't in fact have the disease (999 people) is much bigger than the group that does have the disease (99 people). So even though the test is 99% accurate, if you get a positive result, it's more likely to be wrong than correct – the probability of having the disease is in fact 99/999, which is just under 10%.

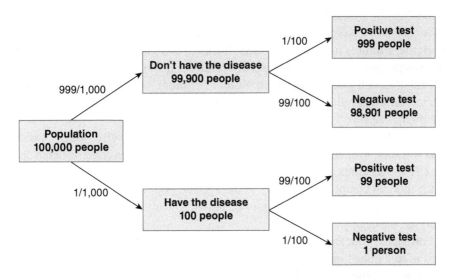

Figure 11.2   Bayes' Theorem in action – how a 99% effective test can get it wrong

This is the principle behind **Bayes' Theorem**, which gives us a way of calculating the probability of something – let's call it A – given something else – let's call it B – if we know the probability of B given A. In the above example, A is having the disease, and B is a positive test result. We know the probability of B given A, the probability of a positive test result given you have the disease: that is, 99%. But we don't know the probability of A given B – that is, the probability of actually having the disease, given you've had a positive test result. What we need to know to do this, though, is the overall probability of A – in the above case, the proportion that have the disease in the population. If that probability is 0.5 – that is, 50% of people have the disease and 50% don't – the probability of A given B is the same as the probability of B given A. In the above case, we know that is not the case – we have 'prior information' which tells us that the disease is rarer than that (it affects less than 50% of the population), and this affects our understanding of the results.

This prior information might be different in different places, which means that where you live could determine the chance that a positive test would be correct. For example, a test for HIV has a higher degree of accuracy (better than 99%) than the hypothetical test in the example above. But the rate of infection is very different in different places. If you lived in Botswana in 2014, nearly 30% of people had HIV, meaning that if you had received a positive test result, you'd have had just under a 99% chance of having the disease. But if you live in the UK, less than 1% of people have the disease, and the chance of having the disease given a positive test result is much smaller – around 40% (one of us has used the software package R and produced some code to work these figures out yourself – see Hartman, 2018). It may sound weird that you would interpret the same test differently in different places, but the prior information that you have in each place is different, so it makes sense that the interpretation should be different too. For more on the maths behind Bayes' Theorem, see Box 11.1.

Bayes' Theorem has been shown to be an incredibly powerful tool. A version of it was used by Alan Turing and others to crack the Enigma code, which helped the UK and its allies win the war (see Box 11.2). It is essential to the development of the modern computer. Its ability to incorporate prior knowledge into statistical inference was a huge step forward for quantitative analysis (for more on Bayesian analysis, see Chapter 8).

Fortunately, doctors are likely to be aware of this. Often, tests like this will be used to rule things out, given that a negative test result is a very strong indicator of not having the disease (in the above example, the chance of having the disease when you have had a negative test result is just 1/98,901 – much better than 99%!). A positive test result would imply that further testing is required, to make sure the diagnosis is correct.

However, in many areas of society, the ideas behind Bayes' Theorem have been greatly misunderstood, and this includes a number of examples in the news media. Let's explore these now.

11.1 The Mathematics of Bayes' Theorem

The logic outlined here was put into mathematical form by Thomas Bayes. The maths he used looks something like this:

$$P(A \mid B) = \frac{P(B \mid A) \times P(A)}{P(B)}$$

Looks complicated, right? Actually, it's relatively simple – we basically need to multiply and divide three numbers. Those vertical lines 'I' mean 'given', so $P(B \mid A)$ means the probability of B happening, given that A has happened. Therefore, if we know the probability of B given A, the overall probability of A and the overall probability of B, we can work out the probability of A given B.

Let's take our medical disease example. There, A was 'having the disease', and B was 'getting a positive test'. We know that the probability of getting a positive test, given you have the disease, is 0.99 (or 99%). We know that the probability of having the disease, with no other information, is the rate in the population (so 0.001, or 1 in 1,000). Finally, we know the probability of getting a positive test from Figure 11.2: it is (999 + 99)/100,000, which is 0.01098.

So we can plug these numbers into the above equation:

$$P(A \mid B) = \frac{0.99 \times 0.001}{0.01098} = 0.090$$

As you can see, we get the same answer as we got using Figure 11.2.

11.2 How Bayes' Theorem Won the Second World War

The Reverend Thomas Bayes (c.1701–61) was a Presbyterian minister, but also a philosopher and, later in his life, a statistician. He published only two works in his lifetime, but he's now most famous for the unpublished notes which formed the basis of what we now call Bayes' Theorem.

The logic of Bayes' Theorem is simple: we can update our initial belief about something with new knowledge or information, and this makes our previous belief more likely to be accurate. In the example used in this chapter, our prior

(Continued)

belief was that 1 in 1,000 individuals had a disease. This was updated based on the results of a medical test (that's the objective knowledge), to produce a new and improved belief about our own situation.

This logic was used, with great effect by codebreakers such as Alan Turing (who was later persecuted by the British state for being gay), to help allied forces crack enemy codes in the Second World War. It was used to track down German U-boats, by assessing the probability of a U-boat being near a particular shipping route, and updating those prior probabilities based on new information as it came in. A similar logic was used to crack the Germans' Enigma code. By finding patterns in coded messages that had a higher probability of being certain letters than others, Turing and his team were able to use that information to update the chance of the code working in a certain way, and reduce the number of guesses a machine trying to break the code would have to make. It is generally believed that this code breaking, backed by Bayes' Theorem, shortened the war by around two years (McGrayne, 2011).

Bayes' Theorem has been central to a huge number of developments since, including the modern computer. Given the importance of computing in the production of this book, you would probably not be reading it now if it weren't for Bayes' Theorem!

11.4.2 Bayes' Theorem in the Media: The Sally Clark Case

One area where Bayes' Theorem, and probability more generally, are important in the news and news media lies in the reporting of criminal cases. When deciding whether or not an individual committed a crime, juries need to consider the probability of whether or not the individual did indeed commit the crime. This is usually done by jurors deciding whether a guilty verdict is 'beyond reasonable doubt' based on their judgment. But often evidence is presented which suggests a specific probability of its being incorrect. It is crucial that those probabilities are relayed correctly.

In 1999, Sally Clark was convicted of the murder of her two children. The defence argued that both deaths were caused by Sudden Infant Death syndrome, or cot death: these terms are used when a sleeping baby's death is unexplained. However, the prosecution argued it was highly unlikely that this would happen to the same mother twice. In fact, they argued that the probability of this happening twice was just 1 in 73 million. They argued, therefore, that it was much more likely that Sally Clark killed her children. It was this evidence that really convinced the jury that it was 'beyond reasonable doubt' that she was guilty.

How was that 1 in 73 million number calculated? Well, it is estimated that, for parents of Sally Clark's demographic, approximately 1 in every 8,500 children dies of cot death, so the probability of a child dying of cot death is approximately 1 in 8,500. The chance of that happening twice, therefore, is 1/8,500 times 1/8,500, which is around 1 in 73 million. It is unsurprising that, given how small these probabilities are, the jury were convinced that it was 'beyond reasonable doubt' that Sally Clark killed her children. However, we know from the above that things are not this simple. The number of 1 in 73 million is the probability of two deaths happening given the accused is innocent – that is, deaths by natural causes and not by murder. That isn't actually what the jury need to know – they need to know the probability of Sally Hunt being innocent, given what they know: that two of her children had died. It's the same as the difference between the probability of A given B, and the probability of B given A. In the evidence presented in court, these two things were conflated (this is known as the **Prosecutor's Fallacy**), but we know from the discussion above that they can be very, very different.

The key difference is that, in considering how likely her innocence is, we need to consider that most people are not child-murderers – just like most people do not have a particular disease in the example above. If we say that 1 in 2.4 million mothers in the UK murders her first two children in their first year of life (Korb, 2012), and apply Bayes' Theorem to this case, we get a very different result. If we plug the numbers into the equation in Box 11.1, we end up with a probability of innocence of just over 3%. That is a much bigger probability than the number of 1 in 73 million presented to jurors. Of course, it is still a small probability, but it might be big enough to instil a bit of doubt in jurors' minds.

However, there are two further reasons why we should be cautious about this. First, we are assuming so far that deaths caused by cot death are random – that is, the chance of one happening doesn't affect the chance of another happening. The causes of cot death are unknown, but it is fairly likely that there could be genetic or environmental factors that make cot death more likely for some families than others. Because if this, if it happens in a family once, it is more likely that it might happen again. It is likely that there is something in the children's genes, or in their home environment, that makes the probability of cot death greater than that in the overall population: a greater chance than 1 in 8,500.

Second, the real question isn't whether the chance of innocence is low, but whether it is lower than the chance of an individual being a murderer. While the chance of innocence may be low, it may not be that much lower than the chance of Sally Clark being a murderer.

Both of these points increase the likelihood that there is reasonable doubt. It is for these reasons that, on appeal, Sally Clark was freed in 2003. Following the

case, a number of other convictions were reviewed and two other people convicted of murdering their children had their convictions quashed.

At the time, Sally Clark was widely reviled in the press as a child killer. It can
be assumed that those who wrote reports did so in good faith. But a greater understanding of statistics, both in the press and in the courtroom, would have meant
that this miscarriage of justice might not have happened. The effects of that injus-
tice did not end with the acquittal. In the subsequent years, Sally Clark developed
psychiatric problems, and died from alcohol poisoning in 2007.

Getting statistics right is not just important for passing exams. It can be a matter
of life and death.

11.5 CONCLUSIONS

We have shown in this chapter that the impossible can be true. Wages can rise
when all education levels experience falling wages. A school can appear discrim-
inatory at the same time as appearing to value equality. A highly effective test
produces incorrect positive results more than correct ones. A test for HIV works
in some countries but not others. Something that has a chance of 1 in 73 million is
actually likely to have happened.

Throughout this book we have seen some relatively obvious ways that statistics can be manipulated in the media. In this chapter, we have seen some
perhaps less obvious ways that the news media, and their readers, can be caught
out by things that seem completely obvious but are not at all as they appear. We
have learned about the perils of Bayes' Theorem and Simpson's Paradox, but
perhaps, more importantly, we have seen that these abstract statistical issues
can have serious consequences on people's lives. Journalists and consumers of
the news, beware!

11.6 CONCEPTS LEARNED IN THIS CHAPTER

Simpson's Paradox: when a relationship between two variables appears overall
in a dataset, but the relationship reverses within a number of different groups
within that data. Simpson's Paradox is often caused by confounding variables that
create between-group effects.

Bayes' Theorem/Bayes' Rule: a method of finding the probability of something conditional on something else, such as the probability of having an illness
given a medical test result, or the probability a defendant is innocent given the
results of a DNA test at the scene of the crime. It can be used to incorporate prior

knowledge (knowledge we have before a particular test is undertaken) to improve the accuracy of the probability it generates.

The Birthday Paradox: the surprising fact that you need only 23 people together in a room than you might think before the chance of two people sharing a birthday goes above 50%.

Within-group effects: a relationship between two variables that occurs within a group that shares a certain characteristic (e.g. education level).

Between-group effects: a relationship between two variables that occurs between groups. The between-group relationship is not always the same as the within-group relationship, in part because of confounding variables that change the between-group effect.

The Prosecutor's Fallacy: the belief that the probability of innocence given some evidence is the same as the probability that a test of that evidence would have occurred if the defendant is innocent. The logic of Bayes' Theorem shows that, in fact, this is not the case.

11.7 QUESTIONS FOR CLASS DISCUSSION

1   The data in Table 11.2 is made up admissions data from the paper on UC Berkeley's admissions rates (Bickel et al., 1975).

Table 11.2   UC Berkeley's admissions rates

	Admitted	Total applications
Department of Machismatics		
Men	200	400
Women	100	200
Department of Social Warfare		
Men	50	150
Women	150	450
Total		
Men	250	550
Women	250	650

Do you think that there is gender discrimination going on at this university? Why, or why not?

2   Can you think of an example of an 'impossible' result in academic papers that you have read or data that you have used? It might be as a result of

(a) Simpson's Paradox, (b) a misunderstanding of Bayes' Theorem, or (c) something else.

3   Suppose that your friend Jamie calls you in a panic after testing positive for HIV. Jamie is understandably upset because doctors assure her that the OraQuick Advance Rapid test is nearly 100% accurate. Below is information about the HIV test from research involving over 12,000 subjects by the Centers for Disease Control and Prevention in the United States.

OraQuick Advance Rapid HIV-1/2

Sensitivity: 99.1% of HIV cases are detected by the test when HIV is present (true positive), but the test misses 0.9% of real HIV cases (false negative)

Specificity: 99.6% of healthy people have negative tests (true negative), but 0.4% of the tests return an incorrect result (false positive)

To help Jamie make sense of her results, you search the Web for official government statistics and discover that there are approximately 110,000 people living with HIV in the UK. Experts estimate that the overall prevalence of HIV is 2.8 per 1,000 inhabitants, or 0.28% of the population.

Using Bayes' Rule, what is the probability that Jamie has HIV, given that she had a positive test result – that is, $P(\text{HIV}|\text{Positive Test})$? Given this conditional probability, how worried should Jamie be about the positive HIV test?

Does the answer change if it turns out that Jamie lived in Lesotho, where one in four people (25%) have the disease, and not the UK?

FURTHER READING

Another good book if you want to go further with your understanding of Bayes' Theorem is:

Stone, J. (2013) *Bayes' Rule: A Tutorial Introduction to Bayesian Analysis*. Sheffield: Sebtel Press.

For more on the Prosecutor's Fallacy:

Harford, T. (2015) Making a lottery out of the law. *Financial Times.* Available at https://www.ft.com/content/b100d86c-a677-11e4-9bd3-00144feab7de?mhq5j=e7

The Inns of Court College of Advocacy, Royal Statistical Society (2017) Statistics and probability for advocates: understanding the use of statistical evidence in courts and tribunals. Available at www.rss.org.uk/RSS/Influencing_Change/Statistics_and_the_law/Advocates_guide/RSS/Influencing_Change/Current_projects_sub/Advocates_guide.aspx?hkey=883603a7-fc93-4921-a2cc-36ac14e1cf82

REFERENCES

Albers, C. (2015) NWO, gender bias and Simpson's paradox. Casper Albers' blog. Available at http://blog.casperalbers.nl/science/nwo-gender-bias-and-simpsons-paradox/

Bickel, P. J., Hammel, E. A. and O'Connell, J. W. (1975) Sex bias in graduate admissions: data from Berkeley. *Science*, 187(4175), 398–404.

Hartman, T. (2018) Lab exercise: conditional probability and global HIV. Available at https://github.com/tkhartman/qss/blob/master/conditional_probability_global_hiv_v2.md

Korb, K. B. (2012) Sally Clark is wrongly convicted of murdering her children. Bayesians without Borders. Available at http://bayesian-intelligence.com/bwb/2012-03/sally-clark-is-wrongly-convicted-of-murdering-her-children/

McGrayne, S. B. (2011) *The Theory That Would Not Die: How Bayes' Rule Cracked the Enigma Code, Hunted down Russian Submarines, and Emerged Triumphant from Two Centuries of Controversy*. New Haven, CT: Yale University Press.

Norris, F. (2013a) Median pay in US is stagnant, but low-paid workers lose. *The New York Times*, 26 April. Available at www.nytimes.com/2013/04/27/business/economy/wage-disparity-continues-to-grow.html

Norris, F. (2013b) Can every group be worse than average? Yes. New York Times Economix blog. Available at https://economix.blogs.nytimes.com/2013/05/01/can-every-group-be-worse-than-average-yes/

Smith, D. (2013) A great example of Simpson's Paradox: US median wage decline. Revolutions blog. Available at http://blog.revolutionanalytics.com/2013/07/a-great-example-of-simpsons-paradox.html

Van der Lee, R. and Ellemers, N. (2015) Gender contributes to personal research funding success in The Netherlands. *Proceedings of the National Academy of Sciences*, 112(40), 12349–53.

12 Conclusion

Through the course of this book, we have seen examples of news stories, websites, adverts, political campaigns, and more, all of which have used statistics to help support the things that they are claiming. In some cases they do this in ways that are really fair, and often very innovative and clever. In other cases, what you end up with is misleading – those statistics are used to make a point that isn't really justified.

This book will hopefully have helped you to spot the difference. It should have helped you to see which statistics are good and which are bad; which graphs help to summarise an important point and which graphs have been made to trick you into thinking something is true when it isn't; which sources of data are representative and how you know when it is or isn't, the importance of experiments in understanding causal claims, and so on.

Of course, spotting the difference is rarely as clear cut as we might hope. While some people might think a league table is highly misleading, others might think it has ranked organisations perfectly. A causal claim might be justified in one person's opinion, and deeply misleading in another. People often think that statistics (unlike other parts of social science) are somehow scientific, objective or truthful. But the truth is that statistics can be as subjective as any other 'finding' in research and in the media.

This might make you think: what's the point? If quantitative data can't unambiguously tell us the truth, isn't it better to just leave it behind? In our view, the answer is no. First, statistics sometimes *can* give us information that is more objective than other information – we just need to know how to read the signs of how it might have been manipulated. And second, even when the information is contested, it is in that contest that our understanding can grow. Through creating statistics we can understand the world, and the different ways of seeing it, much better, even if that understanding is more complicated than a single number. So in fact, the subjective nature of statistics makes it *more* important to understand what statistics is and isn't saying, not less.

Having read the preceding chapters, you will now have found out about a number of ways that data in the media can be critiqued: how you can know when those representations of data are accurate, and when they are misleading. There's a huge range of ways this is done, and we haven't covered them all here. However, the logic that we've used in questioning the claims made in the media using data can be applied to other data sources, media stories and statistical representations as well.

Not only that, but by reading this book you will have learned about a number of statistical methods and concepts that will be useful in understanding statistics both now and in the future. You have learned about averages, variance, uncertainty, regression, p-values, multilevel models, Bayes' Theorem, confounding, representativeness, the ecological fallacy, the modifiable areal unit problem, and more. These methods and ideas are not limited to the news media: a huge host of academic journal articles use ideas like these, and now you understand what they are you will hopefully be able to understand those journal articles better as well.

Let's take one final example that involves a number of concepts that are illustrated throughout the book. In November 2015, the UK newspaper *The Sun* led with the headline: '1 in 5 Brit Muslims' sympathy for jihadis'. It was illustrated by an image of an Islamic State militant, holding a knife. The implication was clear: a large portion of the Muslim community in the UK supports terrorists, not just a tiny minority as is often claimed. If true, this is an important finding. In a world where terrorism is a major fear to a lot of people, and Islamic State continues to cause chaos on an international scale, it is reasonable for the public to want to know who the people are that are supporting it. If false, this example is potentially dangerous, in painting a picture of a whole group in British society that is unfair, and potentially stoking prejudice.

How did *The Sun* get to this conclusion? Well, it was based on a survey conducted by the polling company Survation, and the question that was asked to British Muslims was:

> Which of these statements do you most agree with?

1   I have a lot of sympathy for young Muslims who leave the UK to join fighters in Syria.
2   I have some sympathy for young Muslims who leave the UK to join fighters in Syria.
3   I have no sympathy for young Muslims who leave the UK to join fighters in Syria.

Approximately one in five responded to this question with either answer 1 or 2.

You may already be asking questions about this, based on the chapters you have read.

- Is the survey from a trusted source? In this case, probably yes: Survation is a reputable polling company, although as a one-off poll it is probably less trustworthy than a larger-scale survey.
- Is the survey representative? Again, probably it isn't far off, although, as we know, it is difficult to be sure that the sample is representative, especially for subpopulations like 'Muslims'.
- Is the sample size big enough? Just over 1,000 Muslims were polled – so there will be a margin of sampling error of around 3%. This is not a huge amount of uncertainty, and would suggest the true answer is pretty close to 1 in 5.
- Is 1 in 5 a big number? Well it sounds big, but what we want to think about is what it's compared with. Compared with zero, it sounds big, but it turns out the same survey found 13% of non-Muslims also answered the question with options 1 or 2. Thinking back to Chapter 2, this perhaps isn't as big as it is made to sound.
- Is the question being interpreted correctly? Probably not. The survey question doesn't mention jihad or terrorists at all – so many might have interpreted this as referring to people travelling to Syria to join groups fighting jihadists, or fighting the Syrian regime. Not only that, but it refers to sympathy, and not support; one might sympathise with a brainwashed teenager, while not condoning their actions. The way the survey was interpreted and the imagery that accompanied that interpretation painted a picture that was not supported by the survey, because the survey could be interpreted in a number of different ways.

So, overall, this was an example of a statistic being misinterpreted to create a false impression. But information like this is not just wrong, it can also be dangerous. Lots of people in the UK have fairly low opinions of Muslims in general, and this Islamophobia has increased as a result of the reporting of recent terror attacks. There have been a number of violent attacks against Muslims in recent years. Misinformation that backs up the view that a lot of Muslims support terrorism provides justification to those crimes for those who commit them. While it is impossible to link a specific news story to any specific violent crime, it seems likely that a headline like *The Sun*'s could harden someone's prejudice against Muslims, and potentially make them more likely to commit crimes against Muslims.

12.1 THE MEDIA TODAY

There are a number of reasons why this book has been written, but one of them is that the media are currently at something of a crossroads. First, the media are being watched more carefully than ever before: websites are dedicated to fact checking, meaning it is easier to identify whether stories are real or fake than it has ever been. Second, there are more media sources out there than ever before, and more information, both good and bad, for the reader to wade through. And third, now that there are so many media sources out there, a lot of that media is bad. Many media sources, whether through incompetence or malice, don't check their sources properly, and fail to report information honestly and fairly.

As we write, there are criminal cases being heard about interference by the Russian state in elections and referendums in other countries, with the news media being a key tool of this interference. The claims are that there are multiple news sources and websites, coordinated from Moscow, which present information that is often untrue and misleading, in order to change the opinions of people who live in other countries. It is claimed that Russia was involved in the election of Donald Trump in 2016, the Brexit referendum result, and others. The nature of this interference varies – from downright falsehoods, to misleading presentation of information, to cute cat videos designed to make the news source go viral (and get more followers). In our view, all are dangerous.

At the same time, however, there's a lot of sources of the news that we see as highly effective. There are many journalists undertaking great investigations, and using statistics to make extremely effective and valid points about society. We mentioned some examples of these in this book, but there are more examples coming out every day.

We hope that this book helps reduce the power of the former, and increase the capability of the latter. The tools outlined in the book will help you spot when news articles appear dubious. These tools will help you in being able to question whether a news story is accurate or not, from a sensible or a dubious source, fairly presented or misleading. If we, as citizens, can spot when news is bad, that bad news becomes less effective.

If you are studying on a journalism course right now, we hope this book will help you to become a really great journalist: one who can understand statistics and data without fear, and who can write up new stories based on statistics in a way that is both persuasive and fair. If you are a reader of the news, we hope that this book will help you to decide which statistics are and are not worth paying attention to, and help you to critique the things that you read.

However, this won't happen on its own. We all need to play our part in this, as readers and writers of the media. We need to be quick to call out inaccuracies when we see them. When friends share a misleading statistic on Facebook, tell them why it's misleading. If your boss tells you to publish a statistic without checking where it came from, refuse. We all need to be involved in helping to make statistics work for us, and not against us.

Index